D0209090

"My Husband's Trying to Kill Me!"

"My Husband's Trying to Kill Me!"

A TRUE STORY OF MONEY, MARRIAGE, AND MURDEROUS INTENT

JIM SCHUTZE

HarperCollins*Publishers*

Photographs courtesy Linda DeSilva.

"MY HUSBAND'S TRYING TO KILL ME!" Copyright © 1992 by Jim Schutze. All rights reserved. Printed in the United States of America. No part of this book may be used or reproduced in any manner whatsoever without written permission except in the case of brief quotations embodied in critical articles and reviews. For information address HarperCollins Publishers, Inc., 10 East 53rd Street, New York, NY 10022.

HarperCollins books may be purchased for educational, business, or sales promotional use. For information please write: Special Markets Department, HarperCollins Publishers, Inc., 10 East 53rd Street, New York, NY 10022.

FIRST EDITION

Designed by George J. McKeon

Library of Congress Cataloging-in-Publication Data

Schutze, Jim.
  My husband's trying to kill me! : a true story of money, marriage, and murderous intent / Jim Schutze. — 1st ed.
    p. cm.
  ISBN 0-06-017960-0 (hard)
  1. Attempted murder—Texas—Dallas—Case studies. 2. Wife abuse—Texas—Dallas—Case studies. 3. Edelman, Robert. 4. DeSilva, Linda. I. Title.
  HV6534.D34S38 1992
  364.1'523'097642812—dc20   92-52600

92 93 94 95 96 ❖/RRD 10 9 8 7 6 5 4 3 2 1

To my parents, Bill and Peggy

ACKNOWLEDGMENTS

For hours on end, months on end, Linda DeSilva patiently told me this story and answered my questions. Later, when I went out looking for corroboration, I was astonished by the accuracy and the evenhandedness with which she had recounted these events. It cannot be an easy thing, to remember so dark a time so honestly. I hope there will be moments in the years ahead when she may forget.

There are two people without whom Linda's story would never have been told. The first is my literary agent, Jane Wilkins Manus. She listened to Linda, saw the human value of her story, and then brought the rest of us together to render this story as a book. The second is Craig Nelson, my editor at HarperCollins, whose constant encouragement, patience, and sunny generosity made writing this book a particular pleasure.

This is the true story of Linda DeSilva and Robert Edelman. However, to protect the identity of other people involved in the story, some names (Snubby Ellis, Janet Lesser, Sparkle Masoud, Brian Thomas, Frank Clifford, Patricia Canton, Rabbi Green) and details have been changed.

CHAPTER ONE

M arriage is like a dream: the trick is to notice when the dream changes. Linda knew she had not noticed. At some point the walls of the dream had warped and cracked, and the cracks had spouted blood. But she could not remember when the dream had changed. She sat staring at the glistening, black expanse of the plate-glass window as she had all night, from the moment Ike had left her here alone in the house, alone in the woods, waiting for her killer to appear in the window. She wanted to remember all of the moments, to sort back through them like snapshots in a cardboard box. She wanted to find the moment when she should have known.

She remembered driving.

It had been white-hot outside that day. Everything at lunch had been so dark, so syrupy sweet with the scent of lilies, so very Dallas. Robert was in his element, dressed in a $1,500 suit and bragging about deals. Now outside, through the blue tint of the Cadillac windows, the vast new concrete surfaces of the city were bathed in sheeting glare. The car's laboring air conditioner filled the interior with cold, damp air.

Robert had been happy at lunch, full of himself and charming. He had told the New York stories, how awful it was. He managed to let everyone know how much money he was making. He ate ravenously, smoked like a chimney, and made certain he was seen by people he admired. He was in Robert Edelman heaven.

Now they were driving back to their huge house on Caruth Boulevard. They were approaching the railroad tracks, and the crossing gate was coming down to stop the traffic ahead of them. Linda was belted into the passenger seat. They both had been silent since getting into the car.

Out of the blue, Robert said: "I really hate T-Ball," reopening their longstanding argument about children's softball versus soccer.

She knew she would have to reply.

"I don't know why," she said softly. She could not give up the point, but the last thing she wanted was another fight.

"You know that I want him to play soccer, Linda," he said, his voice already keening upward into an adolescent whine. "I don't understand why you have to get into it with me over these things. Jesus."

"Robert, Stephen is the one who wants to play T-Ball. He likes T-Ball because his friends play T-Ball."

"Well, hell, Linda, then I guess that just about settles it, doesn't it? I mean, Goddamn, if his stupid friends play T-Ball. . . "

"Robert, I don't want to discuss this. I want to wait and talk about it later."

The car was stopped. The crossing gate was down, holding the back of its long white arm against the faces of the traffic. The warning alarm was clanging. The inside of the car was bone-chillingly cold. Robert was still sweating heavily from his three-minute exposure to the sun waiting for the valet parker to bring the car.

Linda looked out the window absently. There was a gleaming, pearl-gray Mercedes in the next lane. At the wheel was a tall man with neatly swept white hair, in a dark blue pinstriped suit. His passenger was a woman with gray-blonde hair, wearing an off-white knit dress and two long loops of pearls.

The man's eyes met Linda's idle glance. His eyes were a piercing blue, his face expressionless but not slack.

The blow smashed her chin upward and simultaneously snapped her head backward against the headrest at the top of the seat. As her head rotated forward, recoiling, she saw the back of Robert's clenched fist retracting.

"Discuss it later," Robert roared, still staring straight ahead at the train, his other hand holding the wheel. "Goddamn you, Linda, you never, ever listen."

The bell was clanging. The fist flew back across the length of the dashboard and swung up backhanded again. The seat belt was holding her so that she could not wrench free to get out of the way. The fist cracked into her partially open mouth and sent spit flying against the window.

Her head was pressed sideways against the headrest by the second blow. She was staring out the window, through speckles of her own saliva, and she saw the man and the woman in the Mercedes staring back in horror.

Thoughts scattered through her mind. "Oh, I am so sorry," she thought. "I am so embarrassed. I am so sorry."

The clanging stopped. The man and the woman in the Mercedes turned slowly away and looked ahead impassively through the windshield of their own car, knitted lines of worry visible above their eyes. The Mercedes pulled away smoothly and disappeared into traffic. The Cadillac lurched ahead.

In the pre-dawn she was still awake, fully dressed, alone in the house in the woods with all of the lights blazing, still staring straight ahead. The lake materialized at last in the first light of day, just where Ike had said it would be. The outline of a cove appeared. She could see a dark bulk, moving up and down on glassy swells at the far right point of the cove. Her heart froze.

It was a small aluminum boat.

The light gathered slowly, like snow.

Two figures appeared, sitting in the boat. Two men. They were fishing. She stared at the boat and imagined what might happen next. She imagined them turning their faces toward her. She imagined that it would be Joe Masterson and Gerry Hubbell. Joe would smile and give her a thumbs up.

She imagined that it would not be Joe and Gerry. Two strangers with cruel faces would steer the boat to shore and come walking toward her with guns lifted to her face. She stared at the boat for more than forty minutes.

Finally she could see the men clearly. They were strangers. They saw her. The one in the bow leaned out over the gunwales and reeled in a wet anchor line. The other reached back over the stern and pulled the starter-cord on a small green outboard motor. The motor made a high rattling noise like an eggbeater and sent up a blue plume of exhaust. The boat swung around, its bow cutting a lacy wake in the still water, and it moved toward the house. Then the boat turned again, out into the lake. It passed around the point of the cove and disappeared. In a moment she could no longer hear it.

There was nothing for her to do but sit. There was nowhere for her to go. After a while, she returned to her memories. She tried to remember when she had first laid eyes on Robert, but she could not.

He was just there. It was at Oklahoma University. She was the darling of the music department, playing the female lead in *Stop the World, I Want to Get Off.* The decision had already been made to take the production to Germany as a USO show. Everyone in the Oklahoma University music school talked about Linda in terms of New York and a career.

It was the summer of 1967. She and most of the cast had enrolled in summer school so they would have an excuse to stick around in Norman and make changes in the show. She never knew if the others saw the show as she did, as a platform from which they would launch their dreams. But that certainly was how Linda DeSilva viewed it.

Robert Edelman was around on the set because, in his never-ending quest to graduate, he had enrolled in a stage-lighting course—something he thought would be easy and might not require much reading. Robert was not good at heavy reading.

He fawned over her, but so did lots of boys at that point. In the boys-named-Brian department alone, she had three that year.

Here, sitting before the plate-glass window in the house in the woods, she could not quite remember their names. Brian This, Brian That, and Brian Something-or-other. She did remember they were all handsome and charming and absolutely in love with her.

Even on the University of Oklahoma's huge campus, amid all those tens of thousands of undergraduates, Linda DeSilva was a standout. She was just under 5'4", with a dancer's lithe body, honey-blonde hair, and hazel eyes that came on like neon lights when she smiled. Her face was a rare combination of beauty, intelligence, and unpretentious friendliness. Boys were always drawn to her.

But Robert emerged. He came forward somehow to the center stage of Linda's attentions. He brought flowers to her dressing room. He was different. His manners were more formal, prouder than the good-old-boy football-jocks who seemed to think they had first call on the campus's most desirable females. Robert was from Dallas. He drove a new white convertible his parents had given him, and he always dressed impeccably.

Her first clear memory of Robert was an ordinary moment, a moment like any other. She was downstairs in the sitting room of her dormitory, looking out through the plate-glass windows in the front of the building, just as she was staring out through this window now. Robert had called earlier and said he wanted to visit. She had said yes. Now she couldn't remember why she said yes. Probably just to be nice.

Life was so happy that summer. She remembered it as a prolonged natural high. There were already a few students at OU who were experimenting with other kinds of highs, like marijuana and barbiturates, and of course there were many students who drank heavily. All of that was out of the question for Linda, given her strict upbringing in Duncan, Oklahoma, but it was also unnecessary and irrelevant. Life itself was so very sweet and so very exciting that summer. She could not imagine wanting life to be any different from what it already was.

And then Robert appeared. He was walking up the hill from the parking lot toward the dorm. The sun fell on his beautiful black hair. Robert, dressed in a black cashmere V-neck sweater and gray flannel trousers, was handsome, tall and imposing, and he moved regally. That was the first moment. She looked out at him from the window of the dorm, and there was an audible ping in her heart.

Sitting here now, she could not repress a little smile. How could she not have seen what Robert represented to her in that moment? Given her family's house full of Disney books, Disney records, Disney sheet music; given the fact she could sing the entire score of *Snow White* by age eight and that one of her sustaining dreams in life was to sing a role in a Disney movie; how could she have sat there in the dorm in Norman looking out at that tall, dark, handsome, impeccable young man striding up the hill to her and have failed to understand that, in that moment and in her young eyes, he was Prince Charming?

She did not know him. She did not know anything about him. From what little she had seen, he was completely unlike her. She was sunny, optimistic, trusting, outgoing, and sure of herself. Robert was brooding, dark, reclusive, and a little paranoid.

But she was twenty-one years old that summer, and life was spinning by in a beautiful dream. Perhaps some people might have found her childhood in Duncan narrow. But for her it had been snug, safe, reassuring, and happy. Duncan was a prosperous town of the Oklahoma "oil patch," with pretty new houses on neatly kept streets. Her mother had arranged private lessons for Linda and her younger sister, Miriam, and had driven both girls to the voice, piano, and dance teachers who would prepare them for life on a grander stage.

Her brief courtship with Robert took place at a moment in her life when it seemed as if that larger stage might already be beckoning. The USO Tour in October and December of 1967 was a huge success at each of its stops, with standing ovations and many curtain calls, especially for Linda.

When Linda and the company arrived at each hotel on the itinerary, there was always a call waiting from Robert. In their long and very expensive transatlantic telephone conversations, this boy who had only known Linda a matter of months told her again and again: "You are the only person in the entire world who cares about me. You are the only one I have. I never had anything of my own before."

The tour was thrilling, but she was also extremely homesick. By the time she returned, she and Robert had already vowed by telephone that they would get married the following June.

Both families had reservations. There was the religious difference: Robert was a Jew, and Linda was a Christian. The parents had barely met, let alone gotten to know each other. Linda was open and cheerful with Robert's parents, but Robert was aloof in the extreme with her parents.

Linda's bright, shy younger sister, Miriam, had more pointed doubts about Robert. Miriam, who was also a student at OU, had run into Robert when Linda was not around. She found him to be cold, arrogant, even mean-spirited.

But it was also clear to everyone else that these two attractive and willful young people intended to take their newly earned freedom as adults and do what they wanted, which was to marry. Both families decided to make the best of the bargain, and in June of 1968, in a ceremony in Linda's parents' home, they were wed.

They immediately moved to Dallas, where Linda acquired an Actors' Equity card for the first time in her life. She quickly landed a job with the Dallas Summer Musicals—road productions of recent Broadway hits, featuring the New York stars and local supporting casts.

Robert made money right away. He went to work selling computers—then a new field—and took to it like a bird to air. Then one night toward the end of that first summer of marriage, Robert came home with exciting news. He had been offered a job selling computer hardware and software for Honeywell in New York.

"So what are we going to do?" she asked.

"What do you mean, 'what?' We're going to New York. What the fuck do you think we're going to do, Linda?"

The moment the Summer Musicals season ended, Linda began to pack. Her mother was delighted. Never shy about pressing an advantage for her daughter, Virginia DeSilva wrote to the mother of the famous soprano Beverly Sills and told her that her daughter Linda, a soprano, was coming to New York to live and needed to find a good voice teacher. Sills herself sent a personal letter back promptly, telling Mrs. DeSilva that her own teacher, Estelle Leibling, would give Linda an audition when she arrived in the city.

"This is so exciting," she said.

"Yeah," Robert said, "maybe now we're going to make it."

Linda and Robert, still in their early twenties, loaded up everything they owned in a U-Haul trailer and drove straight to Manhattan. They checked into the Howard Johnson's Hotel on Eighth Avenue, between Fifty-second and Fifty-third Streets, installed Linda's orange tabby cat, "Dallas," in the room, and walked out to see the city.

Even at dusk the sidewalks were packed with people; the tops of the tall buildings spun around their heads like a roller coaster; taxicab horns honked out a rhythm; the sidewalks were awash in faces and feet. They found a coffee shop with a window, and they sat and gazed in absolute awe at the city. They were there.

The next day they set out on foot to hunt for a place to live. Robert picked several buildings by sight, choosing the largest, fanciest-looking places he could find.

"I don't want to live anywhere where they don't have an awning and a doorman," he said.

They were shown apartments in some of the expensive buildings where they inquired. The rents were more per month than they could afford to pay in a year.

"I believe," one rental agent said, "that you are looking considerably outside the range of what you can afford."

Some of the rental agents gave them advice about where they needed to be looking. They eventually found themselves in the Forest Hills section of Queens, with an impatient landlord standing in his T-shirt in the doorway behind them while they inspected what they could afford—a tiny one-room apartment with heavily scarred walls and an ancient all-gas "alcove" kitchen. After paying the first and last months' rent and a damage deposit, they were close to broke. They set up housekeeping with a television set on a metal folding tray, a card table, two chairs, a bed, and the cat.

Linda went to see Estelle Leibling the following Monday. Leibling was a powerful woman, then in her eighties, who lived in a beautiful apartment off Central Park just around the corner from the Plaza Hotel. She sat on a bench before a grand piano covered with an elegant silk scarf while Linda sang.

The old lady listened carefully, barely nodding her head while Linda worked her way through passages from *La Traviata*. Finally she said, "You have a beautiful voice, my dear."

"Thank you, Miss Leibling. I know that I still have much to learn."

"I will be very happy to teach you."

Linda was thrilled. "I am so honored," she said.

"Good. I will write you your own cadenza, and we will work from that."

Linda studied with Leibling for six months. The lessons gave her barely enough confidence to carry her through the round of auditions she was making in the city, none of which were going especially well.

Robert's own relationship with New York was bumpy. The men he worked with at Honeywell were sharp, tough, fast-moving, and seemed to know everything there was to know about the computer business and about selling. Robert learned a lot about computers from them, but the part he soaked up like a sponge was the selling and the dealing. That part of it—the attitude and the rhythms, the push and the shove, the patience, the coaxing, and the timing that went into closing a deal—that part was elixir to Robert. He drank it down with an unquenchable thirst.

Robert and Linda socialized in the evenings with the Honeywell people and the people with whom Robert was doing business, but not with the theater people Linda was meeting. Robert's business acquaintances in New York were hard-driving and hard-drinking. It was an eye-opening experience for a girl from Duncan, Oklahoma. In fact, it was pretty bracing for a boy from North Dallas, too. Robert had never been much of a drinker. He would much rather lie in his own bed and talk to people on the telephone than sit around a table talking person-to-person for hours on end. But as long as the core of the conversation was about business, he could make himself do it, and he expected Linda to do it with him.

"She's great," a drunk associate said one night in a bar, leering across the booth at Linda. "You got a great wife, Edelman."

"Yeah," he said. "Isn't she pretty? When I found her in Oklahoma, she was barefoot and sassy. Now she sings opera with Beverly Sills."

There were some aspects of life in New York to which Robert was absolutely impervious. On the first Monday, when he was to report for work in Manhattan, Robert walked down the staircase into a subway station in Queens, looked around, climbed back up out of the station, returned to the apartment, and told Linda to get the car and drive him to work.

"I am not going to ride with those people," he said. "Ever."

They had planned on getting rid of their car, since keeping a car garaged in New York was so horribly expensive, but it was clear from that moment on that they would be keeping the car. Every single working day from that time forward, when the rush-hour buses and cabs and limousines poured into Manhattan in the morning and out again in the evening, there in the middle of them all was little Linda DeSilva, fighting her way through traffic in order to drop her husband off for work and pick him up again at the end of the day.

It was a long grueling drive. Of all the people at Honeywell, including the very top management, Robert Edelman was the only person whose wife dropped him off and picked him up every day as if he were commuting the ten minutes that it takes to get from North Dallas to downtown Dallas. But Robert had no intention of allowing it to be any other way, and by now Linda knew not to cross him on certain matters.

New York was a hard life for both of them. Linda was accustomed to seeing her family at least every month or so, and she missed them with an aching heart. Robert talked on a Honeywell WATS line to his own mother in Dallas every day, sometimes more than once a day, often fighting with her, but he nevertheless missed being home. He was learning a lot in New York, but it was in Dallas, where he had grown up an average kid from a normal family, that Robert yearned to shine. Even if he made some kind of a hit in New York, it would never be as sweet, because there was nobody in New York he had always wanted to impress.

One night in the fall of 1970, just after Linda and Robert had come in from their daily motorcross trip from Manhattan, the phone rang. It was Linda's mother with exciting news! The DeSilvas were coming, bringing Miriam, Linda's beloved Aunt Ruth, and the family dog. They knew their girl was lonely. When Linda hung up, there were tears of joy in her eyes.

"What is it?" Robert asked warily. "Was that your mother? What did she tell you?"

"Oh Robert," she said. "I'm so happy. They're coming. In a couple of weeks they'll be here. My whole family is coming to visit us. They're even bringing the dog."

Robert had his back to her. He was looking out a window that opened on a sooty little balcony. His massive back blocked out the light from the window, so that Linda could see him only in a blackened silhouette. When he turned around to face her, his eyes were bulging, and his face was purple and knotted with veins. His mouth clenched and twitched several times before he could spit out his words.

"The hell they are" he roared at last. "What the fuck do you mean, Linda, your Goddamn parents are coming here with half of your relatives and the Goddamn dog? Did you even think to ask me about this before you told them to fucking just come right on and move in on us?"

"I didn't tell them . . ." she began to say.

Robert was moving toward her. His eyes looked as if they were about to pop out of his skull. Linda had often seen Robert angry, but she had never seen him like this. She wondered if there was something wrong, if he might be ill or in pain. He was swinging massive balled fists at his side.

"Robert," she said softly.

The blow came straight on, like a boxer's punch. It exploded into her jaw and hurled her backward. The back of her head cracked against the wall. She slid down the wall, foggy, uncomprehending at first, her face throbbing and crisscrossed by lightning bolts of pain. She collapsed on the floor and tried to call out. Saliva and blood dribbled from her mouth but the only sound she produced was an inchoate grunting.

Her jaw would not move. At first she thought he had knocked it apart somehow, that it was dislocated, broken. Horror raced deep into her soul. She thought of her voice.

Robert was kneeling in front of her. "Oh, Linda," he said. "Linda, oh my Linda. Oh my Linda, what have I done, Linda." He reached forward. She flinched away, but he took her arms firmly in his huge hands. "Oh Linda, Linda, I am so sorry. I just . . . I don't know what came over me, baby. Oh my baby, I am so sorry."

She felt as if she were no longer inside her own body. She was apart, at a distance from what was happening. It was almost as if she were standing on the other side of the room and could see herself sitting slumped on the floor with her mouth open and saliva drooling out, Robert kneeling before her, holding her elbows and speaking into her face so intensely and deliberately. In a strange way, the sense of being outside herself allowed her a measure of control and calm. She could appraise what was happening to her, as if she were a stranger who had happened onto this scene by accident. Robert kept asking her if she could close her mouth, and she kept nodding no.

"Can you get up?" he asked.

She stared at him, then pushed his hands away from her arms and lifted herself to her feet.

"Are you all right?"

She looked away dreamily, not quite able to formulate an answer. Her jaw was throbbing. It felt unhinged and thick. Her tongue lay in her mouth at an odd angle.

"A dislocated jaw," she thought. "He hit me in the face, and I have a dislocated jaw. If they can put it back in place, my face will still be whole."

"Linda," Robert said, "I am going to drive you straight to an emergency room."

As soon as they were moving in the light evening traffic, Robert began talking. "We have a lot of problems to get through, Linda. I know that. New York has been rough on both of us. It hasn't turned out to be your dream. I know that's hard for you. I know you had stars in your eyes.

"I've done okay, but I hate the life. We live like beggars. I can't stand that. It makes me feel cheap and poor. I know there has been a lot of tension building up. I feel so terrible, baby. I wish. . . . I just feel so bad about this.

"Maybe we can go home. Maybe we should just go back. The life is so much better in Dallas. I've learned a lot here. I could make this same money or better back there, and think how much farther it would go. Here, we live like peasants. Back home, we'd live like kings on this money.

"I know you counted on this a lot for your career. But maybe you're ready to face reality and see that it just wasn't in the cards for you. Maybe not. We don't have to go back. Oh, Linda. . ."

A deep wracking sob welled up out of him. He began sobbing in waves that shook his entire upper body. His face was shimmering with a solid sheet of tears. "Oh baby, I'm so sorry."

He reached over with his right hand and squeezed it around the long fingers of her left hand. She allowed his hand to stay there.

"You know, Linda," he said, snorting back the remaining tears and wiping his nose on his shoulder, "if you tell them I hit you, they will take me to jail. And I know you probably think that's just what I deserve. I probably do deserve it. But if they do that, it's just going to be that much harder to get everything straightened out.

"I will lose my job, and we'll have to pay a lawyer and everything. I don't know what will happen. We'll be screwed, that's all. Then we'll really be screwed.

"I want to work all this out. I love you more than life itself, baby. I want us to stay together and work everything out. But in order to do that, we've got to have a . . . if they even see you like this, they're going to think I popped you. They'll just leap to that assumption, you watch. And they'll ask. You know, shit, it's New York, they probably have some kind of truth squad just hovering right there in the emergency room waiting for this kind of shit.

"Linda, I think you should just tell them you were taking a shower in the bathtub, standing up, and you lost your footing and came down on the faucet."

He drove on in silence for a half block or so. She could see the neon sign of the hospital over the roof line of the next block.

"Can you do that?"

She nodded yes.

"You were taking a shower, right?"

She nodded yes.

"You reached back to get the soap. You reached back to get the soap, right, baby?"

She nodded yes.

"And you lost your footing, and I came running, and the next thing you knew you were sitting on the floor, and you couldn't close your mouth. Right?"

She nodded yes.

"It's right here. You're going to be all right, Linda. I'm going to take care of you. From now on, our lives are going to be very different. We're going to be happy again."

They were at the door. An orderly reached down and opened the passenger door of the car to help Linda out. Robert was standing outside the car next to the engine, looking across the hood at her as the orderly helped her toward the emergency room door.

"I have to go park. Are you all right? Linda? Are you going to be all right, Linda?"

There in the cabin by the lake, she could not remember anything after those words. She could see Robert saying them. Are you going to be all right, Linda? Are you going to be all right, Linda? But the scene stopped there.

Are you going to be all right?

The words ran slowly through her mind. She sat very quietly on the sofa in the house by the lake. It was very still in the house. All of a sudden she could not move. She felt her breath rise up high in her throat, and she was paralyzed by fear. She had an overwhelming sense that something was alive in the darkness on the other side of the plate-glass window.

Someone. Someone watching.

She squeezed her hands into fists and forced the fear away. The house seemed to squeeze in around her. The air felt thick and close. She ordered herself to get up and pour a glass of water. She did it.

With the glass in hand, she stood in the kitchen, staring at the pattern in the tiled floor. She reached back into her game of memories to see where she had left off.

Going back to Dallas in 1970 was a blur. Linda was rehired immediately by the Summer Musicals, and Robert went to work for the local Honeywell office.

It was a strange time in Dallas. Other parts of the country, especially the Northeast and the Great Lakes industrial region, were headed into a long, rusty economic depression. But rising prices and shortages of Arab oil had conspired with a boom in the Texas oil fields to make the economy in Dallas brilliant.

Everyone in Dallas who had anything to sell was beginning to make money. There was a sense of optimism, excitement, and even a feeling of superiority, as if the North had earned its troubles by being too soft on unions, too old, too weak.

When politicians in the North complained that Texas was taking advantage of the oil embargo to gouge on heating oil prices, the Dallas radio stations began playing a locally produced satirical song called "Freeze a Yankee." Judging by his gleeful chortles, Robert Edelman was the song's greatest fan.

One day in 1972, Robert came home from a business lunch full of excitement and ideas: one of the men at lunch had said the Dallas banks were chock full of money from the oil boom and didn't know where to invest it. Meanwhile, so many people were moving to Dallas that there was a serious housing shortage. If you walked into any one of the big banks downtown and said you wanted some money to build houses with for resale, the bankers practically kissed you on the cheek.

A week later he tried it. He came away with a bridge loan to cover the cost of a large lot in North Dallas and the construction of a new house.

Almost before he could get the house completed, it sold at a substantial profit. Robert went back to the bank for more money. He was now a real estate developer.

He did well, and quickly. Almost everyone else who was building houses in Dallas did well during that period, too, but Robert did better than many. He had a good eye for locations.

His own ambition, if he and Linda ever built a house for themselves, would be to build one in the "Park Cities"—two island enclave communities called University Park and Highland Park, totally surrounded by Dallas proper. The Park Cities area was where Dallas's old-money elite lived.

But Robert understood that the new people flooding into Dallas wanted new-new-new—brand-new houses on brand-new tree-barren streets, with new shopping centers and new schools nearby. Robert gave them what they wanted, and they bought his houses as fast as he could put them up. By late 1972, Robert had left his job as a computer salesman and now introduced himself to people as "a developer."

Linda noticed that the whininess and the crankiness seemed to be leaving Robert, at least when he was in public, supplanted by a cocksure arrogance. He took to holding his cigarettes with his forefinger and thumb, leaving his little finger crooked and aloft in a puffy little cigarette-holder style. When he didn't like what someone said to him, or when he just wanted to make the person feel uncomfortable, he stared coldly into the person's face while sucking hard on his cigarette, then blew a long stream of smoke in the person's face before speaking.

By 1974 Robert and Linda were doing very well indeed. Robert finally decided it would be all right for them to move to a house themselves. He was not ready yet for the dream house in the Park Cities, however, so he allowed Linda to take over a large house he had built on Pagewood Street in North Dallas. It was one of the first houses he had ever built that seemed, curiously enough, to be taking a while to sell.

Linda was delighted. The early darkness of her marriage seemed to be dissipating. If anything, their early years as home builders were the best they ever enjoyed. She even enjoyed her part of the home-building business.

From the beginning, Linda had been deeply involved in the business. She did all of the decorating for the houses and tried to handle all the relationships with buyers after deals had been closed.

When Robert got involved with home-buyers, the results were almost always disastrous. Even the smallest, most reasonable complaint would send Robert off into a furious rage.

Over time, Linda inherited the job of dealing with subcontractors, for the same reason she dealt with buyers. Rather than pay a contractor to run the jobs for him, Robert acted as his own contractor. Robert refused to pay the subs on time, made them beg for their money, and then picked roaring bug-eyed fights with them.

One of the subs Robert used for a long time was a hardworking, nice cowboy named Snubby Ellis. Snubby, a slender sun-baked man in his late fifties, with short red hair and glinting blue-green eyes, owned a forklift tractor, still carrying caked mud from West Texas, which he hauled around town behind a big, shiny, black, six-wheeled pickup truck with a crew cab and a bumper sticker for the annual Willie Nelson picnic in Austin.

In the manner of country Texans, Snubby would never call Robert by his first name. Since he worked for him, he always insisted on calling him "Mr. Edelman" or "Boss."

Robert had hired Snubby to do the roofing on several of the houses he had built. He had paid him for the first job, but he had not paid him for the next three jobs. When Snubby finally pressed him for the money, Robert went through his routine with the long cold look and the cigarette smoke and then said, "I don't think so."

"You owe me the money, Mr. Edelman."

"Oh yeah? Do I?"

"Yes, sir. You know you do."

"Oh. So you're telling me what I know."

"No, sir. I'm just telling you what you owe me."

"Well, let me tell you something. Fuck you. Get a fucking lawyer. I'm not paying you a fucking cent. Now get the fuck off my job site."

That night, Robert pulled his new white Porsche up into the long curving driveway of the house on Pagewood. Only when he was already most of the way up the driveway did he notice the big crew-cab pickup parked at the top of the driveway. As Robert got out of the Porsche, Snubby Ellis climbed down out of the pickup.

"Hey," Robert said in a high-pitched angry voice. "Just get the fuck out of here, you idiot, before I call the police."

Snubby was walking toward Robert through deep shadows. Robert saw something gleaming in his hand. As Snubby came out of the shadows, Robert realized Snubby was holding a gun straight out at the end of one fully extended arm, pointing it right at Robert's head. Robert heard a click.

"What are you doing, Snub?"

"That's the safety comin' off, asshole."

Snubby's speech was slurred, and his gait was lurching. As soon as he came close to Robert, Robert could smell whiskey on his breath.

"Son of a bitch, Snubby, put that Goddamned thing away."

Snubby gritted his teeth and shoved the blue barrel of a .38 caliber revolver up under Robert's nose. "Write me a check for what you owe me, asshole, or I'm just liable to blow your damned face off."

Snubby was of average height. Robert stood more than a head taller. Snubby had to hold the gun up high to get it right in Robert's face. As Robert stared down the barrel of the gun, his head began pouring sheets of glistening sweat. "Look, Snubby, my checks are in the house."

"Then I guess we'll just go in the damned house."

Robert led the way up the curving sandstone staircase and along the long walk to the front porch. Snubby followed with the gun shoved in Robert's back. Robert opened the door with his key, and Snubby followed him in through the foyer and down the long hallway to the office at the back of the house. Robert could hear Snubby behind him, scraping against the walls as he staggered along through the thick pile carpeting in his muddy cowboy boots.

As Robert flipped through the pages of the large black ring-binder that held the checks, his hands were shaking badly.

"You owe me eleven thousand dollars," Snubby said behind him.

Robert scratched out the check. He fumbled for a long time, trying to tear the check out of the book. He turned and handed it to Snubby, who held it close to his eyes and squinted at the lettering, breathing thickly while he tried to decipher the check. As he read the check, Snubby held the revolver extended in one hand, allowing it to waver around slightly in Robert's face. Robert's eyes were fixed so intently on the end of the barrel that his head rotated unconsciously with the motion of the gun.

"All right," Snubby said, stuffing the check into the pocket of his blue-jean jacket. "Now don't even think about canceling this check or going to the police, asshole." He pushed the gun forward so that the cold steel tip of the barrel grazed Robert's upper lip. "If you do, I will come back here, and I will definitely kill your ass dead."

Snubby turned his back on Robert and walked toward the door. "Thank you, sir, I can show myself out."

Robert watched him leave.

Years later, alone in the woods in the house by the lake, Linda could still see Robert's face clearly as he recounted to her what had transpired, sitting on the edge of the bed transfixed, his face white as a sheet, still bathed in sweat, his hands trembling slightly. She remembered seeing first that he had been badly frightened. But she remembered wondering if there were something else in his face, beyond the fear—a wide-eyed new awareness. It was almost as if Robert Edelman had experienced a religious vision.

Now, here in this black and empty house, frozen with fear every time leaves rustled outside or a clock ticked too loudly, she remembered Robert's eyes in that moment. They were huge and white and shiny. The memory of his eyes made her feel sick in the stomach.

She remembered the gun. The day after the Snubby incident Robert bought the Uzi machine gun. He showed it to her and told her how expensive it was.

But it was an ugly weapon. Linda had been around guns all her life—the proudly crafted guns men and women in the west used for hunting, with burnished wood stocks and beautifully engraved barrels.

This gun, this Uzi, was incredibly ugly, by contrast. It was an awkward, spiny, graceless thing, like a chunk of dirty steel that had fallen off an oil rig. It clearly was not made for hunting, but for massacring human beings.

Sitting here by the lake, she remembered watching Robert sit for hours on their bed on Pagewood, staring at the Uzi with those gibbous white eyes and fingering it.

An image of flesh flying apart and blood spouting from holes forced its way into her mind. She put the back of her hand to her lips and bit back tears. She remembered the lady Robert had tortured on the telephone.

Good Earth Development had sold a house the year before to a wealthy, socially prominent couple who were basically happy with their new home but had small complaints. When they tried to talk to Robert, his arrogant, dismissive attitude especially infuriated the wife, who began spreading the news through the Jewish community that Robert Edelman not only was unscrupulous, but was also a crude and vile person.

When word came back to Robert that the woman was saying bad things about him, he became obsessed. He lay on the bed late at night in his underpants, undershirt, and knee-high socks, smoking cigarettes, watching TV, and muttering to himself almost in a whisper about "that fucking bitch."

Linda lay next to him.

Robert would reach over finally, pick up the phone, and dial the woman's number. If her husband answered, he hung up. But the husband traveled, and the wife was often home alone. If the wife answered, Robert would hold the phone against his lip and breathe heavily into it.

The woman was a perfect target for this kind of torture. She never just hung up. She always wound up screaming and crying into the telephone: "I know it's you, Edelman, you bastard! Stop it! Will you just stop it."

A slow grin would come over Robert's face when the woman began screaming. Linda watched him.

It was an awful expression.

"Robert," Linda said after he finally hung up, "what you are doing is wrong. You have got to stop tormenting that poor woman."

He turned his face to her and said, "Shut up, Linda. Mind your own Goddamned business."

Then one night the doorbell rang twenty minutes after Robert had concluded one of his breathing calls to the woman.

Robert jumped up eagerly when the bell rang, perhaps thinking it was the woman's husband or maybe even the woman herself. He threw a silk bathrobe over his underwear and strode to the door with his cigarette held out in the little fancy-pants, two-fingered gesture that had become his trademark.

But when he opened the door, Robert's pose evaporated. His shoulders sank and his cigarette hand fell to his side. Standing framed in the overhead light outside were two uniformed Dallas police officers.

"Robert Edelman?"

"Yes."

"Would you step out here, sir."

"Why?"

"You are under arrest, Mr. Edelman, for making a terroristic threat by telephone."

They drove off with him handcuffed in the back seat of the squad car. One of his lawyer friends had him out of jail within four hours. The next day the woman he had been calling rushed down to the prosecutor's office in a panic, said she was afraid of Robert Edelman and declared in no uncertain terms that she would not press charges and would not cooperate with any prosecution. No official record of the incident was made, but a slim folder went into the district attorney's files with the heading, "Edelman, Robert Marc."

In the late 1970s and early 1980s, the television dramatic serial "Dallas" became extremely popular in the United States and all over the world. The show made Dallas an international symbol of free-wheeling, no-holds-barred, gut-level capitalism, warts and all. Almost anywhere in the world where Dallasites might travel, people asked them about J. R. and Sue Ellen, the show's main characters, and would express great curiosity about the real city of Dallas.

In Dallas, people had always striven to dress like New Yorkers, considering cowboy hats and boots to be the uniforms of hicks and rednecks. But when Dallas saw that the world loved the cowboy hats and boots on the TV show and thought of the whole western look as exotic and intriguing, people in the real Dallas started dressing the part.

It was a strange process. In its rendering of the city as a center of callous materialism, the TV show had not been a half-bad reflection of the truth. Then, as Dallas saw how much the world liked the show and began imitating it, the real city grew even closer to the program.

In the meantime, equally strange things were happening in the Dallas economy. The solid, job-creating, home-buying growth in the economy had begun tapering off by the late 1970s. There were hundreds of homes still to be built and lots of new companies moving in every month, but the rate of real growth had begun to fall from what it had been at the very crest, when Robert and Linda had been making money faster than they could count it.

There was still a great deal of hype around the city, because of the TV show in part, but also because Dallas had become accustomed to hyping itself. If anything, Dallas now had an image to live up to in the world. Elsewhere people may have taken the show for a silly soap opera and a kind of elaborate send-up, but Dallas always took the J. R. business very seriously.

The problem, as the solid underpinnings of the 1970s boom began to ebb, was finding the money to keep all of this image and fanfare going. The demand for housing was already falling, and the serious people in the office tower end of the real estate business saw that Dallas already had more new office tower space than it could ever use. The bankers with any sense began folding their tents, and all of a sudden the solid money just wasn't there any more.

But Dallas was a peculiar city. There were many people in the real estate business in Dallas who could not stand to stop playing, who did not know any other games, and who adamantly did not want to leave Dallas. In order for them to stay in Dallas and keep playing real estate, they had to find a new source of investment capital, and since it could not be serious money anymore, it was going to have to be funny money.

Fortunately for Dallas, a large supply of just that commodity was suddenly available in the form of huge deposits from shady savings and loan operations. The savings and loan scam, made possible by some very convenient laws passed by some very friendly congressmen, had an incredible effect on Dallas. Instead of slowing down naturally, the local economy took off on another bubble.

Dallas was like a drunk who had just discovered cocaine. Office towers flew up skyward in places that were not even near roads, let alone near any possible kind of traffic or demand. But even that was too slow a game for the real gamblers, who took the funny money from the S&Ls and put it into "land-flipping"—selling raw land back and forth to each other.

The land-flippers tended to describe their game as a form of guts poker, but it was really more like Old Maid. They kited property back and forth between each other at inflated values, each one hoping he wouldn't be the last to buy.

Linda was only peripherally aware of Robert's business practices at the time. Robert made the big switch from residential to commercial real estate in 1978 and 1979. By then he was working from a lavish office in one of his own buildings, with a staff of lackeys to do his bidding. The change from residential meant that the clients and investors who were mad at him were now too big-time to bother harassing his wife over their problems.

But Robert was also becoming big-time enough that his business exploits were beginning to make the newspapers. One of his first major go-rounds with the local press was unpleasant and left him in a rage.

His first major commercial building—a high-rise condominium called The Embassy—was in trouble almost from the moment it was completed. Robert, it seemed, had earned himself an unwanted footnote in local history. He had invented a phenomenon that later would become much more common in Dallas but was then absolutely unheard of—a brand-new high-rise that would never, ever have a single tenant.

It happened with spec houses, of course. Once in a while, the house was too far out in the mesquite or too deep into a bad neighborhood; it was too ugly or too badly built, and no one ever moved in. Eventually some spec houses had to be bulldozed without ever having been occupied.

But it had never happened with a 10-story 100,000-square-foot building before. At least not in Dallas. After The Embassy had stood vacant for more than four years, the *Dallas Times Herald* ran a story ridiculing it. The story said one neighbor had found "a practical use for the building."

"It makes a good landmark," the neighbor said. "It's the first thing I see when I walk out my back door."

Later, when many office towers were completed in Dallas only to stand empty, the reasons were obvious. By then the economy had gone to hell; the bottom had fallen right out of the real estate market; and there were far too many new buildings in town anyway. But when The Embassy opened, it was still early enough in the game that Robert should have been able to land at least a few tenants for it.

The real problem was elsewhere. As in almost every major new commercial development, the city building inspectors had found a number of things they wanted changed. Nothing major. The usual nit-picking things a normal developer would take for granted. But not Robert Edelman.

Rather than fix what was wrong and get on with it, Robert dug in his heels and became more obstinate at every meeting. By the time he might have been willing to make a few concessions, it was already too late. There was no interest in the building.

In a story in *D*, the local city magazine, an unnamed "prominent Dallas builder" was quoted as saying The Embassy was never occupied because of Robert's personality. "That building didn't get a certificate of occupancy because of the asshole factor," the builder said. "It was ninety percent code problems and ten percent asshole problems."

After The Embassy and before the bottom fell out, Robert did receive rave reviews for one of his developments—a major office project on Maple Avenue, replacing a seedy row of bars that had once included Jack Ruby's place. The architecture was odd for Dallas but hardly inventive: it was a duplication of early nineteenth-century commercial architecture in Paris. It was also quite similar to a huge new office and hotel complex right across the street that had just been built by the heirs to the H. L. Hunt oil fortune—people with whom Robert dearly wanted to curry favor.

Robert, the Oklahoma University dropout, stood over an architectural model of the project, posing with his cigarette like FDR, and told a newspaper reporter: "We are trying to make the project blend into the area. We didn't want something that would just be faddish today. When you do a building classically, that's what you get."

It was 1984—the year in which Robert was the biggest deal he would ever be. The embarrassment of The Embassy was behind him. The project on Maple Avenue was a critical success, even if the rental contracts seemed to be coming in a bit slowly.

Robert announced to Linda that it was time for the big move to the Park Cities. He bought a large lot on Caruth—one of the best streets in one of the best sections of the Park Cities—and erected a 7,300-foot brick mansion on it.

In terms of personal style, Robert controlled the front of the house—a sweeping Georgian facade, opening into a lavish foyer and swirling Hollywood staircase.

There was a lot that Robert did not know about style. Linda had collected a roomful of beautiful nineteenth and early twentieth-century wicker furniture, all artfully restored, but Robert made her keep them on the partially finished third floor because he thought they looked "cheap."

The third floor of the huge new home, in fact, became her hideaway, even though Robert steadfastly refused to finish flooring it or put in air conditioning and heat. Where there was finished wall, she put up Laura Ashley wallpaper. She arranged her wicker the way she liked it and spent quiet happy hours up there alone, wrapping gifts, working on holiday decorations for the house, being by herself.

Robert insisted on grand furniture for the public rooms at the front of the house on the first floor, but the rest of the house was Linda's work, designed mainly around family and children, with a huge kitchen and adjoining informal dining and family area, enormous playrooms upstairs and down, and the best bedrooms in the house reserved for the children.

Linda sat forward on the sofa at the front of the house in the woods, near the window, and listened. She heard the eggbeater noise of a motorboat again, out on the lake. She looked at her watch. It was barely 7:30 in the morning. The lake was smooth and quiet. The sound was coming closer. It was definitely coming in from the distance, closing on the place where she was. She felt her stomach constrict. She listened and stared at the lake with a terrible electric clarity. Now it was almost a familiar feeling— the ferocious panic that comes when one senses the presence of one's killer.

CHAPTER TWO

The feeling had visited her off and on all day and night, every day for more than a week now. As she had done every other time when the feeling came, she thought of the children, and, when she did, the panic stopped whirling; her mind stopped screaming; and she gathered herself around an inner core of anger.

He wanted her, the children's mother, shot dead. He had ordered their mother and their grandmother and grandfather shot down dead in front of his own kids—in the middle of Disney World.

He said he loved them. Maybe he believed he loved them. But he was wrong. He was evil. He could not love children. He could not be a father to children. She would not let him kill her, kill their mother.

Linda got up and began moving around the house. The last person she had seen was Ike, her lawyer, and he had taken the only gun in the house when he left. Ike and the FBI had insisted she would not need a gun there in the house, where she would be protected. But what if they were wrong? There was nothing she could do except run through the woods and hope to make it to one of the houses Ike had told her were out there somewhere, out of view in the woods. She stopped moving and listened. She was at the back of the house, away from the lake. The motorboat sound was gone.

Linda moved back slowly toward the front of the house, stepping silently and gingerly on her dancer's legs, ready to spring cat-like toward the back door again. She tried to make her breathing even. There was nothing, nothing in the house, nothing on the lake. She stared and listened, standing by the window. Nothing. Perhaps it had been another fishing boat, moving to try its luck at a new hole. She sat down slowly on the sofa and continued to listen. A tiny voice whispered a song over and over in her mind: "His eye is on the sparrow, and I know he watches me."

It came and it went. When the death-fear came, she thought of the children again. And every time the death-fear passed, she thought of the question. Why had she stayed with Robert?

When she had to go back and tell the family that she was leaving him, her parents and her sister, her aunts and most of her uncles and cousins had rallied to her support immediately. None of them had ever said it to her before, but they had come to fear and detest Robert and to fear for Linda's safety over the years. They hadn't said it before, because in their culture and according to their family values, there were limits to the degree to which one pried into the very personal affairs of another adult family member who did not seem to invite prying.

Maybe they should have pried anyway. Certainly according to the values of the 1980s and popular psychology, they should have confronted Linda with their fears. But they didn't have the values of popular psychology; they were solid, conservative, religious people of the American west, of pioneer stock and small towns. Linda had made it clear to all of them over the almost twenty years of her marriage to Robert that she was handling her own affairs and did not need help. With people of their type, that was where it had to rest, until Linda herself came back to her own flesh and blood for help.

She knew all of that, of course. She had been over it a thousand times in the last week. The hard question was not why the family had kept its silence. The hard question was why she, Linda, had stayed with Robert.

Was it the money? She had never really pressed herself on that question before. But on this night, alone in this place and with what might be only hours left to live, she did.

The money had not hurt, she decided. And after Robert had really hit it big, there was plenty of it around. It was funny about Robert: he cared so much about money, and yet it was the one area in which he could be generous. If anything, he splashed the stuff around as if it were water.

There were trips to the couture salons at Neiman-Marcus that left major craters in the checking account. Robert poured in however much money it took to fill the accounts back up.

When Linda was furnishing the Caruth house, there were days when the backed-up delivery trucks from expensive stores looked like an Arab trading caravan. Linda wrote the checks, and Robert made them good.

Then the children came. Stephen was born on November 5, 1979, at Presbyterian Hospital in Dallas. Little Kathleen arrived on November 20, 1981.

Through it all, Stephen had always been so bright, so tough. Linda smiled when she thought about Kathleen—beautiful, charming Kathleen. The littlest survivor. Kathleen would always find her way. Linda was not so certain about Stephen. Stephen's immediate instinctive response to trouble was to pitch himself straight at it. Stephen was probably the only person in Robert's life who talked back to him. But not Kathleen. She had other less dangerous ways to get her way.

Linda sat on the sofa with her head down, smiling a tiny smile for Kathleen. But the smile fell away, and her mouth began to go numb. She stared down at her knees, and a familiar dread began to grow at the pit of her stomach.

She wanted to believe she stayed with him because of the children, because people in her family did not get divorces, because she wanted her children to have a father. Perhaps that was part of it. Certainly it was part of it.

But, as she had on the other occasions when she had asked herself this same question, she began to sink into depression. She fought it. Here, alone in this death house on the edge of a black nameless lake, the depression was even more of a threat, looming up bigger and darker on the horizon than it had ever been before.

With her head dropped and her eyes unfocused, she heard the words he used to say to her. "You are zero. You are not even a person. You are a waste of space."

She lifted her face up and looked around. Now there was no space at all. It was as if she was standing at the very edge of the very top of a very tall building, and Robert was next to her, staring with those round, watery white eyes, breathing and pushing. Pushing. For an instant she wondered if it was wrong to resist so long.

She wiped tears away. The children were important, she decided. But they were far from the whole story.

Robert was not utterly indifferent to the children. There were even times when he seemed passionately drawn to them. But his feelings for them were like his feelings for everything else. He had no idea what was appropriate, what was in bounds and what was out.

Later during the divorce case, when the parents traded weeks having the children and the absent parent spoke to the children by a court-ordered schedule of phone calls, his calls were always tortures for the children, especially for Stephen. Robert always devoted the first portion of each call to grilling the children about who was present in the house with them and what their mother had been doing.

"What do you have to report, Bubber?" Robert asked.

Stephen, at seven years of age, was wise to his father's tricks. "What do you mean, report? Report what?"

"Anything. What you've been doing. Who's there? Are your grandma and grandpa still there?"

"Yeah."

"Both of them?"

"Yes. No. Only one."

"Which is it, Stephen? Are they both there?"

"Yes. How come you always ask me if my grandma and grandpa are still here?"

"Oh, I just think it's odd that they stay there so much."

"Oh, I'm telling."

"You can tell. Anything you want to."

"When the divorce is over, they're not going to stay as much."

"Oh, they're not? Why is that?"

"I don't know."

Robert cackled into the phone. Linda heard it. She always listened on the extension. Now, alone in the lake house, the memory of his cackling laughter made her shiver, because now she knew what he knew when he made that phone call. By then, Robert knew that Stephen's mother, grandmother, and grandfather were to be killed.

"What's so funny, Dad?" Stephen had asked.

"Oh I just think it's funny. The whole thing's ridiculous."

After Robert had become more open about dating, the children especially dreaded the weeks when they had to go live with him. Robert seemed to enjoy flaunting his sexual conquests in front of the children. He teased Stephen unmercifully about Stephen's nervousness concerning his father's sexual relationship with other women.

One night when Robert made his call to Stephen, he asked Stephen several times what he had done that day. Stephen answered the question several times, only to have his father repeat it a few seconds later, as if he had never asked it before. It was plain his father was preoccupied. Then in the background, seven-year-old Stephen heard the sounds that meant Robert and a friend were making love while Robert spoke to his son on the telephone.

Stephen said: "Who's going, 'Okay,' in there?"

"The TV was on," Robert said.

"Any kissing?"

"Not really. Yeah, I've been doing some kissing. Gross, eh?"

"Gross? You do it all the time."

"So do you."

"I do not." Stephen tried to laugh it off at first. He hated to let his father get his goat.

"You do, too," Robert said.

"I do not." The more Robert said it, the more high-pitched and nervous Stephen's denials became.

"All the time, you do it all the time," Robert said.

"Sure I do."

"You do, too. All the time."

"No I don't. Not any time."

"Mmm mmm mmm. You're always kissing. On the lips."

"I am not!" Stephen shouted.

"You do all the time," Robert said, cackling.

"It's not funny," Stephen said, on the verge of tears. "I do not!"

"Okay, I won't tell."

"I can't hear you."

"I won't tell. I love you, Stephen."

"I can't hear you."

The weeks when the children had to go and live with Robert were especially difficult for Stephen. Free from Linda's interference, Robert was able to behave exactly as he wanted. He spared Stephen nothing.

Stephen lashed out in odd, impulsive ways. One Saturday evening, when Robert was standing by the swimming pool at Pagewood in his tuxedo, waiting for a date to dress so they could go out to dinner, Stephen walked up behind him and pushed him into the pool.

He paid dearly for such pranks. Robert dragged him screaming into his bedroom. Kathleen ran to the locked door and stood outside, saying over and over again in a loud, theatrically sweet voice, "You don't have to hit him, Daddy."

Robert yanked the frail little boy to the back of the room by one arm.

"Why did you do that, you little shit? You fucking little prick!"

"Because I hate your guts, and I hope Mama gets us."

Robert swung as hard as he could with his fist and hit the boy full in the stomach, knocking him back halfway across the room, where he lay in a heap, holding his stomach with both hands, breathing through his teeth and refusing to cry. Robert came across the room as if to kick him, and the boy forced himself to his feet. Robert unlocked the door, yanked it open, grabbed Stephen by one hand, and swung him out of the room hard, so that he hit the wall of the hallway and fell to the floor again.

When the door closed, Kathleen reached down and took Stephen's hand to help him to his feet. "Come, Stephen," she said. "It's time for us to be getting our jammies on."

After the divorce had been cranking along for more than a year and after several hundred thousand dollars already had been spent, the Edelman case became the hottest game in town for people in the divorce business—the lawyers, the judges, child psychologists, private detectives, and all the other players in the industry of marital breakup. Even for those who were not immediately involved in the Edelman divorce, it was the show to watch, the Big Top.

At one point the judge decided to use it as a showcase for his new experimental theory on how to handle child custody during the period after a divorce has been filed and before the matter of custody has been permanently settled. It was an approach that was narrowly tailored toward North Dallas and Park Cities cases, since it depended on each parent owning his or her own nice home near the children's school. The judge called it "house-swapping."

The theory was based on the plausible notion that the children should not have to shuttle back and forth between houses when it was their parents who could not muster an agreement. According to this plan, the parents were required to trade houses every ten days, so that the children could stay in the same house.

It was a commonsense idea that turned out to be disastrous when put into practice. Whether the parents like it or not, the children of divorce always rely on and prefer one parent over the other. The overwhelming choice of Stephen and Kathleen was their mother.

Robert was living in the house on Pagewood, which had never sold. Linda had the Caruth house. The judge wanted the children to remain at Caruth, and he wanted Robert and Linda to take turns living there with them. It meant the children had to watch their mother leave home on a weekly basis.

Merriellen Lehner, who lived two doors down Caruth from Robert and Linda's house, had been warned by her husband, an anesthesiologist, not to get involved in the Edelman divorce. Stephen and Kathleen played with the Lehner kids all the time, and according to Dr. Lehner that was close enough.

That was how most people in the neighborhood felt. By then the word was definitely out on Robert. He was cutting a swath in the Dallas business community. The people who lived near him in his own neighborhood knew he was a potentially dangerous man when angered. None of them wanted to volunteer for a tangle with him.

But Merriellen did not heed her husband's well-meaning advice. On the first day Linda was to move out, in order to begin the house-swapping arrangement, Merriellen came over to the house to ask Linda a casual question. She had no idea the house-swapping plan had even been ordered.

Merriellen let herself in through the back door, as was her habit. Rezilla Williams, the black woman who had been Linda's maid since Pagewood, was standing in the huge family room off the kitchen.

"Hello, Zsa," Merriellen said, using the family name Stephen had invented for her when he was too young to pronounce *Rezilla*.

Rezilla said, "Linda's got to move out today, you know, Miz Lehner. That judge told her she's got to move out of her own house and let that man come in here and live with the children every other week. She's up there trying to quieten that poor little boy. Why don't you go on up there?"

Merriellen bounded up the huge staircase as if she had springs in her legs. On the surface, Merriellen was a typical Park Cities woman— pretty enough to be ornamental, smart enough to talk at parties. But just beneath that surface, she was a blunt-spoken former nurse with an extremely high energy level and a down-home Texas lack of pretension. Her own house was huge, too, by normal American standards, although not as big as Linda's. Something about Linda's house always tried Merriellen's patience. It made her mad to get lost in it.

"Linda, where are you?" she bellowed from the top of the stairs.

There was no answer. She walked tentatively toward Stephen's room at the front of the house, tried the door, and pushed it open. It was empty. She turned, walked down the hallway, turned again down another hall and came to the door of Linda's bedroom. She knocked. There was no answer. She pushed it open.

The room was empty, but she thought she heard something—a hacking rasping sound in the distance.

"Linda! Are you in here?"

There was no answer. She walked through the room and down another short hallway to a huge bathroom and dressing room area. There, seated on an overstuffed chair, was Linda, with Stephen in her lap, his skinny little-boy legs splayed out across her knees. She was holding him, rocking him, and kissing his head, while the little boy sobbed convulsively, his entire body shaking with sobs. He made a terrible noise as he cried—a gut-wrenching noise that came up from the very bottom of a little boy's soul.

Five-year-old Kathleen sat nearby, silently playing with a toy on the floor, murmuring a monotone little-girl song to herself, as if nothing in the world were wrong.

Linda looked up, her face bathed in tears.

"Oh my God, Linda," Merriellen said. "Rezilla just told me. Do you have to do this?"

Linda nodded. "Every ten days."

From that moment on, Merriellen could not stop thinking about what was going on down the street from her. She loved Linda as a dear friend. They had hit it off almost immediately upon meeting. But Linda was an adult, responsible for the handling of her own affairs.

It was the children. It was seeing them that way, little Stephen sobbing as if he really would die, and baby Kathleen, woven deep into her own little cocoon. Merriellen could not put that sight out of her mind.

Linda never stayed in the house Robert was occupying on Pagewood. She took a suite at a nearby Holiday Inn, from which she made her pitiful court-allowed phone calls to the children.

One week she left a brush at the Holiday Inn on the day they all moved back to Caruth. The motel called her and said they would hold it. That afternoon, while she was driving Stephen to a T-Ball practice, she swung by the hotel to pick it up.

"Is this where you stay when you leave us?" he asked.

"Yes."

He made her sit on the parking lot for fifteen minutes while he stared at the Holiday Inn. Finally he muttered, "I want to be able to see it in my mind when you're away."

Whenever she returned to Caruth, she found that Robert had left her a huge mess, especially in the bathroom.On some occasions, when it was Robert's turn to take over the house on Caruth, he brought a date with him. The court had ordered Robert to stay out of Linda's bedroom and dressing room while he was in the house, and Linda had installed new locks on the doors of these rooms. But the week after she had installed the new locks, she returned to the house to find her dressing room a shambles and several of her most expensive dresses and jackets stolen. On the floor was a wisp of insulating material from the attic. Robert, who had built the house and still had the drawings, had climbed through an unfinished area in the attic and had let himself down through a trap door in the dressing room ceiling.

Every week after that, some small thing would be missing from her room or amiss, moved and put down in another position—just enough to let her know he had been back in the room and could return whenever he felt like it.

Eventually, the judge relented. The lawyers on both sides were able to persuade him that parental house-swapping was a good idea in the abstract but a bad plan in reality. Even after she no longer had to move out of Caruth every other week, and after Robert had been barred from even driving down the street, let alone entering the house, she continued to find things moved. They were things just small enough, moved so subtly, that she never could be quite sure.

Linda let herself out through the French doors of the lake house and walked down toward the water's edge. The water was beginning to ripple with the morning's first breeze. There was a white iron bench beneath a willow by the water. She sat on it and looked out at the lake. She wondered what the name of the lake was. It looked huge. The far shore was a barely visible green line on the horizon. She judged they had driven between one and a half to two hours from Dallas to get here.

She was obviously somewhere in East Texas. It was green and there were small oaks and a few stands of pine around the house. If they had driven this far west from Dallas, the land would be arid and dotted with prickly pear cactus.

She never knew she would end up here. She never foresaw this. But she did know at some point how dangerous Robert was. She tried to convince people, but at first no one would take her seriously.

Robert told everyone she was a ditsy little country girl from Oklahoma, with a head full of musical comedy and Disney. Dallas listened to him. In the period from the late 1970s to the mid-1980s, Robert was at the height of his power. He was in the perfect place at the perfect time for Robert Edelman. He was everything Dallas admired.

It was true that no one really wanted to get personally involved in his life. It was not possible to find anyone outside his immediate family who would profess to actually liking Robert Edelman, with the exception of people who were actively making money from him.

In spite of all that, he was admired. He was rich. He had made it himself. He had all the right pretensions to class and cultivation. He was the real-life incarnation of J. R. Ewing—the protagonist of the television melodrama about Dallas. He was what a Dallas man was meant to be. And, as a woman in Dallas, Linda was supposed to be respectful and supportive of her man.

But somewhere there had been a moment when all of the expectations and all of Robert's advantages should no longer have counted. Somewhere, in the fabric of time that bound their marriage to this moment, there was a break.

She was here, and he or someone he had hired might be right out there in the woods, with the Uzi, with some other weapon, just on the very verge of bursting in. The flying flesh and the spouting blood could be hers at any moment. Surely there had been some moment when she could have seen this coming. Surely there was some time and place when she could have escaped, even if it was too late now.

She sat forward on the bench and concentrated on the ripples on the surface of the lake. She had to force herself to find the moment. Maybe it would appear and open into a window. Maybe she could still flee through that moment, flee into the lake and wash herself of this awful stink of fear.

She sat forward on the bench and concentrated on the ripples on the surface of the lake. She knew there was a moment. There was some moment when she had seen it in his eye. She had to force herself to find it.

It was in 1985, after Robert's business had started collapsing but before she had left him and filed for divorce. Dallas was going down in flames. All of the funny money from the S&Ls was starting to stink. The banks and the savings and loans were on the line for huge loans they made on what was rapidly becoming worthless collateral. There was no real-life market for the junk the money had been used to build. Everybody wanted his money out fast, before the bust, and Robert was one of the people from whom they wanted it.

He had grown uglier and more tense as the year progressed. By early April he was explosive and unapproachable. The slightest thing—a single word in what he took for the wrong tone of voice—would send him into a rage.

Between the rages, there were moments when even he seemed to realize that something would have to be done about their deteriorating marriage. One morning, Robert came looking for her in their bathroom—a very odd room that Robert had designed himself. It was huge. In the very center was a gigantic glass-enclosed tub and shower. On either side, facing each other through the glass walls of the shower, were exactly matching toilets, next to exactly matching sink-cabinets and towel racks. Each side was a mirror image of the other, so that a stranger to the room, standing on one side and looking across, might even think he was looking at a mirror image on the far wall of the shower stall.

"Linda!" he shouted.

"I'm here," she said, from her dressing room. She was sitting at her vanity, putting on makeup.

He stepped through the door and stood behind her.

"Linda," he said, towering behind her, "I want us to talk to somebody. You remember Rabbi Green, the guy who used to be at temple that I liked so much? He's going to be back in town this week. I think we should see if he could talk to us about our problems. Everybody thinks he's great. Maybe he can help us."

She didn't know exactly how to respond at first. Rabbi Green was a social figure in Dallas—just the kind of person Robert always wanted to impress.

She had met Rabbi Green and liked him. He seemed like the kind of man who really might be able to help them. This gesture was an amazing change from Robert's black mood of the past several months. She was just on the verge of summoning the courage to tell Robert she wanted a divorce, and now here he was with this offer of conciliation.

She had to see it through.

She waited two days, until Thursday, for the meeting with Rabbi Green to take place. Robert was distant and very quiet during that time. He never told her exactly when on Thursday they were to meet. It was not his habit to provide Linda with specific times for things: He expected her to be more or less on call.

Robert came back into the house Thursday morning at about 11 o'clock. Linda was standing in the kitchen, talking to Zsa. As he walked through, Robert told Linda they were meeting Rabbi Green for lunch.

"Dress up," he said. He disappeared up the spiral staircase.

Linda followed him up the stairs.

"Robert. Robert! I want to talk to you."

She heard the door to their bedroom slam in the distance. She walked up the stairs quickly, walked through the room, and found Robert taking off his coat in the bathroom.

"Robert, what do you mean, 'Dress up?'"

"I mean dress up, Linda. As in wear something nice."

The sharp-tongued, brooding mood was back upon him full force. "You do have a few of the nice things left that I bought you, I hope."

Linda stood in the door of the bathroom looking at him for a moment. "Robert, why do I have to dress up? Where are we going?"

"We're going to lunch, Linda, like I just finished telling you."

"Where are we going to lunch?"

"At the Goddamn City Club, Linda! What fucking difference does it make to you where we go to lunch?"

All of a sudden she was angry. The City Club was one of Dallas's premier power-lunch places, where everyone went to see and be seen. It was part of Robert's little heaven—a half-floor at the top of the tallest skyscraper downtown, with an army of elderly black male waiters at one's elbow and an unbroken view beyond of hundreds of miles of flat brown prairie. At one side of the dining room was a fake-ornate bar that women were not allowed to enter. It was almost de rigeur for the male members of the club to leave their women sitting on leather sofas outside the bar for twenty minutes or so, while they took a drink together before lunch.

The dining room was one big open area with a low ceiling and wooden floors. It had terrible acoustics, so that one could pick up snatches of conversation from tables at the far side of the room, which is exactly what everyone spent his time doing.

"Robert, I am not going to go open my heart at the City Club."

He stalked across the room and thrust his huge face down into her face. "Then don't spill your fucking guts, Linda! I doubt he's really going to be all that fascinated by what you have to say, anyway. But I have reservations at the City Club, and you and I are meeting Rabbi Green there in half an hour, so get ready."

The veins were beginning to show on his neck and face, and his eyes were starting to bulge. A shiver of fear ran through Linda. But the more she looked at him, the angrier she became. She was sure that, through all of that bug-eyed posturing, Robert was studying her. He never took his eyes off her. He seemed to measure every little quake and tremor she showed in her face, as if he were standing somewhere behind the grotesque mask of his angry face, coolly calculating his effect.

"Robert, you go meet him for lunch. I am not going. You bring him back with you to the house if you want. We have a big library right downstairs, we can pull the doors closed, no one can hear what goes on inside, and we can talk things out there with him. But I'm not going to the City Club with you today."

Robert backed away two paces and held his hands out next to his head. "Linda, you bitch! Why do you insist on pulling this shit on me?"

His face darkened another shade of purple, and his eyes were beginning to look as if they might pop out of his skull. He opened his mouth and emitted the first few syllables of a sound somewhere between a moan and a roar.

She had not heard the sound in the last year. It was the savage, blood-curdling scream that Robert made just as he went over the top, just before he gave way completely to his wild smashing rage. Linda drew back involuntarily and brought her hands up before her breasts. She was shaking slightly. But she looked at him, and behind the roar and the wild bloodshot eyes she still saw some part of him back there coolly taking her measure.

He reached out with one hand, grabbed her shoulder and threw her up against the door jamb. He pulled his hands back and stood shaking his head and breathing heavily. "Put your fucking clothes on, Linda. We are meeting Rabbi Green at the City Club."

She was shaking badly now. She unconsciously raised her forearms before her face as she spoke. "Robert," she said softly, "I am not going to the . . . to the City Club with you."

He dropped his huge knotted fists down level with his hips, threw his chin up and emitted a long screaming roar, in a voice that was deep and falsetto at the same time, like two voices shrieking together. The fingers flew open from the hands. The hands flew up.

Linda backed away from him quickly, stumbling slightly on the carpeting in the dressing room. When she reached the bedroom, she was just on the verge of turning to run.

But the hands shot forward. He clutched her neck, squeezing both hands in slowly but relentlessly, squeezing her neck smaller and smaller in the closing ring of his hand, so that the flesh of her neck above and below his hands bulged out around his fingers. As he squeezed, the capillaries in her skin began shattering, and her neck turned black in his hands.

Linda's feet went out from under her, so that the only thing holding her up was Robert's grip on her neck. She reached for the bed beneath her, clawing with one hand. A brilliant flash of fear exploded in her. She saw that she was on the verge of death. In that moment she saw Robert's bulging eyes watching her, watching something deep in her eyes while he squeezed her neck. In the last instant of full consciousness, she saw that he saw her fear and was measuring it, watching the fear go down into her to see how deep it went. Then consciousness came apart in a white electric froth of stars and dizziness. Robert dropped her to the bed.

She shook herself awake in time to see Robert's back, plunging out of the bedroom. She scrabbled to her feet, pushing herself off the bed with both arms, afraid that he might return. She gulped convulsively for air, but none would come. When she got to her feet, a terrible pain flashed across the front of her head, and she began to collapse again forward. She caught herself. She gasped and shook her head and gulped again, but no air would come down her throat. She lifted her own hands to her throat, where Robert's hands had been. Finally a blessed shaft of air broke through into her lungs. She gulped again and breathed. She staggered out of the bedroom and down the hall to the top of the back staircase.

Robert was just pushing out the back door. Linda heard screaming at the back of the house. She staggered down the hallway to the top of the back staircase that led down to the family room next to the kitchen. Zsa was standing at the bottom of the back stairs, screaming, her face alive with alarm.

"Linda, are you all right? What's going on up there? What did he do to you?"

Linda leaned against the wall at the top of the stairs. "He choked me, Zsa," she said. She allowed herself to slide down the wall while Zsa came up the stairs toward her. By the time Zsa got to the top, Linda was sitting on the step with her head between her knees. "He choked me real bad, Zsa." She began to cry. "He choked me real bad."

"Oh Linda," Zsa said, tears springing to her own eyes as she reached down and patted her on the neck. "That man is going to kill you, Linda. You just don't know it. That man will kill you."

It was early August and still very hot in Dallas. People had repaired to the dark shelter of their homes, with shades drawn tight and the air conditioning turned up full blast. At the height of the afternoon, Caruth Street was deserted. A host of cicadas in the trees joined the air conditioning compressors in setting up a loud thrumming roar outside, but there was no human noise and little traffic. It was as if the insects had taken over the city.

Linda stayed in bed for three days. Stephen and Kathleen would come and join her for periods, usually in tandem, as if taking shifts. Zsa brought her soup and other light food that she could force down through her painfully constricted throat. When she went into the huge bathroom, she tried to avoid the large wall mirrors that would show her the hideous black and purple swollen welts that looped around her neck like a boa constrictor.

Robert came home late each night, spent a long time in the bathroom, took a shower, and then came and joined her in the bed.

Even when she was already asleep, Robert always snapped the lights back on, turned on the television, and then lay in bed smoking and making phone calls.

One night Linda rose from the bed after Robert had joined her. She was exhausted. It had taken her forever to fall asleep, and now Robert had wakened her. Dragging her pillow along at her heel, she left the room quietly and walked down the hall to the guest room, where Zsa stayed when she spent the night. The room was empty. Linda slipped into the bed and tried to fall asleep again.

The door exploded open with a smashing crack and a burst of light from the hall. Silhouetted against the door jamb was Robert's massive half-naked figure. He had allowed himself to become grossly overweight in the last year, so that the fat over his pectoral muscles hung down in huge white breasts. His face was sallow and his eyes were sunken and dark in the light from the hall. His mouth was twisting angrily.

In a quivering growl, he said: "Get the fuck back in my bed, Linda. Now."

She rose hesitantly, afraid that he would begin smashing her while she was still trapped in the bed clothing.

"Robert, please. . ."

"Just get back in my bed, Linda. Nothing is going to happen."

She rose and walked ahead of him down the hall, half-turning and cringing. Her hand fluttered up reflexively to shelter the ugly purple scars on her neck.

"Nothing is going to happen, Linda. Believe me, the last thing I want from you is sex. You're about as sexy as a Goddamn cow. Do any of your ditsy friends ever mention to you that you could stand to lose some fucking weight, Linda?"

He stood glowering over her while she climbed back into the bed. She was braced for a rain of smashing blows. But they did not come this time.

Robert retired to a chair across the room and lit a cigarette, staring at her face where she peeked out at him from under the covers.

"God, Linda, you're just . . . look at you. I almost feel sorry for you. You're just . . . you're just nothing. I mean, what are you, Linda? You have nothing to say. You embarrass the shit out of me when we go out.

"You look like shit. You look old. You dress like shit. Don't you ever look at how women dress in this town? Why can't you dress like your high society friend, Janet Lesser? You're a crappy cook. You can't even do that right.

"And let me tell you something, Linda," he said in a higher voice, jabbing at her with the cigarette, "you are a really fucked-up mother to those children. I mean, you are really shit as a mother. You are not preparing those children for anything. What are they good for? What can they do? Go to Disney World and be a bunch of little twerps?

"You and your parents love that crap, that sick, sugary little fakey bullshit crap they put out for the suckers. God, you are dumb. You are one dumb little bitch. I can't even call you a bitch. You're too nothing to be a bitch.

"You're nothing, Linda. You are zero. You are not even a person. You are a waste of space. That's all."

The next day, Linda rose early and helped Zsa get the children off to school. Zsa mentioned to her, after the children were gone, that she needed to be paid and that the milkman needed to be paid, too.

Linda took a cup of coffee and climbed up the long spiral staircase to her desk on the landing. She opened the desk and took out her checkbook and a sheaf of bills. She arranged the bills on the desk.

Half an hour later, she realized she had been staring at the bills with eyes only half-focused, sitting motionless at the desk. Her back hurt. She straightened. What was she thinking about?

How could Robert be what he was? How could he behave so savagely? Outside the house, he was a normal and even prominent member of the business community. Inside the house—in her house, with her—he was a hideous beast, a thing from hell itself.

He must be right. That must be the answer. It must be she. She must be what he says she is. Ugly. Stupid. Horribly embarrassing. Unfashionable. Laughable. A thing like a scar on his life. A hideous thing that drives this otherwise successful and admired man to madness. What other answer could there possibly be? How else can he be what he is?

If she leaves him, what? Will he kill her? Beat her to death? She knows what that will feel like. She can taste the blows. What if he allows her to leave? Where would she go? What would she be? She is nothing. She is no one. She has been given everything, and she has allowed it all to turn to rot and stink—a hell on Earth.

"Linda," Zsa said sharply behind her.

She turned suddenly.

"Linda, you been sitting here for almost two hours, not moving. What's the matter with you?"

She stared up at Zsa, her lower lip barely quivering. "I don't know, Zsa. I just don't know."

Two weeks later, Linda summoned the courage to tell Robert she wanted his secretary to buy tickets for her to take the children to visit their grandparents in Duncan for a week. It was a request that almost always invited a terrible fight. In the end, if he gave in at all, it was only after he had managed to make her cut in half the time that she would spend with her parents. He always had to know exactly when she would be leaving and on what flight she would return. Typically, by the time she arrived in Duncan, Robert would already be waiting on the telephone to talk to her.

He would call her each day, sometimes more than a dozen times, each time reciting to her what he had been doing in the last hour or so and then asking her to tell him again on what flight she and the children would be returning. When they did return, Robert was never waiting at the airport. It was Linda's job to get the kids into a cab and bring them back to the house. When they returned to the house on Caruth, Zsa invariably would be at the door to tell them Robert was holding on the telephone, waiting to make sure they had come back as promised.

But this time, when Linda told Robert she was going to Duncan, he said nothing. He and Linda had not really spoken in weeks. Their only contact was in bed. When they passed during the day, he avoided looking at her face or neck. When Linda told him she was taking the children to Duncan, he did not ask for details of the trip.

Linda called Robert's secretary and said that she needed tickets for herself and the children to Oklahoma City on Southwest Airlines. When the secretary asked about the return, Linda paused and then said, "I want one-way tickets."

Robert came home that evening and said that he wanted to take her and the children to Padre Island for a weekend by the ocean, before they went to Oklahoma. It was the first time Robert had ever proposed a family trip anywhere. She was afraid to say no. She suffered through an awful weekend at Padre with him and then came home. A week later she took the children to Oklahoma.

When she finally called him from Duncan and told him she was not coming back, Robert sobbed on the telephone and begged her to reconsider. But he did not roar and threaten.

In the house by the lake, waiting for her killer to come, Linda remembered the moment when the plane taxied out onto the runway at Love Field in Dallas, preparing to carry her and the children away from him.

The words had come back to her then. You are zero. You are not even a person. You are a waste of space. Speeding down the runway, she looked out the window and watched the marker lights flying by, the withered grass melting into a solid sheet of yellow-green. The plane lifted off and nosed up into its sharp banking ascent over downtown. She looked down and watched the shining new high-rise towers spinning beneath, sparkling in the ferocious southwestern sun.

She was zero. There. In that place, in that time, with Robert, she had become nothing. An encumbrance. A worthless, withered thing. She had allowed herself to become, in her own heart, what he had said of her over and over, sometimes shouting it, sometimes hissing.

A waste of space. Something worn out. Something to be cast away. Something no longer new enough, shiny enough.

When the plane leveled, it was headed north. The vast plains of North Texas had faded below to a huge chessboard of fenced squares. Linda put her head back against the seat and found, to her surprise, that she was dry-eyed. There was not a drop of sadness in her. It had all been replaced by a searing anger. He had tried to talk her out of her place in life. Now she wanted it back.

Robert called her friend Janet Lesser. Janet later told Linda Robert had said, "She's leaving me, Janet. She's throwing away sixteen years of marriage and breaking up our family." He had sobbed loudly on the telephone—a deep, wracking sob.

Janet listened. Janet always listened. If a Martian jumped out of a flying saucer and said he was going to turn her into green slime, Janet would listen politely to what he had to say first. She was the product of one of Dallas's oldest families—a mercantile family that had made its fortune in the last century brokering cotton to New England and manufacturing hats. The Lessers had been sending sons and daughters to Rice University in Houston or east to college ever since. There were streets and parks in Dallas named after her family.

On the surface, and when she chose, Janet could give the impression of being fragile—a porcelain belle. She was the kind of person Robert always fawned over and tried to impress, then sneered at behind her back for being weak. But Robert had never bothered to get to know her well.

Janet had survived a bruising divorce before the age of thirty. For all her outward gentility, she had gone right out there after the divorce and supported herself in the same real estate jungle where Robert made his money. She used her brains, charm, and an indomitable will to sell legitimate properties—property actually worth something in the neighborhood of what it sold for, unlike the funny-money land-flipping deals Robert preferred—so that she had not been affected by the savings and loan collapse and was actually doing quite a bit better than Robert at the moment. She had even done some business with Robert, profitably. She knew Robert saw none of her strengths, envied her social standing, and thought of her only as a silly rich woman, and it never occurred to her to say anything about it.

Before this conversation, she certainly had never heard Robert Edelman cry on the telephone before, but somehow she was neither surprised nor impressed. He didn't sound any more sincere to her in tears than he did when he was leaning across a table at the Mansion restaurant or the City Club, smirking and bragging. She listened to him for a while but said nothing in response. After a few minutes, Robert stopped crying and changed his tone completely.

"Janet," he said, "I know you and Linda talk a lot, and she's probably already called you from Oklahoma. If she hasn't, she will soon. But I would like you not to talk to her for a few days. I want to keep calling up there and see if I can handle her and get her to change her mind. I don't know what's the matter with her."

Usually she said whatever it took to steer a conversation with Robert to an early conclusion. This time she decided to speak directly.

"Robert," she said, "what's the matter with her is that you have been beating her up black and blue. And I can't promise you that I won't talk to her. I will talk to her. She is my friend. You are not."

Robert was silent for a moment, then said good-bye and hung up. As soon as she was off the phone with him, Janet called Linda in Duncan and reported the phone call.

"No, my mind is made up," Linda said. "I told Robert I'm not coming back to Dallas with the children until he moves out of the house."

In the house by the lake it was 8:00 A.M. exactly. Linda walked to the wall phone in the kitchen and waited next to it. It rang. One ring. Two rings. She began to lift her hand toward it. Three rings. She held her breath. Four rings! It stopped ringing.

Four rings. Why four? Would it begin to ring again now? Yes! After a pause of less than a minute, it began ringing again. What on earth could that mean? Ike had been so adamant. Three rings only. The signal was three rings. Do not pick the phone up after that if the signal call was any other number of rings. The phone was ringing and ringing now. She stood next to it, staring at it and growing angry and perplexed. He was the one who set the signal, now he had screwed it up. How could it be wrong? She could not answer the phone. She absolutely could not. It stopped ringing.

She walked over and sat down on a stool at the bar that divided the kitchen from the living room. The phone rang again. One ring. Two rings. Three.

Four rings. It was wrong again. It stopped ringing. Forty seconds later the phone began ringing again. It rang and rang. She sat on the stool with her back to it, tears flowing down her face.

It was wrong. The signal was wrong. Just as they had feared. Something had happened. She was stuck in this place, by a lake she did not know the name of, isolated in the middle of the woods without a car, without even a boat.

Her heart quickened. A hot crackling little nerve-fire began racing through her system. It was something beneath the level of thought—a gut-voice that said, "RUN." She looked at the door. The voice said, "RUN OUT THE DOOR! RUN! RUN."

She sucked in a deep breath and clutched her arms around herself. They had told her so adamantly not to leave the house. She had to wait. The FBI might be watching the house even now from somewhere out there. But how could she be sure? They had told her so many times how they were afraid her killer might kill Gerry. What if Gerry, the FBI agent, was lying out there in the woods somewhere with his head hacked halfway off? He might have been killed last night as he left. The killer could be moving toward her at this moment. Why on earth was the signal wrong?

She did what she always did when she had to get control. She thought of the children. If she screwed this up, if she let herself get killed, then the children would go to Robert.

That was not a bearable thought. Even here in this hiding place, with her own death perhaps only moments away, ready to spring at her through a door or from behind or from around a corner, the thought that made her breath come short and her heart pound was the thought of the children going to Robert.

Little Stephen was so smart and so tough, always taking his mother's side even when he knew it would bring on Robert's rages. But the last two years had taken a savage toll on him. At the end of a long exhausting day of either battling with his father himself or watching Linda go through it, seven-year-old Stephen would disappear to the playroom upstairs, where Linda would find him later, curled in a fetal ball in the corner, sucking his thumb. There were weeks when Stephen regressed so badly that Linda and Zsa worried he might be on the verge of a psychological collapse of some kind.

Whenever she had been out of his sight for more than ten minutes, the only thing Linda could think of was to break loose from whatever else was holding her, go find him wherever he was hiding, hold him in her arms, and rock him.

And Kathleen. Kathleen was a very different piece of work. She was always cheerful and gay on the surface. Sometimes her happy little Snow White demeanor was almost frightening: the time Robert came raging into the front door of Caruth, absolutely out of control over something, and smashed Linda so hard with the door that he knocked her flying and bloody all the way across the foyer, sliding and scrambling on the marble floor to stay out of the way while he kicked, into the open doorway of the library.

Merriellen Lehner's children were in the house that day and saw it all. They ran screaming across the front lawns to their mother and were inconsolable for hours. Pretty little Kathleen, in her fluffy white dress and black patent leather shoes, flew up the stairs and joined Stephen in his hiding place under his bed. She lay next to her brother, solemn but calm.

It came out of Kathleen in the deep of the night, beginning with a low choking sound that opened and widened into a strangely deep, unchildlike moan, exploding finally in sobs. Linda sat on the bathroom floor rocking her while she sobbed, but Kathleen could not stop sobbing, nor could she be awakened. With her eyes shut smoothly in sleep, she sobbed sometimes for as long as three hours in the middle of the night. When she awakened in the morning, she remembered none of it.

Linda made a tape of the sobbing one night for Dr. Dan A. Meyers, the psychiatrist to whom she was taking both children. He listened to it and was noncommittal about what it meant.

In the process of the divorce, the children had been hauled around to various shrinks, both psychologists and psychiatrists, all over Dallas. Dr. Meyers, when the children finally got to him, had been a godsend. He did not always tell Linda what she wanted to hear, by any means. Eventually, when he heard the children describe Robert's rages, he realized that Robert was a genuinely dangerous person, and from that point on, he tended to be more sympathetic with Linda's position. But even after that point, Dr. Meyers was just as likely to be critical of Linda as not, depending on the issue.

The point was that, of all the practitioners who had seen the children, Dr. Meyers was the one who clearly had the children's interests first at heart and was willing to make any and all of the adults in the situation mad at him if he thought they were hurting the children.

Not long after Linda played him the tape of Kathleen sobbing, Dr. Meyers called the lawyers on both sides of the divorce, Ken Fuller and Ike Vanden Eykel, and told them he wanted to see them in his office. They were the kind of men who were accustomed to having other people see them in their own offices, but they knew Dr. Meyers's word carried weight with the judge, and they knew better than to make Meyers angry.

When Dan Meyers was first establishing his practice in Dallas, he found a deep commercial lot on an obscure cul-de-sac by a railroad track, right on the border of the Park Cities. It was a little lost world, overgrown with bamboo and hackberry trees, surrounded by the service entrances of sleek modern office buildings on one side and the railroad embankment on the other. He and his father built a cozy little log cabin on the lot, which he used as the clinic for his child psychiatry practice. Deeply shaded, surrounded by bird-feeders and flowers, the clinic had a wonderful Hansel-and-Gretel aura that helped ease the fear many children felt on their first visit to a psychiatrist.

But inside, in the timbered and vaulted room that served as his office, Dan Meyers was all business with the two tough divorce lawyers.

"This situation is very bad and very damaging for both of these children," he said. "You have got to bring these people to a settlement so that this can stop. I insist that the situation be resolved in whatever manner it takes to get these two children out of harm's way."

Both lawyers took him very seriously. When it got down to it, they were really on his side on this issue. Neither of them liked to see children torn apart. They both went back and advised their clients that something was going to have to be done to end the custody portion of the battle soon.

But for Robert, the additional pressure to bring the divorce process to a close meant only one thing—that Linda would win the children. By then, it was what everyone was telling him.

"Prepare yourself, Robert," they said. "She's going to get the kids."

But not if she were dead.

It was that simple. If she died, he won. In fact, that was what this was all about. As long as Linda might sit here in Ike's lake house and search back through all of the ugliest moments, the beatings and the mad rages, it was not there where she would find the moment she was seeking. It wasn't there, not in that realm. Not in rage.

She remembered his eyes that day he had choked her unconscious. Robert was puffed like an adder, purple in the face with his eyes popped out like Bela Lugosi, ranting and roaring like something out of *The Exorcist,* but she saw through all of that, down through a tiny pinpoint of extreme self-control in the center of his pupils, behind which the bastard was doing all of it on purpose and with extreme calculation, in order to get his own way. In order to win.

He was a con. A ruthless con. Robert had a pathological need to get the advantage and have his way. It was probably what made it possible for him to be such a bastard and such a success at the same time in business. Robert would lie in that bed and smoke and talk on the phone and scheme and never sleep until he got what he wanted. He would say or do anything, make or break any promise. Sooner or later, his adversary, whoever it might be, would make the mistake of taking his family to the movies one evening or even just going to sleep on time one night, and Robert would get him. The only way anyone could ever even the score with Robert was to do what Snubby Ellis had done—come shove a gun in his face and make him believe it might go off.

It was such a joke, Robert suddenly deciding that he wanted the children. Robert had barely been aware of their existence for years at a time. Linda looked out at the water on the lake and smiled bitterly, thinking of the beach in front of their hotel on that last-minute trip to Padre Island, a week before she packed up the kids and left for Oklahoma. The trip had been God-awful and sort of laughable at the same time, in a very dark way. In a strange sense, she almost felt sorry for Robert that weekend.

He had proposed it as if it were the Grand Tour. For all the millions of dollars Robert had packed away, it never occurred to him to take the family anywhere.

Padre Island was nice enough—a long sandy barrier island along the southern Gulf Coast of Texas, running down almost to the border of Mexico. A large portion of the island was given over to a federal wildlife preserve. The southern tip of Padre, where they stayed, had been the site of an intense real estate boom in the late 1970s and early 1980s. Robert had made reservations for them in one of the newest, biggest, and flashiest hotels.

That Friday morning they flew down on American Airlines. When Linda took the children to Oklahoma, Robert's secretary always made reservations on Southwest, the inexpensive, bare-bones commuter line. Since Robert was along this time, they had to fly first class. As soon as they were off the plane and ensconced in the huge rental car, Robert picked up his cellular telephone and began talking and smoking non-stop, all the way from the airport to the hotel. He talked on the phone while he stood at the desk checking in, talked all the way to the elevator, signed off for the elevator ride up to the room, then hurried to the room, slipped off his shoes, lay on the bed, pulled up an ashtray and fired up the hotel telephone. He gestured with one hand for Linda to turn on the television so the children could sit on the floor and watch cartoons in the cloud of smoke from his cigarettes. Stephen and Kathleen, who had not the slightest idea what a trip to the beach was about, dutifully did as their father bade them and took positions Indian-style on the rug, fully prepared to watch television until dark.

Linda had been embarrassed about the whole idea of a trip to the beach, because her neck and upper right arm were still horribly bruised from Robert choking her. But she looked at the children, their little faces bleached white by the moon-flicker of the TV set in that over-blown disinfectant-smelling hotel room, and she decided they were going to put on their swimsuits and at least go see the beach.

When Robert saw what was happening, he looked irritated at first, then made a great show of enthusiasm and went into the bathroom to put on his own swimsuit. When he came out, Linda was struck by how he had changed in recent years. She seldom saw him standing without a shirt in the daylight. He had been so big and so powerful-looking in college. Now in middle age, he was puffy, saggy, and very overweight. His skin was mottled and corpselike.

He looked at her. She had on large sunglasses, shorts, a loose-fitting blouse, and a silk scarf around her bruised neck. "Aren't you going in?" he asked.

"No, Robert, you go in with them."

"Fine. That'll be fine. I will. Come on, children. To the beach!"

The hotel was separated from the surf by a high natural dune, over which a wooden stile had been built. Linda, Robert, and the children climbed up the stairs, and when they got to the top, Stephen and Kathleen both clutched their mother's hands and drew in their breath. As far as they could see, a gleaming green sea was rolling in under pearly clouds that softened the glare of the Texas sun. Fifty yards out from the beach where the sea hit the first shallow sandbar, a roaring white lace stretched from one side of the planet to the other.

"Oh, Mother," Kathleen whispered. "It's so beautiful."

Linda took a position under one of the hotel's umbrellas, nodding for Robert to go ahead and take the children into the water. He led them down, holding each by the hand. When he got to the water's edge, it was clear Robert was just as confused as they were about what to do next. They all waded out a few feet into the water. Robert reached down and made an awkward scoop at the water to splash Stephen. Stephen shrieked, reached down with both hands, and splashed Robert.

"Okay, Stephen, let's not overdo it," Robert said. A minute or two later, he left them playing in the water's edge and came back up, lurching clumsily across the sand in his tender bare feet. He sat down next to Linda. She wondered if they were about to have a talk.

But Robert reached into the little kit of things he had brought out to the beach with him and extracted cigarettes, a lighter, and the cellular telephone. Linda rose and walked down to the water to watch the children.

Robert did not spend all of his time talking on the telephone to people back in Dallas. Some of it was spent calling the desk at their hotel and insisting that the hotel get him dinner reservations at the finest restaurant on the island, all of which took a considerable deal of doing and negotiating and provided Robert a satisfying opportunity to treat the hotel staff like dirt.

In late afternoon, when the children were just warming to the whole idea of sand castles, Robert announced it was time for them to return to the room and to get ready to go out to dinner. The children were very disappointed, which caused Robert to become angry. As soon as they saw he was becoming angry, the children stopped objecting and marched back up to the hotel with little slumped shoulders and downcast expressions.

Robert slept late on Saturday morning. Linda took the children downstairs for breakfast. By the time they got back to the room, Robert was awake and on the phone. When he hung up, he told them something had come up in Dallas and they would have to return that morning. The children said nothing. They sat on the floor and watched cartoons while Linda packed.

Sitting on the stool in the house by the lake, Linda remembered the Padre trip and thought to herself that the trip had been Robert's one stab at a family experience. She smiled. It was funny. She was amazed to hear herself laugh. It was ridiculous. She thought of Robert lurching across the beach on his tender white feet, flailing for his telephone like a man swimming for a life preserver, and she laughed out loud.

The phone rang. She sat on the stool and counted. One ring. Two. Three. Four! Maybe Ike forgot. It had to be Ike calling. It didn't make sense otherwise. Now it was ringing again. She ached to pick it up. But someone could be there with him, she thought, holding a gun to his head. She turned her back to the telephone and let it ring.

During the divorce, Robert succeeded in his long campaign to make Stephen play soccer instead of T-Ball. Once Stephen was playing on a Park Cities team, in front of all the right parents, Robert suddenly took a great interest in his son's athletic endeavors. It was such a ludicrous joke—this huge fat man with a terrible cigarette wheeze, stumbling around the field shouting encouragement at the boys but never quite getting even that right, since he didn't really know what one said in order to shout encouragement at boys. And the photographer. Robert hired one of the society page photographers from the newspapers to come on his off-hours and take pictures for the court file—portraits of Robert Edelman, Devoted Soccer Coach.

Linda climbed down off the stool. The phone was ringing again, but she was barely aware of it. She walked to the front of the house and let herself out through the door. All night the door had been a barrier between her and the terrors lurking outside, but now she stepped through it as if it were not there.

She was close now, in her search for the important moment. She was getting hot. She walked down to the edge of the lake, staring ahead as she walked to the water. There was no sand, of course. The green grass of the lawn grew straight down to a red muddy line where the water lapped. Out by the point, there were the remnants of huge old trees sticking out of the water, rotted down to their trunks and larger branches. It was probably one of the older man-made lakes of East Texas—a huge reservoir, probably built by the Army Corps of Engineers some time during the 1950s, probably named after some mean, bald, dirty-talking little congressman.

It was during the process of the divorce. Robert saw that Linda was fighting for the children, not the money. The moment was somewhere in there. Yes, he was a horrible man before then. He beat her. Their marriage was awful. But unfortunately, that sort of thing happens. There are such men. There are such marriages. Lots of them. Yes, she should have left him, but she did not. No, she should not have had the children, but she did.

In spite of all the dark elements in her life and all the wisdom that said she should have abandoned her life, there were things about Linda's life that were wonderful. The children were an immeasurable joy; she cherished and enjoyed her family, when Robert allowed her to; she continued to sing and derived great satisfaction from it. They had a lot of money. Somewhere along the line she had decided that she had it better than many people and that she should make a go of what she had.

It wasn't in any of that. The answer was not there. It was in the process of the divorce itself, when Robert realized that all she wanted was the children, and that she was going to get what she wanted. She was going to win on that point.

Her first attorney had been terrified of Robert. He had spent all of his time telling Linda how bad she was going to look in comparison with Robert and how important it was for her to disguise her true nature. The career on the stage would make her seem like a flibbertigibbet. Her parents' conservative Christianity would make her look like a fundamentalist bigot. No one would believe Robert was violent. Robert was a prominent developer, a man who appeared on the society pages, a winner in a city that worshipped winners and hated whiners.

Robert had hired Ken Fuller, one of the smartest, toughest divorce lawyers in the Southwest. Every time Fuller cruised around Linda's first lawyer with his dorsal fin just cutting the water, Linda's lawyer collapsed into jelly, and then he took it out on her, railing at her about all of her flaws.

In a sense, her lawyer was right. Dallas had never been a city favorably disposed toward wives, and the current circumstances would make everything that much tougher. Since the divorce had been launched, the savings and loan crisis had gone national, and the real estate market in Dallas was starting to look like London during the Blitz. The powers-that-be in Dallas were all in it up to their necks, and they were all in a very bad mood. Linda's lawyer feared Ken Fuller would know just how to paint her—as the spoiled Park Cities nitwit wife, up to her neck in diamonds and fur, out to dump her hapless hubby because he was no longer rolling in dough.

Pressed on all sides by lawyers and terribly afraid she might lose her children before it was all over, Linda felt more and more helpless. Finally it was Janet who helped her find the will to change things.

They met for coffee one mid-morning in a little deli in Highland Park Village, a small but tony shopping center where some of the most expensive, most conservative clothing stores in Dallas were located.

Away from the company of men, Janet dropped a lot of the Southern belle mannerism. "Linda, you have a second-string lawyer," she said.

"I guess you're right," Linda said.

"Robert has Ken Fuller. Ken Fuller is first-string. Your lawyer is scared to death of both Robert and Ken Fuller. This is Dallas. The courts and the juries are only pro-woman if you get raped by a poor person. They're anti-woman if you're rich and you ask for a divorce. Linda, did you sign that consent decree or whatever it was he brought you?"

"Partial summary judgment."

"Did you sign it?"

"Yes."

"Oh, Linda. Why did you . . . how could you do that? The one you showed me? The one we talked about?"

"I had to. I had no choice. They told me I would lose the children if I did not sign it."

"But you've given up everything, then."

"The lawyer told me I had to sign it or I would lose the children."

"But it doesn't guarantee you the children. You don't have the children, Linda. Robert has just snookered you out of everything else, and now he'll go after the children, too."

"Why would Robert want the children?"

"He doesn't want . . ." Janet stopped and drew a deep breath. She looked off over Linda's shoulder. The long aristocratic lines of her face were tense, impatient.

"Linda, it's not about the children for Robert. It's about winning. Robert intends to win. The purpose of getting you to sign the summary judgment on the kids was to deprive you of leverage. The agreement takes the kids out of play."

"Out of play?"

"You can't hold them over his head. You can't use them for leverage, when it comes to the money. Then, once he has what he wants in the money agreement, he will go back after the kids. He wants to win, Linda. He wants you to lose. That's what this is all about."

"I have got to do something, Janet. I know that. But I don't know what."

Janet reached down into her purse and extracted a leather-bound memo pad with a little gold mechanical pencil that slipped into a holder inside. She took out the pencil, turned it until the lead protruded from the tip, and then hastily scrawled out a name. She tore the sheet from the pad and shoved it across the table at Linda.

Linda picked it up and read it aloud. "Ike Vandermichael."

"It's Vanden Eykel."

Linda held the paper in her hands and searched Janet's face. Janet replaced the pencil and the pad in her purse and looked up at Linda. She stared at Linda without speaking for a moment. Then she said, "Dump your lawyer, Linda. Hire Ike."

Ike Vanden Eykel came out from behind his huge desk with both hands extended, one to shake Linda's hand and the other to take her elbow and guide her to a chintz-covered sofa at the end of the long narrow room that was his office.

She judged him to be somewhere between thirty-five and forty years old. He was as big as Robert. He was handsome, with an actor's square-cut jaw and strong mouth. In fact, he reminded her of Van Johnson, with whom she had performed in *Bells Are Ringing* in the Summer Musicals.

He wore his silver-blond hair in a conservative businessman cut, swept neatly over a broad high brow. Even though he was big and mid-dle-aged, he looked athletic—not dissipated and hollow-eyed like Robert. The eyes were light blue—strong eyes, she thought, without being tough or hard.

She began telling him her story from the beginning. He took notes himself and, at one point, asked his secretary to come in and take her own notes.

He took one phone call during their talk.

"Is that right?" he said on the phone. "Well, I'm sorry to hear that. What did you do? That's good, you did the right thing. How did it go on the way there this morning? Well that's good, anyway. When I get home, I'll go down there and have a talk."

He hung up the phone and shrugged. "My son got a new bicycle for his birthday, and this was the first day he was allowed to ride it to school by himself, so, of course, the neighborhood bully had to catch him on the way home and knock him over."

"Oh no," she said. "The poor thing."

"Yeah," he said, smiling. "I think the neighborhood bully did the same thing to me the first time I rode my bike to school. Part of growing up, I guess."

"But it's so sad. You can't help feeling sorry for them."

"Oh yes. Well, I'm sorry to interrupt. Please go ahead. You were telling me about the court's appointment of a lawyer for the children."

She plunged ahead with her story. All of a sudden, she felt very good about her new lawyer. She worried that some of what she was telling him might sound unbelievable, however.

Two hours later, when Linda had finished, she said, "I hear myself telling all this sometimes, and I sound like a crazy person."

"Mrs. Edelman . . ." Ike began.

"Please call me Linda."

"Linda. You should know this. Most of the people who come to see me sound like crazy people the first time. It's usually because they are half-crazy from what's been done to them. I specialize in taking these very complicated, very high-stakes divorces that other lawyers have allowed to drift along forever. And I fix them.

"That is what I will do for you. I will fix it. When it gets fixed, you will no longer sound like a crazy person to yourself. Or to anyone else. Believe me. All right?"

"All right. Fine. I hope so."

"There is one other thing."

"What?"

"You will have to come up with twenty thousand dollars for me before I will take the case."

"I don't have any money," she said. "Robert has all the money."

"Linda," Ike said. "You will have to come up with twenty thousand dollars for me before I will take the case."

When she left Ike's office that first time, Linda felt more sound and whole and steady on her feet than she had in months.

The money, however, was a problem. She had already paid the first lawyer $40,000, which had pretty well cleaned her out. She called her parents in Duncan. They certainly did not have that kind of money readily available, but they had excellent credit. Her father went to the bank the next day and borrowed the full $20,000.

It was not four days before Ike's secretary called Linda and said that Ike was eager to speak to her. Linda called back at the appointed time, and the secretary put her right through.

"Linda," Ike said, "I'm looking at this partial summary judgment you gave me with all your stuff."

"Yes."

"Is this the only copy you have?"

"Yes."

"All right, I need you to think back. Was this document presented to you . . . under what circumstances did you sign this?"

"At my lawyer's office."

"Who was present?"

"Just his secretary. He left it for me out front, in the front office, and I dropped in and signed it one morning. She witnessed my signature."

"No one else was there?"

"No. No one."

"How many copies did you sign?"

"I don't remember. Several. Three or four."

"Did you ever see Robert sign it? Sign another copy of it, perhaps?"

"No. I've never seen Robert sign anything since all of this started. Believe me, I would remember that, if he had ever signed anything."

"Linda, did you ever see the judge sign this thing? Was it ever presented to the judge that you know of?"

"The judge? No. I mean, I don't think so. I couldn't get my lawyer to even talk about the judge. He didn't seem to want to go near the judge. Why?"

"Linda, I need you to keep this absolutely under your hat for the time being. I mean, I don't want you to discuss this with anyone, not with your parents even, not with anyone."

"What is it, Ike?"

"I don't think Ken Fuller ever got Robert to sign this thing or ever took it to the judge to sign off on it, either."

Linda was silent.

"I've been down to the court to see the file. I talked to the judge. He knows nothing about it. This thing's not valid," Ike said. "Legally, it's nonexistent."

"Why didn't they sign it?"

"It was probably Robert. Ken Fuller is one of the best attorneys in Texas, maybe in this country. He doesn't miss things like this. But from everything I hear, Robert never wants to do anything anybody wants him to do."

"No. Even if it was the best deal in the world for him. . . "

"Which it was."

"Robert wouldn't sign it, just because he's so ornery, and he'd worry that he might be able to get something better later."

"Well, he's screwed himself up good this time, if you'll pardon my French."

"But what if he signs it now?"

"That's why I want you to stay quiet about it. We're going to get rid of this mess before they have a chance to notice their mistake."

Sitting on the iron bench by the water's edge, she remembered that conversation on the phone with Ike almost word for word. That was only four months ago. She rose slowly from the bench, almost unaware of her body, and walked down to the water's edge, staring at the ripples with unseeing eyes.

It was there. Right in there somewhere. That was when it happened. The thing she missed, the thing she should have seen.

*   *   *

Ike Vanden Eykel composed a letter that afternoon to Ken Fuller and to the judge. The partial summary judgment had never been signed by Robert Edelman and never had been submitted to the court. Since then certain things had happened that changed the picture. The failure to execute the instrument had caused unforeseen changes in Mrs. Edelman's circumstances. Mrs. Edelman could not make the same decision under existing circumstances that she made when she signed the judgment. The agreement was null and void. There was no agreement between the parties at all.

As soon as his secretary had plucked the finished copy out of the laser printer, Vanden Eykel signed several copies and had them hand-delivered to all of the parties.

So Robert lost a round. A big one. The first time, she thought. She stared at the ripples in the lake, holding her breath and thinking. It was right in here. She was very close.

Even before Ike wrote his letter, a meeting had been scheduled in Ken Fuller's office to discuss Linda's request to take the children to Disney World with her parents for two weeks in July. She had made the request a year earlier. It was one of the first things she had done when the divorce proceedings began.

The Disney World trips were too important to allow them to stop. It might be difficult to explain to someone else, she thought. But the family treks to the Magic Kingdom in Orlando were a light that beckoned her and the children forward through the long dark tunnel of each year.

The Disney movies, books, and the television show had always been important, even when she and Miriam were little girls. They memorized the scores of the movies before they could read sheet music. When John retired from Haliburton in 1977, he and Virginia bought the first in a succession of recreational vehicles that would carry them, their daughters, and their grandchildren on vacation trips to Disney World over the years ahead.

Robert, of course, did not provide any alternative. He never wanted to go anywhere. He hated leaving Dallas and being away from work and the Mansion. The grand Padre trip had been the one exception.

Linda worked hard to provide Stephen and Kathleen with shelter in their lives. Their rooms, both at Pagewood and then at Caruth, were sun-drenched childish fantasies, full of color, toys, and soft edges. She knew, try as she might, that she could not protect them from the menace that sometimes pervaded the rest of the house, but she wanted to make sure each child always had his or her place of safety, of innocent repair.

Robert's terrible antipathy for her parents had become so pronounced over the years that it had become a torture for them to come down and spend time at Caruth. They did it anyway, to see their daughter and their grandchildren. But there was always a black cloud hanging over them when they were there in his house.

It was on the visits to Disney World that the family had been able to open up, relax with each other, and share the tremendous joy of the children in being there, mainly because Robert was never there. They always invited him. John and Virginia made all of the plans and reservations for the trips. They had become old Disney World hands and knew just how to do it, where to make the dinner reservations, how far ahead of time, and so on. In the months before each visit, when they were pulling together the arrangements, they were always careful to make seven reservations at each place they would visit—for John, Virginia, Miriam, Linda, Stephen, Kathleen, and for Robert.

Robert would always hold open the possibility that he might come along, more or less as a threat. At the same time, he would spend the weeks before each visit wheedling and negotiating with Linda to pare down the amount of time she would actually spend there with the children. John and Virginia had learned to expect a last-minute change in which it would be announced that Linda and the children would not drive to Florida with the rest of the family in the RV but would fly later, meet them, and leave early.

It meant unhooking the huge vehicle, leaving the Fort Wilderness campground, and driving to the Orlando Airport to pick them up. But it was a small price to pay, and they were always afraid the least sign of balking or resistance from them would bring down a decree from Robert forbidding Linda to take the children at all.

Given the long history of difficulties associated with the Disney World visits, John and Virginia had pressed Linda to begin negotiating for the next year's trip as soon as the divorce process heated up.

Her first lawyer had ignored the entire matter as a trivial side issue. Now the time was drawing near. But when Linda explained what the trip meant and what kinds of problems she anticipated from Robert, Ike Vanden Eykel grasped the importance of the issue immediately and scheduled a meeting with Fuller.

Linda watched the ripples on the lake move in toward her in hypnotizing sheets. Somewhere in the far distance there was a faint buzzing noise, like a fly, but she ignored it. The meeting came back to her as if it were taking place all around her, as if this patch of grass by the lake in East Texas was a ghost dimension and she was actually there again, watching it, watching herself.

✿   ✿   ✿

She was nervous on her way there. She started up the Cadillac, pushed the button on the remote control to open the garage door, shoved the car into reverse, and tromped on the accelerator.

It was Linda's patented reverse-flying-start—a topic of whispered awe all over the neighborhood. It was not that Linda was reckless or casual about the way she drove her Cadillac. She had children in the car with her too often for that. It was more that she was extremely practiced and expert at maneuvering her car through the narrow confines of the alley and managed to accomplish it at speeds that might make a Formula One race driver blanch.

The meeting took place in Fuller's office. Vanden Eykel and Fuller were direct with each other, but businesslike. Each was a tough bargainer, but they both knew the difference between business and personal feeling.

Ike sketched out the ground on which they could negotiate. The judge was going to grant Linda the right to take her children to Disney World with their grandparents. There was no need for anybody to pretend that was not going to happen. The only questions they could resolve in their meeting that day were the basic logistics.

Robert chose an overstuffed red leather chair at an awkward distance from everyone else, most of the way across the room. He turned the chair as he sat down on it, so that he was able to present his side and not his full face to the others in the room. He lighted a cigarette, which he held in his most exaggerated Greta Garbo cigarette-holder pose, and began puffing away with his head tossed over the back of the chair as if he were about to receive a shampoo.

"Linda and her parents plan to leave on July 14," Ike said.

"I don't believe so," Robert said from inside his personal cloud of smoke at the end of the room.

"Pardon me?" Ike said.

"That won't be satisfactory," Robert said.

"Okay. Well, let me just lay out our position here, what we want, and then we'll hear what you all want to do about it," Ike said.

Robert snickered. Vanden Eykel looked him over carefully, then began reading again from notes, listing the days they would be gone, where they would stay, what arrangements might be made so that the children could call home to their father.

"That's all just a bunch of bullshit," Robert said. "This whole Disney World thing is a bunch of crap. I say they're not going."

"But they are going, Mr. Edelman."

Robert leaned forward. "Fuck you. They're not fucking going anywhere unless I say they are."

Vanden Eykel shrugged haplessly at Fuller, then began slipping his notes back into his briefcase. He rose.

"I can see we're not going to get anywhere with this. This is a waste of both our clients' money. I'm going to say good-bye, and we will be on our way."

"Sit down." Robert shouted, rising from his chair. "What's the matter, can't stand a little give-and-take, Mr. Hotshot-Lawyer? You can dish it out, but you can't take it, is that it?" Robert came forward across the room as he spoke. His face darkened, and his eyes were beginning to bulge. "Well I want this shit settled. I'm paying for this Goddamned meeting, and I want all this crap settled before anybody leaves."

When Robert had pulled this same act with Linda's first lawyer, the man had almost begun crying. But Ike stood his ground, briefcase in hand, with absolute equanimity.

"Good-bye, Mr. Edelman. We have nothing more to say to you."

Linda walked back across the green lawn and let herself in through the front room of the lake house. She walked to the sink and poured herself a glass of water. When she turned off the tap, her ears caught a new sound. It was the motorboat sound again, coming toward the lake house. She walked back to the plate-glass window and looked out. It was a small green fiberglass dinghy with an outboard motor on the back, headed straight toward her. There was one man in the boat. He was staring ahead at the house. Straight at her? Yes. She felt her heart quicken. It was coming.

It began in that instant, when Ike turned his back on Robert and walked out. Fuller must have told Robert afterward that Ike had been right, that the judge was going to grant the trip and there was nothing Robert could do about it.

But it was not Disney World in his eye that day. It was the summary judgment. By then, Fuller obviously had told him that the summary judgment was out the window. Robert had just lost a big one. Now his strategy was slipping from his grasp. Linda was slipping from his grasp. He was going to lose.

He was going to lose.

He was going to lose.

That was it. That was the moment. When Ike turned his back on Robert. When she looked into Robert's eyes and saw that he knew he was going to lose. In that instant he decided to send someone to kill her.

CHAPTER THREE

t was raining. The wheels of Colonel Young's modest American sedan hissed as he passed over the steeply pitched streets of an old Mexican-American neighborhood on Dallas's west side. He pulled into the parking lot of the Howard Johnson restaurant on the Stemmons Freeway, not far from Parkland Hospital, where President John F. Kennedy was declared dead in 1963. In mid-afternoon on a Saturday, a third of the booths and tables in the restaurant were full, mainly with nurses, doctors, and staff from Parkland. Colonel Young waited at the door to be seated by the hostess.

He was an unprepossessing man, of slight build, in his late fifties, with thin black hair combed straight back. His face and smile were Asian. When he spoke, there was barely a trace of accent. He had grown up in Chinese communities in the United States. While he waited for the hostess to notice him at the door, his eyes flitted nervously around the restaurant. He smiled and then recomposed his face several times, folding and unfolding his hands at his waist.

Finally the hostess saw him and came to him. She was holding a large menu in both hands.

"Meeting someone," he said. "I can look around."

"Yes, of course. Who is it?"

"I will look around and see if I see him," he said, smiling and nodding. He slipped past her and walked quickly to a back room that was partially out of view from the door.

Robert was sitting at a booth in the far back corner. He scowled at Young and then looked away from him irritably. Young turned, nodded the hostess away, and then joined Robert at his booth.

"You're late, Colonel."

"I'm very sorry, Mr. Edelman. I came right away when I got your message."

They both ordered coffee. As soon as the waitress was gone, Robert lifted a briefcase up from the floor and put it next to himself on the seat. He clawed clumsily at the brass latch with his large fingers and finally popped it open. He looked around the restaurant quickly and then pulled a thick folded blueprint from the briefcase. He held the blueprint in one hand in the air next to his head and stared at Young.

"Colonel, do you understand that I need this thing done?"

"Yes, sir."

"You have two weeks."

"I know. I am working on it."

"Do you have a plan?"

"I am working on it."

Young smiled at Robert.

Robert's face was a stone mask.

"Look, Colonel, I want you to see something." He took his right forearm and pushed the salt and pepper, napkin-holder, and other restaurant detritus roughly out of the way, spilling sugar on the table and sending the pepper shaker to the carpeted floor. Then he unfolded the blueprint over the table.

"I built this house. The house she's in on Caruth. I know every of inch of it. I want you to see something."

Robert took a ballpoint pen from his coat pocket and began drawing rough little rectangles here and there across the floor plan of the house. "These are motion detectors, under the carpeting," he said. "If you stay off these, and, uh . . . watch out for this, don't even go through this doorway . . ." He drew an X in one entryway. "That's a seeing-eye deal," he said. "If you avoid that stuff, you can go anywhere you want in the house."

Young smiled. "Why do I want to go in the house?"

Robert stared at him with iron eyes. "Why do you want to go in the house? Why do you. . . Look, try to follow me, here. She comes in here." He drew a line of dots where Linda would drive down the alley and approach the garage door. "She pushes a deal in her car, and the garage door comes up. She drives in.

"Now, once she's in the garage, she has to get out of the car and walk back over here." He made a mark on the side wall of the garage. "And she has to turn off the alarm system at a panel here. You could kill her then. If you were waiting outside by the air conditioning.

"Or, you can get in the garage, because it's not alarmed. The alarm is between the garage and the house, but there's no alarm on the outside garage door itself. And once she's in the house, she won't turn the alarm back on. So you could be in the garage, and then, if you don't want to kill her there, you could come in the house, here, once she's in."

Robert reached over, picked up the blueprint and folded it. He brushed some loose sugar from the paper and then put it back down.

"Here," he said, making X's with his pen, "and here, is where she sleeps and where her parents sleep, when they visit. There are no motion detectors upstairs. You could come in the house, come up these stairs here, and kill them all up there."

Robert looked down into Young's face for a response.

Colonel Young sat on both of his hands and hunched forward over the table with his face bent low, studying the blueprint intently.

"So," Robert said, "what do you think you'll use?"

Colonel Young looked up. "Use, Mr. Edelman?"

"Use. To kill them. Like a gun, or, I don't know, a knife. What?"

Colonel Young smiled meekly and looked away as if embarrassed. He looked back at Robert, wide-eyed and earnest. "If it's okay, I'd like to use a kind of army knife," he said. "It's real sharp."

Robert returned his gaze for a long moment. Finally he nodded. "Army knife. Great. Whatever. You're gonna make it look like a robbery."

"Oh, yes, sir."

"Great. Just get it done. It's got to be done soon. There is a deadline. You do understand that, right?"

"Oh, yes."

"Here," Robert said, handing him the blueprint. "You take this." He slapped it against Colonel Young's chest.

Colonel Young looked down at the blueprint, still in Robert's hand. He frowned suddenly. He looked up very slowly at Robert with an exaggerated, almost childish scowl.

"Put it down," he said petulantly. "It has sugar spilled on it."

Robert looked at him for a moment, then laid the blueprint down carefully on the table.

Her parents were visiting when she found out. Ike was on vacation in Wisconsin. Linda didn't expect him back in Dallas for two more weeks, shortly before the divorce was scheduled to go to trial. But his paralegal called in the middle of the week.

"He's cutting his vacation short," she told Linda, "and he'll be back at the end of the week. He would like to meet with you to go over the case at 8:45 A.M. Saturday in his office."

"At 8:45?"

"Yes."

"In the morning?"

"Yes ma'am."

"This coming Saturday?"

"Yes."

"All right. Fine. Good. I'll be there. Eight thirty Saturday."

"I'll tell him to expect you then."

On Saturday morning the children needed tending. Stephen had T-Ball. John and Virginia would drive Stephen to his game, but Linda had to pick out clothes, help Zsa with breakfast, call to check on the location of the game, draw a map for her father, and stop to have a brief conference with little Kathleen, who wanted to know why she had to go to the T-Ball game, too. Linda bustled around the huge house getting things in order and getting herself ready. By the time she walked toward the back of the house to get in the car, it was already 8:45. She wasn't worried about being a little late, because she knew Ike wouldn't show up until at least 9:30.

Colonel Young eased the car down the alley toward the garage door of Linda's house. He stopped a few yards clear of the property line.

"That's it," he said.

Fred Zabitosky looked. His eyes, deep-set in a craggy face, flew around the perimeter. He had spent a good deal of his life doing reconnaissance of places where blood was to be shed. Zabitosky looked for cover, for points of exposure, ingress, and egress.

"You think Jack hides where?"

"There," Young snapped impatiently, pointing with a nervous finger. "Behind the air conditioning thing."

"The compressor."

"That Goddamned thing right there."

Fred shrugged, his own temper fine-tuned. He never flashed back. Someone else's impatience always made Fred Zabitosky slow down and watch even more carefully.

"I'm getting out" he said, easing the door open.

"What the hell you getting out for?"

Zabitosky held up an old Leica 35-millimeter camera. "Snapshots," he said. He let himself out of the car. Moving swiftly, fluidly, he passed around the double garage door in a smooth arc, snapping pictures as he went. In bare moments he was back in the car next to Colonel Young, not having broken a sweat in the ninety-eight-degree heat outside.

Young had kept the engine running with the air conditioning on full blast.

"So?" he said.

"Nah," Zabitosky said. "Not the air conditioning compressor. She'd see him. The bushes. Over there. He's got room there, and he'll be in position to slip in around into the garage while she's pulling the car in. That okay with you?"

"You tell him about the alarm?"

"What about it?"

"No alarm on the garage, but he's got to wait for her to punch in the code over on the garage wall to disarm the system. Then he can get in the house and get her."

"Yeah, yeah. He and I will figure that all out. Jack's an experienced guy. He'll have his own thoughts."

"Good," Young said, "I'm glad he has thoughts. But you tell fucking Jack this. I don't give a fuck what kinda thoughts he's got, if he don't kill this bitch this week, we're out of business. The guy, my banker, he wants it done now. Later is no good. This weekend, her kids will be gone. That's when to do it. He don't want the kids taken out."

Over the white roar of the car's air conditioning, neither man heard the whirring noise outside. The garage door was coming up.

Linda, as usual, was staring straight out the windshield of the Cadillac at the wall of her garage, thinking about everything that was happening in her life. When she saw daylight in the rear-view mirror, she threw the Cadillac into reverse and jammed down on the accelerator.

"Holy shit!" Zabitosky shouted. "Somebody's comin' out of there fast!"

"Oh man," Colonel Young muttered, wrenching his car into reverse. "She's gonna hit us! Oh man."

He floored the car backward down the alley. His tires screeched and sent up a cloud of dust. The car wobbled and bumbled on its wheels as Colonel Young fought to get out of Linda's way in time.

When Linda had finished backing out, she stopped. She had made her usual adroit swoop into the alleyway. Her rear bumper was perhaps ten feet from Colonel Young's front bumper.

Linda put the Cadillac into drive and drove off down the alley to the side street.

Young and Zabitosky sat on the seat staring at each other.

"Damn!" Zabitosky said. "I don't think she ever noticed us."

Colonel Young snapped back around and looked down the alley. There was no sign of her.

As her beige Cadillac bounced out of the alley in a puff of dust and wheeled around to go north, a nondescript, tan, full-sized American sedan pulled away from the curb on the side street and fell in behind her. She didn't notice it, either.

She drove a favorite route of shortcuts down the long tree-roofed streets of University Park until she came to the North Dallas Tollway—a broad, steep-walled, beautifully landscaped private highway serving the affluent neighborhoods of the Park Cities and North Dallas. The hoi polloi of Dallas were reduced to finding their wretched ways from south to north and back again along the foul-smelling miles of perpetually jammed, aging, packed, and pollution-clogged Central Expressway, a few miles east of the tollway. The dual road system, First Class and Second Class, was a typical Dallas arrangement and not one to which Linda ever gave a moment's thought.

The plain tan car with black sidewalled tires and a tiny little aerial poking up from the center of the roof followed her to the tollway. One of the two men in it paid a toll a few cars behind her in line. The car followed her part of the way up the tollway but fell out of view before she exited.

Ike's office was on an upper floor of an office building in an area called the Galleria, at the intersection of the North Dallas Tollway and the LBJ Freeway. The Galleria area was a strange little planet of its own, locked up inside a rim of freeway ramps and access roads like a gleaming satellite spinning within rings of deadly gas. The Galleria area had been the focus of some of the era's wildest, most other-worldly real estate speculation. Only five years earlier, all of it had been brown-stubble, black-dirt prairie pasture, on land that had grown wonderful cotton briefly after the Civil War, until the soil was ruined.

At the center was the Galleria—a huge, totally enclosed, ferociously air-conditioned shopping village, from which the whole little area took its name. Clustered in around the shopping center like spires of a martian stronghold were glass-walled office towers and a hotel. At night, the entire district was occupied by half a dozen security guards mumbling to each other through walkie-talkies like geese honking. At daybreak on business days, an incredible din of humanity jammed into the area.

The district was almost entirely without connecting thoroughfares and absolutely without sidewalks, paths, or means for pedestrians. If a person who occupied an office in one of the towers hoped to eat lunch somewhere in the shopping center, he had to peel off his coat and make a bullfighting dash for it through a jumbled hell of parking structures, open lots, and service alleys, where the sun was always blazing hot and the motorists short of temper.

But on this early Saturday morning, when Linda found her way to the parking structure that served Ike's office tower, hers was almost the only car she saw. The huge, sloping, densely pillared floors of the parking structure loomed off into the gray ahead of her, empty and endless. She saw the tan car in her rear-view mirror.

Linda drove to a spot near the elevator that went down to the ground-level walkway to Ike's office building. The tan car followed her and parked in the next row, down about six empty spaces. There were two men in the car. As Linda pushed open the door of her own car and clambered out, struggling to scoop up the thick stack of files and documents she had brought for Ike, she looked up and caught one of the men watching appreciatively while her long dancer's leg pawed for the pavement.

They got out of their car with briefcases. One was taller, in his early forties, with prematurely white hair cropped close to his head and a square Lee Marvin jaw. He was handsome and well-dressed, with an unmistakable thread of tough-guy running through the face and upper body.

The other man was somewhat shorter, stockier, a little older, and strikingly good-looking. He looked like the tanned, bicycle-trained president of a Fortune 500 company, with strong dark features, level eyes, and a tangible aura of power and control about him.

They both looked away from her, speaking quietly to each other, ignoring her. Linda locked her car and hurried, juggling the files in both hands, to the elevator. The door closed behind her, and she rode down alone.

The appearance of the men and the way they had looked at her was disquieting. She disliked being here, almost alone in the parking structure. She wondered why on earth Ike had insisted on a meeting at such an odd hour. Parking structures around the shopping centers in North Dallas were sometimes dangerous places. There were rapes and robberies.

She hurried off the elevator and started down the walkway toward Ike's building. When she was two-thirds of the way, however, she was suddenly overwhelmed by the sensation of being watched from behind. She turned and looked back.

The faces of the men snapped back out of view behind the barrier on the upper level of the parking structure. They had been watching her.

Why? Waiting for the elevator? Nothing else to do? Admiring her from behind? Why did they pull back from view so suddenly? They hadn't looked like types who would be easily embarrassed. The appropriate thing would have been to smile. In the instant when she caught them, both had looked grim.

She hurried on across and entered the building. She walked down the long hallway and pushed a button for the elevator.

The men were coming. They were walking toward her on the walkway. They looked like normal people. They were walking slowly. Very slowly. She wondered what they would do when they came to the elevator. Speak? Nod?

But they stopped outside the door. They were speaking to each other. They were both watching her. She had the uncanny feeling they were waiting for her to get on the elevator. They did not want to ride with her.

The elevator arrived. She stepped on quickly and pushed the button. Her finger was trembling slightly. How silly, she thought.

Then it occurred to her that Ike might be late. He often was. Was she going to be stuck in the corridor outside his office, alone in this huge empty building? Alone except for those men?

But the moment she got off the elevator, she looked down the long corridor and saw Ike standing there in front of his door, watching for her and examining his wristwatch. She smiled when she got close, but Ike shook his head impatiently.

"Linda, I said 8:45. Where in the hell have you been, pardon my French."

"Ike," she said, laughing, "I'm only fifteen or twenty minutes late. Boy, your vacation didn't do you much good, did it?"

"Well, I said 8:45." He pushed the door open and took some of the files from her. "Go on straight back to my office, please."

She began trudging down the half-lit beige corridor toward Ike's office. "I hope you didn't have to interrupt your trip because of something to do with my case, Ike," she said.

"Where were you, Linda?"

They kept walking toward the back.

"This morning? Oh, Ike, I don't know. I'm sorry. What is the big deal, anyway?"

"Just go in my office," he said, nodding through the door.

Just as Linda stepped in through the door, she looked back quickly down the corridor behind her. She couldn't be sure, but she thought she caught a glimpse of the front door coming open and someone else beginning to come in from the corridor.

"Did you have a good vacation, Ike?"

She was standing inside the office. Ike paused out in the hallway, looking back down toward the door. "I was having a good vacation," he muttered, "until something happened."

Linda's heart sank. It was Robert. Robert had pulled something. He and Fuller had come up with some new maneuver. The custody was threatened. Linda spent most of her time trying not to play out dark mental scenarios in which she lost the children, but when something like this happened, all of her worst imaginings and fears raced through her mind in an instant.

"What is it, Ike?"

He came in from the hall but left the door open.

"Sit down."

"What is it?"

"Please sit down."

She was impatient. She didn't want to sit down. She wanted to know what was wrong. But if Ike was going to insist on being chivalrous, then the fastest way to get him to talk was to do what he said. She looked around quickly, picked a little gray chair in a corner, and went to it and sat.

"What is it, Ike?"

He walked over and stood in front of her. He gave his large head one shake, sucked in his breath, stared at her for an instant, and then said, "Robert has taken out a contract to have you killed."

She stared back. The words had flown by. "Oh, Ike," she said, smiling. "That's not funny."

He gazed back at her, trying to figure out what it was she did not understand. "Linda," he said, "this is not a joke. I have been informed by the FBI that your husband, Robert Edelman, has taken out a contract with a professional killer or killers to have you and your parents assassinated. There has already been an attempt."

She stood up and moved toward him.

"A what, Ike?"

"An attempt."

"An attempt. An attempt to. . . ?"

The two men from the parking garage came in through the open door of the office. Linda was startled by their sudden appearance here. She saw, at this closer range, that the shorter man, the Fortune 500-type, had thick salt-and-pepper hair. Both men put briefcases down by the door and walked toward Linda. As they approached her, they both made identical gestures with their hands, reaching inside their suit coats. For an instant, it occurred to Linda that these men might be about to kill her. She looked up quickly at Ike, who was calm. She looked back at the men, who were now close in front of her, each of them holding something up in front of her face with both hands, the way communicants hold the wafer in their hands before swallowing it.

"I am Special Agent Joe Masterson of the Federal Bureau of Investigation," the Fortune 500 one said. "This is my associate, FBI Special Agent Gerry Hubbell. These are our identifications."

They continued to hold their badges up in front of Linda's face. She could not read the badges because her eyes were blurred. She realized they were not going to take the badges away from her face until she made some gesture that it was all right, so she nodded and said, "Thank you."

They dropped the badges, but they continued to stand and look at her.

She realized they were waiting for her to sit back down.

She sat down.

Joe Masterson walked over to the door, picked up a slim, smooth, brown leather folio-briefcase, came back and sat down in a chair facing her a few feet away. Gerry Hubbell, the taller one with short white hair and the Lee Marvin jaw, turned and walked to a chair farther away in the room and at an angle that was almost out of her range of vision, off one shoulder, so that she had to turn her body to see him. Ike walked back behind his desk and sat down.

Masterson opened his briefcase into a flat lap-desk, which he arranged neatly, almost fussily on his knees. He plucked a pair of horn-rimmed, half-moon reading glasses from a pocket in the briefcase and slipped them up over his nose. With the glasses on, he looked like a cross between Mr. Chips and Humphrey Bogart. He pulled a sheaf of papers from the lap-desk and arranged them so that he could refer to them while he spoke.

"Mrs. Edelman," he said, "on June 25 of this year, I received information from a cooperating witness who was not an employee of the FBI but has been employed and associated with other federal branches and agencies and has been found to be reliable. . . ."

Linda watched him talk. He was well spoken, but he was not a southerner. He had a vaguely eastern accent, with a hard *th* that came out almost as a *d,* as in "dat," instead of "that." On the surface, his voice was soft and measured, but beneath the surface there was an undercurrent of toughness.

"The witness advised me that an individual known to him as James Young, a retired United States army colonel, was seeking to carry out a murder contract that he, the witness, had accepted."

The sun was beginning to flood in through the single large window at the end of Ike's office. Something down near Masterson's foot caught the light and gave off a barely perceptible glint. Linda's eye ran down the length of his thick leg until she saw the barrel and the end of the cylinder of a small revolver, strapped to the leg and protruding from the pants cuff.

"These are men with guns," she thought, while Joe Masterson continued to read from his official statement to her. The thought kept ticking back around and around in her brain like a loose fly-wheel. "Men with guns, men with guns."

Suddenly tears sprang to her eyes.

Masterson was still reading: "The cooperating witness advised Young in so many words that he was not interested in that sort of activity, but he might know someone who might be interested and used the name, Jack, as this someone."

Behind the shell of tears, her eyes went out of focus. She felt herself lifting, floating, as if leaving her body. It was as if she could look down and watch while these FBI agents informed Linda Edelman of a plot on her life. She was not really here. She was away from what was happening to Linda.

All of it raced through her heart—the years of fear, the beatings, the mounting pressure of the divorce, the terrible breathless panic she felt whenever she thought Robert was about to get the children.

But now Robert really was about to get the children! He was going to kill her! There were men with guns here in this room, and it had to do with murder.

Ike had gotten ahead of the game with Robert. He had leapfrogged over Robert and Fuller. He had leapt ahead of them and taken the advantage, and now Robert was taking it back.

A blackness began to grow at the back of her head. It was a rage that flowed down her arms like a painful injection and made her fingers curl up into claws.

This was how Robert intended to do it, how he intended to win. This was how he intended to take the children. She thought of the children; her eyes dried and she came back into focus within herself.

When she looked up, she saw that all three men were silent, staring at her.

In a quiet voice, Masterson said, "Are you going to be all right, Mrs. Edelman?"

Ike spoke up. "Are you okay, Linda? Do you need to . . . stop, or something?"

She reached in her purse for a Kleenex, wiped her eyes and nose and then sat up straight. "I am all right."

Her voice was strong, but her breath was a little short. "I have been telling people for a year now that Robert was dangerous. No one would believe me."

"We believe that your husband is a very dangerous man," Joe Masterson said.

She looked at him. It made her feel better for him to say he knew Robert was dangerous. His voice wrapped around her.

"I appreciate that," she said. "I appreciate what you are doing. What kind of danger is there right now for my children and for my parents?"

Gerry Hubbell cleared his throat at the back of the room. Masterson turned around, shot him a look, and then turned back and fixed his gaze closely on Linda's face.

"Based on the information we have, the man your husband has hired to kill you is an experienced professional assassin. We do not have enough evidence at this point to arrest him."

Linda stared back at him. The words were like blows, but she held her composure. "He is free? The killer?" she said.

"Yes."

"What about my parents and my children?"

"Your parents are at risk."

"What kind of risk?"

"Great risk. You are in danger, and they are in danger. They are included in the contract. Especially your mother. We think there may have been an attempt while you were at Disney World."

Linda stared back into his face without speaking for a long moment. "What?"

"You and your parents and your sister and your children went to Disney World last month, some time in mid-June?"

"Yes. We were supposed to go this month, right about now. But we had to go earlier to get Robert to agree, to make it jibe with his schedule."

Masterson waited patiently for her to finish.

"The assassin," he said, "stalked you and your parents while you were at Disney World. He had instructions to shoot you, your mother and maybe your father, at Disney World, in front of the children if necessary."

"In front of the children?"

"That's the information we have."

"He was there? The killer was there? Stalking us?"

"Yes. We believe so."

Linda looked around at them, turning to see Gerry Hubbell, who was silent in the far corner of the room. She turned back to Joe Masterson. She raised her eyebrows and held out her palms in a question.

"He wasn't able to do it, because of the crowds," Masterson said.

"They didn't know Disney World was crowded?" she said. "I wonder how smart a hit man he is. Of course, I can understand Robert not knowing."

"Mrs. Edelman," Masterson said, "I told you a moment ago that we believe your husband is a very dangerous man. We also believe Colonel Young is an extremely dangerous man. It was sheer good luck that a witness came forward in time. We want to arrest these men and any accomplices they may have and see them tried and punished for their crimes. We want to get to them before they get to you or your parents. But we do not have enough evidence to make a conviction stick at this point. We need your help in order to bring your husband and his accomplice to justice."

"What do you want me to do?"

There was a long pause while Joe Masterson leafed through some papers on the lap desk. Finally Ike could stand it no longer. He stood up brusquely behind his desk and said, "They want you to fake your death, Linda."

"Fake my death?"

Joe Masterson looked up over the upper rims of his little half-glasses at Ike. It was not a professorial expression. He was not happy with Ike for blurting that out. Ike looked at him and then sat back down with a boyish shrug.

"Mrs. Edelman, we need to build a very strong case to show a jury that your husband is involved in what we call a murder-for-hire or murder solicitation conspiracy. In order to make that charge stick, we have to have certain elements in our case, particularly against a man like your husband. . . "

"Who has a lot of money," Linda said, finishing the sentence for him, "and who will hire the best lawyers money can buy."

"There is that," Masterson said.

"And if this does not stick, he will use it to take my children away from me," she said, turning to Ike for confirmation.

Ike gazed back at her, expressionless.

"What is it that you want me to do?" she asked again.

Masterson explained the legal ins and outs of the case. He sketched, in very general terms, a scheme for catching Robert and the assassin and convicting them.

Linda would have to disappear for a period of time. It could be a week. It might be a month or more. They would not be able to push the pace of the operation beyond certain limits.

The FBI, Masterson said, already had infiltrated a secret agent into the situation. Colonel Young, it seems, had stopped doing his own killing some four or five years earlier. He was now in the habit of subcontracting his hits.

"Who does he work for?" Linda asked. "Who does he do these hits for?"

"We think it's mainly business people," Masterson said. "Possibly some organized crime, but probably not a lot. It's mainly your bigshot Dallas guy who wants to get rid of a business partner. . . "

"Or a wife," she said.

"Or a wife."

Colonel Young originally had approached the cooperating witness to ask him about doing the hit. But the witness had come to the FBI instead. The FBI had sent the cooperating witness back to Colonel Young to tell him he could not carry out the hit himself, for various reasons, but that he had an associate who might be interested. Through this mechanism, Young eventually was introduced to "Hitman Jack"—actually an FBI agent. Young had subcontracted with Hitman Jack to carry out the murders. Joe Masterson told Linda he did not know yet whether Young had informed Robert that he had involved either the cooperating witness or Hitman Jack. Young might want Robert to think instead that he, Young, was going to do the "heavy lifting" himself. It was all a way for Young, an experienced criminal, to insulate himself from criminal exposure and to control the operation, by making sure neither his client nor his own subcontractors ever saw the whole picture.

In this plot, Hitman Jack would inform Young that he had killed Linda after she had disappeared. When Young went to Robert to be paid for the job, the FBI would find a way to watch and capture the transaction with cameras and recorders. Then, with that kind of evidence in hand, they would seize Robert, Young, and anyone else who showed up in their net.

"How will I disappear?" she asked.

"We will take you to a safe place, where you will be protected and kept secret for the duration of the operation, until we actually make the arrests."

She gazed levelly at them. "I don't quite understand how it works," she said. "How do we explain this? How do we do it? What do we tell my family?"

She looked around the room again, and they all stared back in silence at her for a while. Finally Ike jumped up again from his chair.

"They have to tell everybody you're dead, Linda."

Masterson didn't move a muscle, but his eyes shot up over the rims of the glasses again at Ike. Ike sat down.

"In order to make this operation work, Mrs. Edelman. . . "

"You're not telling my parents I'm dead," she said. "No. No. Forget that. They are too old. My daddy is seventy-two. It would kill him."

"I share these concerns, Mrs. Edelman," Masterson said.

"You cannot tell my parents that I'm really dead."

"There is another set of considerations to keep in mind, Mrs. Edelman, as we approach this operation." He put the lap desk down on a little end table and rose to his feet. He began pacing slowly back and forth, walking with a smooth, pneumatic, muscular motion as he spoke, gesturing slowly but effectively at the air with one finger.

"Colonel Young, Mrs. Edelman, is what we in this business call a stone cold killer. He does this for a living. Your life is at risk. Your parents' lives are at risk. But we also now have an FBI agent who has presented himself to Colonel Young as an accomplice in murder.

"That agent is there to save your life. He is a man with a family, a wife, children, and his own life to live. And his own life is at serious risk every second this operation runs, until Young and your husband are behind bars.

"There is also the cooperating witness, who I must tell you has already dealt with a lot more danger than the average person could take, in order to save your life, and he doesn't even know you.

"If Young catches a single whiff of a burn, and this type of individual has got a very sensitive nose for such things . . . if either your husband or Colonel Young figures out that you are not really dead and that this is a sting operation, then somebody will get killed. Real fast. You can count on that.

"It might be you, and I don't want that. They might decide to change plans and get rid of you quick. Or it might be the one who is closer to them, which is my agent, Hitman Jack, who gets killed. And believe me, I do not want that, either. It might be our informant."

"I appreciate what you all are trying to do for me," Linda said, tears beginning to form again.

Joe Masterson sat back down and stared deeply into Linda's eyes. "I know you do, Mrs. Edelman. But I want you to appreciate something else. I want you to appreciate that this is very serious business we're dealing with here."

She looked up, wiped her eyes, and nodded yes without speaking. She continued to nod while he stared at her.

"Nothing must go wrong, Mrs. Edelman. Nothing."

She nodded.

"This is life and death."

She wiped her eyes.

Masterson looked at Ike, then at Gerry Hubbell. Another long silence was beginning to loom out over the room like a shadow.

Speaking quickly and softly, Ike said to Linda: "What about your parents?"

Masterson's shoulders slumped slightly, but he turned to Linda and waited for her response.

She looked around at them all and was quiet for a moment. "No," she said. "If you tell my daddy I am dead, it will kill him."

"Linda," Ike began.

"No," she said. "We are not telling my parents that I am dead."

"Then they will have to be in on it," said Masterson. "Do you think they can handle that?"

Linda considered the question without speaking.

"You understand," Masterson said, "how tough that's going to be. It won't be hard for you, not that part of it, because you won't be there. You won't be anywhere near anybody you know. But as far as your parents are concerned, life will have to go on for them exactly normal, the way it would happen if you really did get killed. They will have to stick to the story. If they tell anyone, then you could wind up dead and so could our agent and our informant. And maybe so could your parents. Do you think your folks can handle that?"

"What do you think?" Linda asked.

"Well, Mrs. Edelman," he said. He stopped and looked at his notes, then looked back up. "Before we ever took this case, and before we ever came up with the idea of a sting, we did some preliminary checking on you and your family. We have a research assistant at the FBI, Kathy Hagen, who is about as good at checking people out as anybody I have ever known in the business. She tells me your parents are solid people. Probably pretty strong people, I imagine."

"Yes, they are."

"Good Oklahoma blood," he said, smiling.

Linda smiled. "My mother is from Oklahoma. My daddy came to Fort Sill from Chicago during World War II."

"Met the town beauty and never left town, eh?"

"Something like that."

"They might be able to do it," he said. "It will be up to you to impress on them how important it will be for them not to slip up, not even once. But they can probably do it."

"Oh, thank God," she said. She let a deep sigh escape and put one hand to her breast. "I am so glad to hear you say that. We just could not have told them I was dead."

"The ones who can't do it are your children," Masterson said.

"Oh no!" Linda said, half shouting as she came up from her chair.

"Linda!" Ike said sharply.

"No! No! You cannot tell those children. . .!"

"Mrs. Edelman, please," Masterson said, both hands in the air and his voice flowing around her in a river of reassurance. "Please! We do not have to tell them that you are dead. That normally is not what would happen anyway."

"What do you mean?"

"You will be missing for a period of time. That way we don't have to come up with a body."

"I see."

"In real life, during that period, when there was still a ray of hope that you might be found alive, the children probably would not be told anyway that you were already dead."

"I am not quite following," she said. "I thought it was going to be announced that I was dead."

"They'll say you're missing and they're looking for you," Ike blurted from behind his desk. "Everyone will assume Robert has killed you."

Masterson looked at Ike, then turned back to Linda. "Yes. But during that period, if this were really happening, the children would naturally be given some story, such as that you decided at the last minute to go visit a friend or something in Oklahoma."

"No, no, you don't understand," Linda said. "You don't understand what our life has been like, what kind of shape these children are in. Stephen won't let me out of his sight. He asks me constantly whether I will ever leave him or whether he's going to be taken away from me."

"We'll tell them you're just visiting," Masterson began.

"No, no, you're still not . . . you don't understand what I'm telling you. My little boy is very bright, and he's also very suspicious and skeptical. I never go anywhere without telling both of them exactly where I will be and how long. I don't even go to the grocery store. They're just too fragile. They won't believe anything you tell them. If I'm gone and I haven't told them where I am. . . "

"Robert is going to grill them, Linda," Ike said.

"Robert?"

"Yes," Masterson said.

"Robert will be there."

"Robert will be free until we get the evidence we need," Masterson said. "Mr. Vanden Eykel is exactly right. The first pressure point he will use to test the story will be the children. He will figure if there's anything flaky about the story and, if they know, he'll be able to get it out of them. In order to protect your life and the life of my agent, the children must not know any detail or aspect of this operation at all."

He took off his glasses. "Mrs. Edelman, that aspect of the operation is not negotiable."

Linda sighed.

Masterson changed the subject. He put the lap desk back in position, square on his knees, and began asking Linda questions and noting her answers. Gerry Hubbell rose from his chair for the first time, came over, and stood behind Masterson to watch him jot down Linda's responses.

Masterson wanted to know exactly what Linda's normal schedule was supposed to be for the next several weeks. He took down each hair appointment, doctor's appointment, manicure, church service, and shopping trip.

Linda told him Robert was slated to pick the children up the next Friday at 4:00 P.M. and keep them for five days, until the following Wednesday at 8:00 A.M. As soon as he brought the children back to Caruth, Linda had planned to drive them up to Oklahoma, where she and her parents would then get in their new thirty-five-foot Pace Arrow motor home and drive to Silverton, Colorado, to ride the popular narrow-gauge tourist railway up into the mountains.

"We'll have to keep it that way," Masterson said. "We don't want anything to change suddenly. As far as Robert can see, it's all standard operating procedure. Life goes on." He turned to Gerry Hubbell. "Maybe we can work this into the deal."

Hubbell nodded.

Masterson said, "We have to get this thing going just as fast as we can. As long as they're out there, your husband and Colonel Young . . ."

"What kind of Colonel is he?" Linda interrupted.

"Rogue military," Masterson said. "Retired, big deal in Viet Nam, goes way back, Special Forces, we think. Had a partner up until recently who did the hits for him, but the guy had cancer or something and died. He's Chinese."

"Who is?"

"Colonel Young."

"Chinese? But he was in . . . what? The American army?"

"He's Chinese-American. Born here."

"I have to interject something here," Ike said quietly.

Masterson shrugged. "What is it?"

"The children cannot wind up in Robert's hands."

Everyone stared at Ike.

"If Robert has possession of the children when Linda is reported missing, then I think Robert will use that as an excuse to move very quickly to get the children out of range of the court, probably out of the country. I'm sure that's already an important part of his plan. What Robert wants to do is to win. What he wants to win is custody. Killing Linda is only step one. Grabbing the kids, getting them out of Dallas where nobody can get to them and keeping them there, that's step two."

No one said anything for a while.

"How will you handle Robert," Ike asked, "when this goes down? What is his position? What will your posture be, vis-à-vis Robert, once Linda has been reported missing?"

"Oh, he's suspect numero uno," Joe said. "That's always going to be the case in a situation like this. Messy divorce, lots of money in play, lots of animosity. Lots of motive for the husband to have his wife murdered. If we didn't treat Robert as, at least, a major suspect, it would look very odd. It wouldn't make sense. They'll be looking for Robert to be interviewed, and he'll have a hell of an alibi all fixed up."

There was another long silence.

"When will I be reported missing?" Linda asked.

"Pretty quick after you disappear. We have to have a report made so that the FBI can get in on the deal logically."

"How is it an FBI matter?" Ike asked. "I mean, I know how it is really. It's because the cooperating witness came to the FBI. But why does Robert think the FBI is involved?"

"We'll handle that. We'll probably disappear Linda across a state line or something."

Linda asked, "Then when will Robert be told?"

"Well," Masterson said, taking off his glasses and rubbing his eyes with his fingers, "that depends. It depends on how it goes. It's like a lot of this. We have to leave it loose and play it by ear. What we need to do is have you disappear, make a report, but then let as long a period of time go by as we can when you're just gone, but Robert hasn't been told yet."

"Why?" Ike asked.

"We want to have a period when Robert knows . . ." Masterson began. He got up from his chair, walked to a position midway between Ike and Linda, and lectured with his hands: "It's like this. Mrs. Edelman, you disappear. Hitman Jack tells Colonel Young the job's done. Whatever proof they want, they'll ask our double agent for something, he will give them the proof. So Colonel Young believes it's done.

"Colonel Young goes to Robert, says, 'It's done, she's dead, I want the rest of my money.' Robert still feels like he has a certain amount of freedom of movement, because nobody has come to him yet to tell him what's what. He's not under the microscope, so he feels okay, we hope, about meeting Colonel Young to pay him off. . . "

"Which you tape," Ike said.

"Which we hope we tape," Masterson said. "There is another reason for allowing a period of time when Robert knows Mrs. Edelman is dead but nobody has told him."

Linda and Ike waited.

"There are certain things a guy would only do if he knew he was under suspicion and about to be nabbed," Masterson said.

"Like make reservations to get out of the country?" Ike asked.

"Well, maybe, but mainly just changing his plans all of a sudden. That can provide us with evidence that will help make a case. Mainly, we want him and Young to have some time when they can run around acting like criminals who think they're smarter than everybody else. We want them to think they've pulled off the perfect crime."

Masterson was sitting again, going through notes on his lap desk.

From the back of the room, Gerry Hubbell said, "It has to go down while he's got the kids."

Linda turned to look at him. She realized it was the first time she had heard his voice. It was a nice voice, smoother and more polite than what she had expected of him. He looked tougher than his voice.

"Why?" Masterson asked.

"If it goes down while she's got the kids, and it takes a while, then the natural thing is for him to come get the kids when it rolls around to his turn for them again."

"Which the court is going to support absolutely," Ike said. "Believe me. The last thing this judge is going to do is change the deal in any way. Will the judge be in on it? Will he know what's really happening?"

"The divorce judge?" Masterson asked. "No. No way. No one, no one but us right here in this room and now, I guess, Mrs. Edelman's parents."

"No one in local law enforcement?" Ike asked.

"We have one guy in the University Park police department we might use," Masterson said. "The chief. He's solid. But we have problems elsewhere."

There was a long silence, during which Ike stared at Masterson with raised eyebrows.

"Problems?" Ike asked.

"Oh, well, Ike, you know Robert," Linda said. "He brags all the time about how he's got the City of Dallas cops in his pocket."

"We have problems," Masterson said. "We'll leave it at that. But no one outside our circle is to know, and that includes the judge in the divorce case."

Ike allowed a deep breath of air to escape. "Man," he said. "This is . . . this is awfully dicey, it seems to me. You can't trust the local law enforcement agencies, and yet you're going to have to report Linda missing to them. I mean, it seems to me as if there are an awful lot of points along the way when things could slip between the cracks."

"It's a very dangerous business, Mr. Vanden Eykel," Masterson said, "life and death."

"Then, uh, Agent . . . the other agent," Ike stammered.

"Agent Hubbell," Masterson said.

"Then Agent Hubbell is right. If you start this while the kids are with Linda, and if it takes a while, then Robert will come pick the kids up on his day."

"Whereas," Masterson began. He stopped to think. "If we start it when he's got them, and we let it run a few days before he is officially informed, then he would have to bring the kids back."

"Why?" Linda asked.

"Because he's not supposed to know you're gone. Just like we can't change any routines to tip our hand to him, he's locked into his routines, too. If he fails to bring the kids back on time, he knows that will be proof he knows something. He's got to act like he doesn't know anything. So he has to bring the kids back. . . "

"As if everything is normal," Linda said.

"Right," Masterson said.

"Right," Ike said.

"That's right," Gerry Hubbell said.

They all looked at each other for a while, blinking like surprised chickens.

"Who would be in the house Wednesday, the way things stand?" Masterson asked.

Linda thought for a moment. "Only Zsa. Rezilla Williams. My house-keeper. She's very close to the children and extremely responsible."

"That's not enough," Ike said. "If we're going to do this, then we can't have any periods when the children are not in the custody of family."

Joe Masterson stood up and reassumed his professorial position at the head of the room. "All right, everybody, here's the deal. We have some FBI-type pieces we have to put into play this coming week anyway, before the deal will be ready to go.

"Next Friday, Mr. Edelman comes to get the kids. The following weekend, we're going to disappear Mrs. Edelman. We will keep the thing low-key and quiet until after the following Wednesday, when he brings the kids home.

"We will go ahead and use the Silverton narrow-gauge trip to get the grandparents down here, instead of you going up there to join them. We can afford that much of a change. You tell the kids before they go to stay with Mr. Edelman that you changed your mind, the grandparents are going to come down here in the motor home and pick you all up here in Dallas for the trip. So your parents could come down Tuesday and be here already when Robert drops off the kids. Would that be normal?"

"Yes," Linda said. "Very normal. Typical, in fact."

"Great. Do you have any questions?"

"Yes. Where will I be?"

"When?"

"When I'm dead."

Joe and Ike exchanged a worried look.

"You mean when you're in custody, Linda?" Ike asked.

"Yes, I mean when I'm in custody, Ike."

Ike and Linda laughed. Joe was expressionless.

"We haven't settled that," Joe said. "We'll probably take you to a hotel in another city."

"How far away?"

"Pretty far."

"I don't like that," she said. "If something goes wrong with the children, I want to be within a few hours' drive of them."

"Well, what's going to go wrong with the children?" Joe asked.

"I don't know," she said. "But I do not want to be that far away from them in case something does."

"The problem is, we don't have anything that close that I would consider safe, given your husband's means and his connections and so on around Dallas."

Ike came forward. "I've been thinking about this," he said. "My wife and I have a nice lake house in East Texas, about two hours from here. It's extremely secluded, and nobody knows we have it. It's our hideaway."

Gerry Hubbell looked up. "What lake?" he asked.

Ike gave him the name of the lake. It was a typical East Texas body of water, created as an enormous reservoir for Dallas in the 1950s, with a complicated shoreline of coves and niches and a forest of dead trees still sticking out of the water in places. Many Dallas people used it as a weekend destination.

When Ike named the lake, Joe and Gerry exchanged sharp looks.

"That might be good," Joe said.

"Be great for me," Gerry said, snickering.

"All right." Masterson looked at his watch. They had been at it for over two hours. The instant Joe Masterson glanced at his watch, Linda realized that she was exhausted.

"Mrs. Edelman, here is what I need you to do. I need you to go home. Your parents are there now, is that right?"

"Yes. How did you know that?"

There was a silence.

"They have you under surveillance, Linda," Ike said.

"Oh."

Masterson squinted at Ike, then said: "I want you to tell your parents that Ike needs to see you and them first thing Monday. To go over their testimony." He looked to Ike for approval.

Ike nodded. "Sure. We're supposed to be two weeks away from trial."

"By that time, when we all get back together Monday, Agent

Hubbell and I will have a detailed plan worked up with every little part of it all planned out. We will be burning the midnight oil between now and Monday morning, believe me."

"When do I tell them?" Linda asked.

"Your parents?"

"Yes."

"You don't, Mrs. Edelman. We do. When they get here. We still have a whole lot of details to work out."

He got up, walked to her, stood before her, bent forward, and put his hands on her shoulders.

"Mrs. Edelman," he said, "can I call you Linda?"

"Please."

"Linda. If you say anything to anyone, someone may be killed as a result. It may be you. It might be our informant. It might be our agent. It could be one or both of your parents. Do you understand me?"

"Yes."

"No one must know."

"I understand."

Ike tapped a pencil on his desk, thinking. "Joe," he said, "I have a question. How does Robert plan to have it done? Do you know? Do you have any idea when or how the hit man is supposed to do it?"

"Not yet," Masterson said. He straightened up. "Nine o'clock Monday morning sound okay to you, Ike, for the next meeting?"

Ike nodded and shook his head at the same time. "Oh, that sounds wonderful," he said.

Linda rose, thinking she could leave. She wanted to leave. But as soon as she rose, a terrible chill ran down her spine; her forehead broke out in sweat; she felt flushed; her breath was short, and she sat back down.

"Linda?" Ike asked. "You okay?"

She waved them all away. "No. No, I'm not okay. I'm scared to death. What happens to me now? Who is going with me? Do I go home alone? Is someone out there going to try to kill me? To shoot me? With a gun? Is that how they'll do it? Or stab me? Or blow me up with a bomb?"

"You will be protected at all times," Masterson said quickly. "You will not see us. But we will be there. You will be safe."

"I go home alone then?"

"Yes. But we have one last detail to ask for your help with."

Masterson explained he and Agent Hubbell would leave Ike's office first. On the way in that morning, they had scouted a position from the parking structure from which they wanted to take a picture of Linda.

They needed a photograph of her for Hitman Jack, who would supply it to Colonel Young as a surveillance shot, to prove he was on the case.

They wanted Linda to follow them out of the building by a few minutes, pause and look up at them in the parking structure. They would take her picture, and then they would leave. She would not see them again until Monday.

Masterson asked her again if she would be all right, and she said she would. Then Masterson and Hubbell left.

Ike came around from behind his desk and took her by one arm.

"Linda," he said. "Can you do this?"

"Yes, Ike. I think so."

"Linda, I want to tell you something. If you can do this? If you can do it right, and not get killed or get somebody else killed?"

"Yes."

"And not get anybody killed?"

"Yes."

"Including me?"

"Yes."

"Your custody worries are over."

She looked at him in stunned silence for a moment. He stared back into her face, wide-eyed and sincere. Then it dawned on her.

"Oh my gosh, Ike, you're right, aren't you?"

"You bet I am. Robert loses. Big time."

"Oh. The children would be mine?"

"Totally. Forever."

"Wouldn't that be wonderful?."

"You better go. They're waiting."

Ike helped Linda slip into her raincoat. He walked her back down the long corridor to the reception area, then reached forward awkwardly and squeezed her arm as he saw her out the front door.

"You're going to be all right, Linda. They're watching you. I grilled them about that. I made sure you will be protected."

She smiled, then walked to the elevator and rode down alone. It was a short distance from the bank of elevators on the ground level to the door to the outside walkway. She pushed open the door, walked out, and looked up. She gasped.

Two men were looking down. One was pointing something at her. She recognized Joe Masterson. Was this the moment when she would die? Who were they? They were men with guns. They showed her identification; she didn't see it; it meant nothing. She didn't know what to do with identification offered by men with guns. There, standing stupidly with her face upturned and both hands clutching her purse, her legs and arms shaking, with two men looking down and pointing a thing at her, she saw that her life was entirely in their hands: They could take her picture or they could blow her head apart like an overripe melon.

They took her picture and disappeared. When she got up to the level where her car was parked, she saw the brake lights of their car flash as they slowed to go down the curving ramp.

Her hand was still shaking slightly as she tried to get the ignition key into the slot. Her foot trembled on the accelerator, and the car lurched and squealed backward a few feet, then coughed and died. She got it going, got it turned around the right way and followed them down the ramp. They were nowhere in sight when she got to the bottom. She negotiated the complex webwork of narrow service roads that led out to the North Dallas Tollway, then headed south, back to the house on Caruth.

Traffic was light. A car came up fast behind her, then whizzed past. It was a large BMW with two gray-templed golfers inside, off to begin their weekend. Another car eased up next to her—an expensive Japanese sedan. Linda looked over and saw a well-dressed grandmotherly woman at the wheel and two young children in the back seat.

"Oh my word," she said out loud to herself. Her lips barely moving, she mumbled, "Robert wants me to be dead." Tears began streaming down her face. "I shouldn't be out here," she thought. "I can't see to drive, because I'm crying. I am scared to death. I am afraid every person I see will lift a gun to the window and blow my brains out. They shouldn't have let me drive home alone."

Her hands began trembling, then her arms, then her shoulders. The steering wheel vibrated, and the car began to wobble slightly. Then, just as suddenly as the tears had come, they stopped. She lifted one arm of her raincoat and wiped her eyes on it, smearing mascara all over her sleeve. She gripped the wheel hard, and the trembling went away.

"All right, this is it," she thought. "This is the deal. Robert has just changed the deal, and now this is what the new game is. If I die, if I let him kill me, or if I get in a wreck and kill myself or mess up this FBI business in some way, then he wins the game. He takes Stephen and Kathleen, and they spend the rest of their lives living in whatever version of hell that means.

"If I win, he loses. But I have got to do this right in order to win."

She began drifting back again to the thought that Robert wanted her to be dead. The instant she allowed her mind to move in that direction, she could feel the trembling just on the verge of returning. She realized she could not afford to dwell on what any of this meant. All she could do was go ahead. And win. And live.

Her mother was sitting in the large family room adjacent to the kitchen, watching the children finish a late Saturday morning breakfast. Virginia's ears pricked up when she heard the car roll into the garage and then heard the door from the garage to the back corridor open. She could tell exactly how each visit to the lawyer had gone by listening to the sound of Linda's footfall coming down the back corridor afterward.

This visit had gone very badly, her ears told her. There must have been bad news about the children. She filed this insight away. She never pressed Linda for news, but now she would know exactly what to listen for as the day wore on and as Linda began volunteering small bits and pieces.

Linda's father came walking through the family room with his slightly hesitant gait, gazing at Virginia through his spectacles.

"She back?"

Virginia nodded.

"Hi, Daddy," Linda said, coming into the room, still in her coat, peeling off the scarf. "Hello, Mama."

John walked up to her and stared into her face.

"How'd it go?"

"Oh, it went all right. Just a bunch of lawyer things, sort of depressing, but it's all okay. I'll tell you later. When were you all going back up to Duncan?"

"Just right now," John said. "Soon as you got back. Been waiting."

Linda took off her coat and laid it over a chair. Zsa swept by in the background, picked the coat up, and disappeared with it.

"I think you should stay," Linda said. "Ike needs to see you Monday morning, to go over your testimony."

"Linda," Virginia said, "are you all right?"

Linda looked back at her limply. She was not eager to go through an examination. "Yes, Mother, I'm fine. Just tired. We worked hard."

"You look puny."

"I'm fine."

John was staring at her, still weighing what she had said. "He wants us to what?"

"Go over our testimony, John," Virginia said. "He's going to rehearse us."

John considered it, then shrugged. "Huh," he said, with a tiny smile. "Says on Perry Mason they're not supposed to do that."

"Yes," Virginia said, rising to get Linda something to eat. "But Perry Mason never met Robert Edelman."

She said to Linda, "We'll just stay, then. Can I get you something to eat, honey? You don't look well."

Virginia busied herself putting together a light lunch for Linda. John sat down at the long table in the center of the room and gestured for Linda to come sit across from him. He held his hand out to her and squeezed her hand.

"Are you all right, Linda?"

For all his tenderness and sensitivity to her, John had never awarded her a pet name like "Honey" or "Baby." He was always formal in his outward manner—informal and loving in his eyes.

"Yes, Daddy, I'm fine. I'm so sorry to interrupt your schedule."

He waved a hand at her. "What did Ike talk to you about all this time?"

"Just details. Getting ready."

Virginia came back to the table and put a plate down before Linda. "You go ahead and get some food in your stomach. The kids have eaten. I think they're both planning on running down to the Lehners' to play there."

Linda was toying with her food, half listening. Virginia explained that she and John had been planning on stopping off on their way home at the Target discount department store to pick up some things John needed for his shop. "So we may just go on ahead and do that now," she said

Linda looked up. "I'm sorry? Do what?"

"We're going to go to Target and pick up some things. Is that all right, John?"

"Certainly. I'll go get the car out of the garage." John rose to his feet and headed toward the back hallway that led to the garage.

In an instant Linda was on her feet and standing between her father and the door to the back hall. "No, Daddy, I don't think you should." She put her hands lightly on his shoulders and tried to turn him back toward the table.

"You don't think I should what?" John said. The slightest shadow of crankiness flashed across his brow.

"Mother," she said, speaking around her father, "I don't think you should go to Target right now." Her voice was just half a tone too high and a barely perceptible bit forced.

John looked at her hands on his shoulders and turned around to Virginia. "What's the matter with her?"

"What is it, Linda?" Virginia asked, squinting across the large room to see Linda's eyes.

"Well," Linda said, with forced cheeriness, "I just wish we could all stay together today and have a nice family day, here in the house."

"Yeah," John said. "That's what we'll do. After we get back from Target." He reached up and decorously removed her hands from his shoulders and began moving around her to get to the door.

"No!" Linda said, her voice inching toward stridence. She moved and put herself between him and the door again. "I don't want you to go to Target. I want you to stay here. It will upset me very much if you go to Target without me."

John stopped and regarded her for a long silent moment. "It will upset you very much if we go to Target without you. Then why don't you finish eating, and then you can go to Target with us?"

"No, no. I don't want anyone to go to Target. I want us to stay here in the house today and just be together and spend a day together and not run off shopping. . ."

"Not running off shopping," John muttered half to himself. He was beginning to be indignant. "Just going to Target."

"John," Virginia said, "I think Linda's right. I think we should just stay in today. We can go to Target tomorrow, after church." She came over, put her arm around Linda, and led her back to her chair at the table. All three of them sat down.

"You're right, honey," Virginia said. "We'll just stay in."

Linda sat at the table and stared at her food. "Mama," she said.

"Yes?"

"I don't . . . uh, I really don't feel like going to church this weekend, either."

John looked up sharply, then turned and exchanged a long meaningful gaze with Virginia.

"That's fine," Virginia said. "We won't go to church either."

John looked from one of them to the other and back again, saying nothing. He rose slowly, walked over to the sofa beneath a large window at the outside wall of the room, opened a newspaper, and settled in to read for an hour or so.

Virginia said, "John can just take the children to Sunday school and drop them off."

"No," Linda said quickly, "I don't want them taken to Sunday school. We'll all just stay together here tomorrow."

John dropped his newspaper just enough to barely peek over the top at Virginia, who barely acknowledged his glance. He put the paper down and went to the utility room at the back of the house where supplies and a small stepladder were stored. It had always irritated John that Robert was so incapable of taking care of anything in his own home. The house was full of recessed ceiling lights, upstairs and down, at least half of which were burned out.

There was a small mountain of replacement bulbs in yellow corrugated packages on a shelf in the utility room. John tried to read the packages, but the poor lighting in the utility room made it impossible. He grabbed a stack of packages off the top of the pile, wrestled the stepladder out into the hallway, and busied himself for most of the rest of the day replacing bulbs in the ceiling.

The minute it was settled that they would all stay close to the house, Linda found that she had a new problem. She had no idea what to do next. Time slowed and flowed in around her, trapping her as if she were a beetle in amber. The day barely moved ahead from minute to minute, hour to hour. The grandfather clock in the hallway tapped out the minutes one by one like a snare drum in a funeral parade. Every time the children ran out the door and down the street to the Lehner house, Linda stepped out onto the lawn to watch them go. And every time a passing automobile whizzed by, something in her consciousness cringed in anticipation of a blow.

Linda's friend Janet called in late afternoon.

"I'm so tired of these four walls," Janet said. "Are your parents in town?"

"Yes."

"What about going shopping with me this evening? There's a new place a friend of mine was telling me about at North Park. . . "

"Thanks, Janet, but I don't think so. I'm not in much of a shopping mood."

"You're not? Well, all right. Is everything all right at Casa Edelman? Has that monster been causing any more mayhem lately?"

"No, everything's fine. We're just having a cozy family weekend together."

"Good. Well, maybe next time."

"Yes, Janet, thanks for thinking of me."

"When does Robert pick them up?"

"Next Friday. He has them for five days."

"Ike got the judge off that thing of house-trading?."

"Yes."

"No more trading houses. No more Holiday Inn. He just takes them to Pagewood on his time?"

"Yes."

"Ike's great, isn't he?"

"Yes."

"It sounds as if he's turned your whole case around."

"Yes."

"All right. Linda's not feeling chatty."

"Sorry."

"Perfectly all right. I will just check back with you. Maybe we can go see a movie while he has the kids."

"Yes. That would be nice."

She hung up.

Linda and her mother put the children to bed early. Virginia went back downstairs to join John, who was watching television in the family room. Linda went into her bedroom and sat on the edge of the huge, flouncy four-poster bed for a while.

She stared through the open door into the dressing room. The bathroom was on the other side of the dressing room. An image popped into her mind: it was of tufts of insulation on the carpeting in the dressing room. She rose and walked into the dressing room. The floor was clean. But she remembered where she had seen the tufts of insulation, the day she had come back from a weeklong sojourn at the Holiday Inn, back when the judge was still making her vacate the house during Robert's time with the children.

She had unlocked the bedroom door that morning. The judge had granted an order allowing her to keep the bedroom and dressing room locked while she was out of the house and ordered Robert to stay out of that part of the house. She had looked in the dressing room then, as she was looking now, and she had seen the insulation on the floor. She had looked up quickly, realizing Robert had broken in. She had scanned the racks and seen that a good deal of clothing had been taken. And then she had looked straight up at the ceiling, as she was looking now, and she had seen the trap-door to the attic, left slightly ajar.

Now she stared up at the trap door and saw that it was perfectly in place. A shudder went through her.

The FBI agents had told her that she must do everything exactly as she would under normal circumstances. The killer would be watching, to see whether she knew. The slightest deviation, the least little tip or clue might be enough to give it all away. What would happen after that was anyone's guess.

She went downstairs to the family room. John was watching football, and Virginia was reading *Time* magazine.

"Y'all, I've been thinking," Linda said, "and I guess I think I'd like for us all to go to church together tomorrow."

Virginia looked up and stared at her for a moment before answering. "You do want to go to church in the morning?"

"Yes."

"Fine," she said. She leaned over to John, who was hard of hearing anyway, and was almost deaf when the television set was turned up loud. "Linda wants to go to church tomorrow," she said.

"What?" he said.

"LINDA WANTS TO GO TO CHURCH TOMORROW!"

"Go to church?"

"YES. GO TO CHURCH."

"I'm watching football."

"No, tomorrow, John. She wants to go to church tomorrow."

He reached over, flipped off the television, and smiled up at Linda. "Good, Linda. I think that's a good idea. Fix what ails you."

It was a special and difficult Sunday at Park Cities Baptist Church. A cloud of grief had been lingering over the huge parish on Northwest Highway in North Dallas for a week, since the death in a private plane crash of three men prominent in lay religious circles in Dallas, one of them an elder of Park Cities Baptist. The pastor of the church, Dr. James Pleitz, had been in Switzerland when the accident occurred. He had just returned a few days ago. The service, attended by Linda, her parents, and her children, was an unofficial memorial for the dead men.

In his sermon on this Sunday, Dr. Pleitz referred only obliquely to the freak crash over the Dakotas that had taken the lives of the elders. He pointed out that on the day before this crash, two large commercial airliners had passed within a few hundred yards of each other off the California coast. The hair's-breadth escape from disaster, he said, had been a miracle.

While it was not in man's ability to understand everything God did, he said, it was in God's ability to give man the strength, hope, and faith he needed to carry on.

"Sometimes," he said, "all we can do is go from this day to the next, barely plodding ahead, barely able to walk and not faint. In those terrible moments, we must remember the words of the prophet, Isaiah, when he said, 'but they who wait for the Lord shall renew their strength, they shall mount up with wings like eagles, they shall run and not be weary, they shall walk and not faint.' "

It was a short drive from Park Cities Baptist to Caruth. They rode the several blocks in silence. John drove. Linda sat in the back with the children, peering at every car that passed them. When they were all standing back in the family room, Virginia said, "Well, Linda, it looks like we are the ones who are walking and not fainting."

Linda smiled and reached out to take both of her mother's hands. A tear leapt to her eye. "Yes, Mama, we are. I am so lucky. . . ." She choked up for a moment. "I am so lucky to have all of you. You and Daddy. And. . ."

She turned and looked at her children. "My darling Kathleen," she said, kneeling to hug her. "And my brave little Stephen," she said, pulling him to her by one hand.

Above her and out of her line of sight, John gave Virginia a sharp look and then shook his head solemnly. Virginia shrugged and held out her hands to show she didn't know what it was.

CHAPTER FOUR

S he rose early that morning and went down to the kitchen. Linda
made coffee so that it would be ready for Zsa when she got there.
Then she went back upstairs. She could hear the sounds of her
mother and father stirring in the guest room at the back of the house.
She found her mother in the guest bathroom.

Linda held her hand forward and opened it. In her palm were three
prescription pain relievers. "Mother, I want you to take these."

Virginia stared at the pills. "Linda, I'm not nervous about seeing
Ike."

Virginia and John had already met with Ike Vanden Eykel several
times. They respected him and had even grown a little fond of him.

"I don't care, Mama. I want you to take these. Just take them.
Please. For me."

Virginia swallowed the pills a little glumly. Then Linda found her
father, who almost never took medication of any kind.

"I don't want that, Linda," he said.

"I want you to take these pills."

"Why?"

"I just do."

"I don't want to."

"Daddy, just take them. Please. I insist."

"You insist?"

"Yes."

"You insist!"

"Yes. I do. I insist. Take them. Please. Right now."

John swallowed them, but he was angry about it.

Zsa would feed the children when they rose. Linda and her mother climbed into John's car. John drove them to the Galleria. As each new mile ticked by on the North Dallas Tollway, Linda could feel her stomach knotting tighter.

Linda pushed open the wide door that opened on the reception area of Ike's law firm and ushered in her parents. The receptionist smiled at Linda and said good morning.

"Mr. Vanden Eykel will be with you in just a moment," she said.

Joe Masterson and Gerry Hubbell were already there, waiting in the reception area. Gerry was sitting at one end of a leather sofa. Joe was sitting across from him in an overstuffed chair. Both were staring off into space, as if they had never seen Linda before in their lives—as if, in fact, they had never seen each other before in their lives.

Linda attempted to steer her parents toward chairs and a love seat at the far end of the reception area. Her mother walked in the direction Linda indicated with her arm, but John balked. He stepped out of the way of Linda's arm and walked right over to the sofa where Gerry was sitting. There were fishing magazines on a coffee table in front of the sofa. John sat down next to Gerry Hubbell, picked out a magazine, and settled in to read while he waited.

Ike appeared. Ike was always natty and extremely neat—"smooth as a jelly bean," Virginia liked to say—but on this Monday morning he was especially impeccable. Each shining silver-blond hair was in place; his white shirt was starched smooth as marble; his blue eyes gleamed like stained glass; and his face was bright with a beaming, absolutely joyless smile.

"Good morning," he said.

"Good morning, Ike," Virginia said.

"Hi, Ike," John said, boyish behind his magazine.

"Good morning, Ike," Linda said.

"Why don't you all come back with me," he said. "I'm all ready for you."

As soon as Linda and her parents were in the corridor, Joe and Gerry rose. The receptionist started to speak to them, but Ike lifted a hand and nodded slightly to her, to show that it was all right. The three men followed Linda and her parents down the hall.

When they were almost at Ike's office, John noticed the two extra men following. He stopped and turned to look at them.

"Ike's office is right here, Daddy," Linda said, steering him through the door.

John looked up at his daughter through his thick spectacles and brushed off his sleeve where Linda had been tugging at him. He stepped through the door and stood waiting. When Ike and the two men followed him through the door, John took a standing position, with his legs spread apart, staring at the two strangers, waiting for an explanation. Linda was able to get her mother into a chair.

"Would you please sit down, Daddy?"

There was an awkward silence while John stared at her and stared at the two men. Ike smiled helplessly at John, whose face never cracked. Finally John shrugged, walked over, and sat next to Virginia. Gerry and Joe remained standing by the door, briefcases in hand.

The receptionist appeared, uninvited but obviously curious.

"Coffee, anyone?" she asked.

Ike looked around the room. "Would anyone like coffee? Use the bathroom? Because then I'm going to close the door," he said, looking pointedly at the receptionist, "and ask that we not be disturbed by anyone, for any reason."

Virginia said, "Yes, I'd like a cup of coffee, please."

A barely audible sigh escaped from Ike. He stood watching nervously while the receptionist took orders and then left. The room was silent. Virginia smiled at the men standing by the door. Joe Masterson smiled back. In his early fifties and with a strong, vigorous face, Joe had a smile to which women of all ages instantly warmed.

John sat silently and continued to stare at the two men, his own face stolid and emotionless.

Ike sat at his desk, staring at the open door, waiting for the receptionist to return. Finally she came back in with the tray. Ike reached forward hurriedly and unloaded the two cups of coffee, sloshing coffee into the bone saucers in his haste.

Then he whirled to find the receptionist still standing behind him, looking on expectantly, as if she intended to stay.

"Thank you," Ike said, nodding for her to leave. "That will be all. From now on, I do not want to be disturbed. Tell my secretary that, when she gets in."

The receptionist smiled and nodded.

"At all," Ike said. He gestured toward the room and the meeting about to begin. "It's private."

The receptionist withdrew. Ike reached over, closed the door, and clicked the lock.

Linda was standing behind her parents, staring at Ike.

Ike cleared his throat. "Mr. and Mrs. DeSilva," Ike said, "I would like you to meet Special Agents Joe Masterson and Gerry Hubbell of the FBI."

Joe came forward first, with Gerry just behind him. Each had his FBI identification in a folding wallet held in both hands, as if in prayer. Virginia craned around and looked to Linda for an explanation. John stared at the identification and then stared at the faces of the two men.

The men took seats near John and Virginia. Ike, who was standing, stepped to the center of the room.

"Mr. and Mrs. DeSilva," he said, "these gentlemen are here because Robert has taken out a contract on Linda's life."

The room was quiet.

"Taken out a contract?" Virginia said softly.

Ike paused. Linda stepped around and knelt in front of her parents. She heard a faint high-pitched ringing somewhere, like the tinkle of broken glass jumbled together. She looked down and saw that her mother's coffee cup was shaking as she held it on the saucer. She put the fingers of her left hand on her mother's wrist and took John's left hand in her right.

"Mama. Daddy. Do you know what Ike means when he says Robert 'took out a contract?' "

Virginia murmured, "To kill you."

John was silent.

"Daddy, were you able to hear what Ike just said?"

John peered at her. "Yes," he said quietly. "I understand."

Ike said, "Agent Masterson would like to speak to you now about this situation."

As soon as Ike had spoken, Joe Masterson stood up, returned to the doorway where he had left his briefcase, and retrieved it. He came back to his chair and sat down facing the DeSilvas. He opened the flat leather folio and spread it across both of his knees. He reached in and withdrew his half-lens reading glasses, which he installed and adjusted tidily on his nose.

While John and Virginia listened intently, Joe recited the chronology of the case so far. He told them about Colonel Jimmy Young, and his "subcontracting" of killers for hire. Robert had hired the retired U.S. Army colonel to kill Linda. Young, he said, was a rogue former special forces officer, a Chinese-American with extensive combat and intelligence experience in Southeast Asia. The FBI believed Young to be an extremely dangerous, highly skilled, well-established procurer of professional murderers.

Young did not do the killing himself. He subcontracted that work. Robert might not realize yet that Young was not going to kill Linda himself. Young had worked for years with an associate who had done the actual killing. Young was extremely well-connected in the shadow world of mercenary soldiers and mercenary murderers. He had always been in charge of seeking new business rather than carrying out the "heavy lifting" himself.

Jimmy Young's long-term associate had died of cancer a few years ago. Since then, Young had been forced to farm out work to professional killers on a freelance basis. In this particular case, he had picked the wrong freelancer.

Reaching into his contacts in the world of mercenary soldiers, Colonel Young had come up with the man who then became the FBI's "cooperating witness" in the case. His name was Fred Zabitosky. He was a retired army sergeant who, until a few years ago, had been running a mercenary operation in Laos, in support of anti-communist guerrillas.

Outwardly, at least, Zabitosky was just the type of man Colonel Young was accustomed to recruiting—a trained killer with a lot of military experience, capable of planning and carrying out a clandestine mission, capable of thinking for himself, and willing to accept cash in payment for his services.

The difference—what Colonel Young's practiced eye had failed to note—was that Fred Zabitosky was several cuts above the quality of man with whom Jimmy Young was accustomed to doing business. Fred Zabitosky was a real, bona fide, card-carrying hero.

While in the Special Forces in Viet Nam, Zabitosky had helped lead small Special Forces reconnaissance teams deep into enemy territory. On one such mission, his team had been attacked by a much larger unit of the North Vietnamese Regular Army.

Zabitosky ordered his team to retreat to a helicopter landing site for evacuation while he stayed behind to cover them. He single-handedly held off the entire enemy force with grenades and small arms fire until his team had escaped. Then he worked himself back to the landing site, where he deployed the team in defensive positions. Diving from man to man through a hail of automatic weapons fire, Zabitosky urged his team on while they waited for the helicopters to arrive.

He helped direct the approach of the choppers and dispatched the team members to them one by one. By the time the team had been boarded, the enemy guns were thick and close, and the air was gray with bullets. Last to board, Zabitosky dove into the side of the gunship and took a crouching position in the open door, continuing to fire at the onrushing enemy. But in midair during lift-off, the helicopter was struck. It crashed and burned. Zabitosky was thrown clear, but suffered several broken bones and severe burns.

Ignoring his own wounds, Zabitosky dragged himself back to the flaming wreck and pulled the unconscious pilot clear. He attempted to go back for the bodies of his team members but was driven back by the intense heat. He returned to the pilot, whom he dragged through enemy fire to another clearing, where a second helicopter was able to approach. Zabitosky helped the crew of the second chopper load the pilot, and then he himself collapsed unconscious on the ground. Others of his team, who were already on the second helicopter, retrieved him. For this episode, Fred Zabitosky was awarded the Congressional Medal of Honor.

It was true he had worked in Laos as a mercenary after his military retirement, but the Laos operation had been supported with American dollars, probably from the CIA. His motives for going back to Southeast Asia to risk his life had been more idealistic and ideological than pecuniary.

Colonel Young approached Zabitosky when Zabitosky was in Dallas to take part in a special Green Beret alumni memorial service at the monument to President John F. Kennedy, creator of the army Special Forces. At first when Colonel Young had approached Zabitosky about doing a hit, Zabitosky had dismissed him as a nut—typical of a tough-talking adult male groupie who tends to be attracted to former Green Berets.

But after the second conversation, Fred Zabitosky's antennae told him Colonel Jimmy Young was no joke.

"The cooperating witness became concerned," Joe Masterson said, reading from his notes, "that his contact was serious about finding someone to carry out the murder-for-hire contract and would lose interest and go find someone else if the cooperating witness did not come up with a response. Therefore, the cooperating witness said that he knew someone, whom he referred to as 'Jack,' who might be willing to take the assignment."

Joe Masterson took off his glasses and leaned forward to explain to John and Virginia what had happened since then. Fred Zabitosky had only come to the FBI two weeks ago. In that time, the FBI had managed to insert an undercover agent into the Jimmy Young murder-for-hire plot. Picking up on the name Zabitosky had suggested for his friend, the FBI undercover agent was being presented to Young as "Hitman Jack."

Young, meanwhile, was putting extreme pressure on Zabitosky to get the job done immediately, within the next two weeks.

Linda's father listened intently. "He wants it done before the divorce gets to trial," he muttered, almost to himself. "Robert wants her dead before the divorce is final."

Whatever the rationale, Masterson said, the point was that the operation he was about to propose had to proceed immediately. If it was not launched right away—if Young could not be assured that a hit was underway and would be accomplished within the next week—then Young might shift gears and hire someone else.

Masterson paused and sat up straight. He surveyed the family carefully. "There is also the possibility, I must tell you, that he has already hired someone else."

"What?" Linda said.

Masterson explained that Young could have offered the job to more than one hitman, figuring he would pay whichever one got it done first. There was also the possibility that Robert might have done the same thing: he might have hired one or more agents other than Young to get it done.

"So," Ike said, hearing this point for the first time, "you don't know for sure how many killers are out there stalking her or who they might be."

"No," Masterson said. "We do not."

All anyone could know for sure was that Robert had made a decision to have Linda killed, and that he had involved a professional assassin or assassins in his scheme. Therefore, it was imperative that the authorities move to build a case against Robert and get him under arrest as soon as possible.

"Why don't you go arrest him, then?" John asked.

"We could," Joe said. "We probably have enough to get a magistrate to sign a warrant. What we don't have is enough to make a case on him."

"A case?" Virginia asked.

"Right now we don't have any direct evidence linking Robert to a plot to kill Linda. All we have is our cooperating witness's word that Colonel Jimmy Young told him that Robert Edelman had hired him to carry out a hit. If that's all we took to the U.S. Attorney, we'd never even get into court."

Ike, who had been sitting behind his desk, stood up and paced out into the room. "Robert's divorce attorney, Ken Fuller, is tough, and he's tops. If we make a run at Robert with this, and if Robert slips free, then I think it will be used against us in the divorce case."

"I could lose my children," Linda said.

Ike shrugged.

"What do we have to do?" John asked.

Joe smiled at John, then grew somber again. "There is one other thing I need to talk to you about, before we get into the sting itself. One of my fellow agents is going to be out there, with his life on the line every second of the time."

Speaking slowly and deliberately, Joe explained that both Robert and Young would be watching every move the family made in order to gauge whether their plot had been discovered.

"We will operate on the assumption that the house phones and the house itself are bugged," Joe said.

"Linda's house?" John asked.

"Yes, Daddy," Linda said. She had thought about this already on her own. "He's had plenty of opportunity to be all over that house, or someone he hired has. That business where he kept stealing my clothes, crawling in and out of the attic, that could have been a cover-up for hooking up some kind of microphones."

"Then why don't we go stay somewhere else?" Virginia asked.

Joe immediately shook his head no. "That's exactly what you cannot do. You have got to continue to do exactly what you would be doing normally, including staying in the house when you would normally be staying in it."

"But he can hear us in there," John said.

"Who can?" Virginia asked. "This man?" she said, nodding toward Joe.

"No, Virginia," John said impatiently, "the hitman—the man . . . Young! Whatever his name is! The Colonel."

"Or Robert," Ike said.

"What about here?" John said.

"We have swept Ike's office," Joe said.

John waited for Joe to explain what that meant.

"It's safe to talk here," Joe said.

"Well, if Robert's been all over that house. . . ," Virginia said, trailing off. "You know Robert has keys." She turned to Linda. "Do these people know that Robert has machine guns? Do they know how violent Robert is?"

"I think they do, Mother."

"Well, we'll be in danger in that house," Virginia said.

There was a long silence. Joe Masterson was shaking his head no.

"No, no, Mrs. DeSilva, you won't be. We will be watching the house every minute. But my undercover agent will be in extreme danger. He will have to be alone with Robert and Young at certain points in the operation. One wrong word in that house, and it could cost my undercover agent his life."

John and Virginia looked at each other. John turned back around and stared through his spectacles into Joe's face.

"We understand," he said. "There won't be any wrong words."

Joe nodded. He opened the lap desk again and flipped pages on a yellow legal pad until he came to a clean page.

"Mr. and Mrs. DeSilva," he said, "I am going to write out exactly what you must do, step by step."

The hardest part, he said, was that they would have to take Linda back to Caruth after this meeting, pack their things, and return to Oklahoma as they had planned. The children knew that the grandparents were scheduled to go home today. Robert would grill the children, searching for any telltale shift in plans or circumstances. John and Virginia would have to stick to their schedule.

The drill—assuming that every word they said was overheard, that every move they made was watched—would begin immediately, the moment they stepped out of Ike's office into the corridor, and it would last until Robert was behind bars. During their long week alone in Oklahoma, John and Virginia were to say nothing to anyone. They were to call Linda as they would normally. Robert, who might be listening to the Caruth phone line, might notice if they changed their normal pattern of calls.

Joe had worked out the timing of the sting, he said, around the regularly scheduled return hand-off of the children, from Robert to Linda, a week from Wednesday. The object was to arrange things so that, on the Monday before the Wednesday when Robert was to bring the children home, Robert would hear from Colonel Young that Linda had been killed. Robert would know, then, from some time on Monday night, that she was dead. But he would not be informed officially by police of her disappearance until Wednesday afternoon.

He would have to continue to appear to act normally, in order not to betray his knowledge of the murder. He would have to bring the children back to Caruth on Wednesday morning. The purpose in setting up this period when Robert would believe Linda had been murdered but would not yet have been informed by the police was to exert a psychological pincers effect on him. On the one hand, he would believe he was getting away with it. On the other hand, there would be a great deal of pressure on him.

The object was to watch him like a bug under glass—but prod him to scurry. There were only so many directions toward which he would be able to scurry. He could get sloppy and try to hit the trail with the children and his girlfriend. He could pay off Young and count himself a genius. He could panic and bolt. He could lose his famous temper and get into a fight with Young. Whatever direction Robert Edelman tried to scuttle, the FBI would be standing there, waiting with a net.

As long as no one made a mistake.

Linda would be taken into custody a week from today, on Monday evening. A week from tomorrow, on the following Tuesday, John and Virginia were to load up the motor home for their trip to Colorado. They were to drive down to Dallas and time their arrival precisely so that they would arrive at 4:00 P.M. At that time, Rezilla would inform them that

Linda had not been at home that morning when she arrived for work and had not been present in the house all day.

"Will Rezilla know the truth?" Virginia asked.

"No," Joe said.

"Why?"

"Because every person who knows the truth is another chance that this thing will blow up on us."

"So Rezilla will believe that Linda is missing," John said, "but we won't be able to tell her the truth?"

"Right."

All at once and simultaneously, the full dimension of the challenge was beginning to dawn on John, Virginia, and Linda. Joe had been waiting patiently for it to settle in.

"At some point," Linda said, "my friends and my family are going to get the picture that Robert has killed me . . ."

"No, no, no, they will not," Joe said. "At least, nothing your parents say to them will give them that idea. Your parents and Rezilla will simply know that you have been away for an uncharacteristic period of time and that you appear to be missing . . ."

"Everyone will assume Robert has either killed me himself or had someone else kill me."

John and Virginia began nodding their heads vigorously in support of what Linda had just said.

"Well," Joe said, smiling, "that may be a conclusion that you yourselves would leap to . . ." He turned to Ike for support.

"Anybody who knows Robert very well is going to wonder," Ike said.

Joe shrugged. "Well, we can't control that, but certainly you are not going to say to anyone that Robert has killed Linda or had anything to do with killing Linda."

"Why . . . why is it four o'clock?" John asked.

"Why is what four o'clock?"

"Why do we have to arrive at four o'clock exactly?"

"You have to arrive at four o'clock," Joe said, "because we have made certain arrangements with the University Park Police for a certain officer to be on duty when you come in that afternoon to report Linda missing."

"It has to be just that officer?" Virginia said.

"Yes."

There was a silence.

"They're afraid," Linda said to her parents, "that some of the other police may not be safe. Robert has always bragged about paying off so many police around Dallas. So they can only trust a few."

John stared at Joe and Gerry. "Can you trust yourselves?" he asked, unsmiling.

Joe smiled and turned around to nod at Gerry. "Can we trust ourselves?"

Gerry gave Joe a tight unamused smile. "I think so."

Joe turned back to face Linda and her parents. Linda looked over his shoulder and caught Gerry staring icily at the back of Joe's head.

Joe had already written out the arrival time on his legal pad. Allowing them an hour to settle in and talk to Rezilla, he wrote out 5:00 P.M. next, as the time they were to go to the University Park police station and report Linda missing.

"Then what?" Virginia asked.

"Then you return to Caruth. And you stay there. As you would if you really believed your daughter was missing."

"And what do we tell people?"

"You tell people the story."

No one said anything for almost a full minute.

"People are going to go through the roof," Linda muttered. She looked up quickly. "What happens at eight o'clock on Wednesday morning when Robert brings the children home? What do my parents tell Stephen and Kathleen?"

Joe turned to John and Virginia. "You lie to them."

"We lie?" Virginia said.

Joe put his lap desk down and stood up. He held up both hands like the conductor of an orchestra.

"I want you to understand one thing clearly. The children are Robert's window into the house. He will call them, as is his right, and he will grill the hell out of them. He will be listening for hints in what they say. They must know nothing."

"All right, Agent Masterson, I understand that," Linda said.

"Please, it's Joe," he said.

"All right, Joe," she said, smiling warmly at him, "I understand what you're saying. I understand the strategic reasons for keeping the children in the dark. So I understand the need to lie to them. What I don't understand is what lie to tell them."

Joe looked puzzled. "Just, uh . . . just tell them Mommy has gone off to visit a friend for a few days, something like that, she'll be back soon. Isn't that what you would do normally? You wouldn't tell them she was missing, would you?"

"No, of course not," Linda said, "but, Joe, you have to understand who these kids are. You have to understand what they've been through with Robert and this divorce and this whole mess in the last year. I told you this Saturday when we met. Stephen will not let me out of his sight."

"Yes, you explained that. The boy does live half the time with his father."

"But he calls me at seven o'clock on the dot every night when he is with Robert, as soon as the court order says Robert has to let him call me."

"Well, Mrs. Edelman. . ."

"He has nightmares about being separated from me. So does Kathleen. When they're at Caruth, they won't let me leave the house to go to the corner without grilling me first about where I'm going and when I will be back."

Ike said, "What if your parents tell the kids you're visiting a friend in Oklahoma?"

"Stephen will not leave it at that," she said. "He will figure out that I would not have gone to Oklahoma without telling him first. He knows I would not leave Dallas without taking him and Kathleen with me. He will understand that I left without telling him, and he will figure out that that means Robert has done something to me."

"That's a lot of figuring for a . . . how old is he?"

"Eight. He'll be nine in November. Kathleen is six. Stephen is very smart and very suspicious of adults. He is pushy and asks questions."

Joe held up his hands. "We have no choice. They cannot know the truth. Therefore someone will have to tell them a lie."

"Meaning we will," Virginia said.

"Yes," he said. "You will."

"Oh my," she said. She turned her face away and stared out the window. No one spoke for a while.

"Joe," Linda said quietly, "I know that you know what you are doing, and I know you have a lot more experience at this kind of thing than I do. But I just don't . . . I don't think this is going to work. The kids will figure it out. My friends will figure it out. They will go through the roof."

"They will figure what out?" Ike asked.

"That . . . that it doesn't add up."

"They will figure out," Joe said, "that your husband has killed you. And they will act accordingly. That's exactly what we want."

An edge of frustration and alarm crept into Linda's voice. "But my children will figure it out, too," she said, "and they will not be able to take it."

Joe Masterson gave Linda a long appraising look. He twisted in his chair, considering his next words carefully.

"Linda," he said, "I am a father. I have children. You have my word. If the children are ever in any danger, either psychologically or physically, we will break it off. We will take care of them and then do what we can do with Robert at that point. We will not allow anything bad to happen to your children."

She looked deep into his face.

"You have my word," he said.

She sighed. "Does it have to be this way?"

"It has to be this way, Linda," he said. "Think about it. What other way is there? You tell me."

They all stared at Linda.

Virginia said, "All of our relatives, the minute they hear about this, will get in their cars and drive straight to Dallas."

Linda managed a small laugh. "With casseroles," she said.

Joe was shaking his head adamantly. "You stay on that telephone, Mrs. DeSilva, and you tell them not to come. That's the last thing we can afford, is a bunch of unusual activity around that house and people meddling. That would be extremely dangerous. It will be your job to keep them away."

"My job is sounding worse every minute," Virginia said to John in a whisper. She turned to Joe.

"There is another problem here, which is Linda's sister, Miriam, in Oklahoma City. Linda and Miriam are very close. They always have been. And Miriam does not miss a thing, believe me. Wouldn't you say that's true, Linda?"

Linda nodded. "She's quiet on the outside, but she's very smart and intense, and she knows me like a book."

Joe was shaking his head no.

"Well," Virginia said, "I am just trying to tell you that. . . "

"No," Joe said, "I'm sorry. I said this would be hard. It will be. But we've got more people in on it now than I like already. You will just have to do it. You will have to lie to her and make it stick."

Linda and her mother exchanged worried looks.

John concluded that the meeting was at an end. He stood up abruptly and gave Virginia his arm.

"It's not a good situation, Mr. Masterson," he said, "but I guess that's Robert's doing. You know what you're doing. We will do whatever you tell us to do."

Virginia said, "How close have they been to us?"

"Young?" Joe asked.

"The hit man."

Joe looked back at Gerry, then shrugged. "The alley."

"What alley?"

"They've been in the alley on Caruth while you came in and out of the house, behind the air-conditioning compressors there."

"My air-conditioning compressors?" Linda asked.

"Yes."

"To kill me?"

"Not yet. Surveillance. Setting it up. You almost wiped them out Saturday morning when you were coming here for your appointment."

Linda and her parents were motionless, speechless.

"You have to be very careful," Joe said. "And you have to behave as if you know nothing. Nothing at all."

On the way back from Ike's office to Caruth in John's car, they all sat staring out the windows, not speaking, John and Virginia in front, Linda in back. Every time Linda leaned forward across the seat to try to speak to John or Virginia, they looked at her in alarm and then turned away.

Linda thought, "My parents are watching the cars that pass us. They think Robert can hear us in the car."

She wondered if he could hear them.

As they neared the house, Linda said, "Are you two going to be all right?"

They didn't answer.

John was going down Caruth toward the house. He passed the house, turned right on Turtle Creek, and then turned right again up the alley to the garage behind the house.

They could see Stephen and Kathleen coming out of the Lehner house. Andrew Lehner, Stephen's friend, was with them. Then little Maggie Lehner, who played with Kathleen, came out. Stephen caught sight of John's car. All of the children waved from the lawn as John passed them. The other children went back to their play immediately, but Stephen ran forward to the parkway and stood close while the car passed, peering into it.

The car bumped up into the alley. All three of them stared at the air-conditioning compressors as they passed. Virginia lifted up the remote control device and pushed the button. The right garage door whirred up out of the way. Lights came on in the garage. John drove in, and the door came down behind them.

Linda and her parents were motionless, speechless.

"Are you two going to be all right?" Linda asked again.

They turned toward her but would not speak. Only then did Linda see the film of tears in her father's eyes.

They went in through the back corridor to the family room. Rezilla, who was working in the kitchen, dropped her work and came forward to meet them.

Sixty-three years old and gray-headed, Rezilla was still a vigorous-looking woman, toughened by a life of hard work. She was born on a farm between Henderson and Kilgore, in the red-dirt East Texas farm country where many black families acquired land and settled during the Reconstruction Era, after the Civil War. It's country that produces conservative, religious, family-centered people, both black and white, and Rezilla was true to her roots.

Drawn first to Kilgore by the promise of domestic work, then eventually to Dallas, she worked for a wealthy Park Cities family for twenty years before coming to work for Robert and Linda. She had an excellent reputation as an employee and frequently received offers to come to work for other families.

Robert had always treated her badly, refusing to pay Social Security for her, and paying her irregularly as he did everyone who worked for him. But she had grown extremely close to Linda and the children. She had witnessed the aftermath of some of the beatings Robert had given Linda, in terms of the effect on both Linda and the children.

Rezilla could take care of herself. She always paid her own half of the Social Security tax, and she knew, through her network of friends and relatives who worked as domestics, that Robert would get hit with a lump-sum judgment for the rest of it when she decided to retire. If he wasn't smart enough to figure that out for himself, that was not her problem.

But she could not leave Linda and the children. Not yet.

"Linda," she said, as they came in slowly from the back, "that cat is sick. I think it needs to go back to the vet."

Linda slumped. The cat was the most recent in a line of orange cats—called Amber Tabbies—that had begun with "Dallas," the one she had taken to New York. Her cats were always important to her. They were soft little friends who came to her in quiet and lonely moments. This cat had been with her for several years. In the last few weeks, it had begun exhibiting all the symptoms of feline leukemia.

"I can't do it today," she said.

"Well, we'll keep an eye on her," Rezilla said. "She might get better."

Linda helped her parents pack their things and load the car. In an hour they were ready to leave. Not a word had passed between them.

In the family room, John sat down and discussed the plans for Colorado with Stephen, who wanted to know whether they were coming to pick them up in the motor home or whether he, his mother, and his sister would fly to Oklahoma City to meet them. John explained the plans in detail.

"How will Aunt Miriam get to be with us?" Stephen asked.

"We will pick her up in Oklahoma City on the way back up toward Colorado," John said.

"Why do you want to drive all the way down here in the motor home and then drive all the way back up there to get Aunt Miriam? Why not just have us meet you at Aunt Miriam's house?"

John looked up in alarm at Linda and Virginia. It didn't make sense. Viewed on a map, it was all the long way around. Stephen, an eight-year-old, had figured it out, and now he was insisting his grandfather explain it while sitting under God only knew how many listening devices. John was flustered.

Linda stepped forward quickly. "You know how I hate to carry all that stuff on the plane," she said. "Grandpa has agreed to come down here with the motor home so we can get it all ready here."

"Plus I'm having some work done on it," John said, "and I want to give it a little shake-out drive before we start on the trip."

"Oh," Stephen said, shrugging. "Great. I love the motor home. I can't wait."

Linda stood in back, waving at her parents as they pulled away down the alley. She remembered the time they had visited her in Queens. They had brought Miriam and Linda's Aunt Ruth. By the time they arrived, Linda's face had recovered, and they had no idea.

Robert had been horrible to them, staying away from home and refusing even to eat with them during most of the visit. When they had pulled away from the apartment building in Queens, waving from the windows of their big American car with plates on the back that said "Oklahoma is O.K.," Linda had felt as if she were freezing to death and utterly alone in the universe. Now, watching them pull down the alley, she felt exactly the same way.

The next morning at eleven o'clock, Colonel Young pulled into a Union 76 Truck Stop in Rowlett, a distant suburb of Dallas. He waited in the hot parking lot at the side of the station with his motor running and the air conditioner on. Two minutes later a car that had been parked on the shoulder across the road pulled across the street and parked next to him.

Hitman Jack climbed out. Colonel Young got out of his car. The two men nodded curtly to each other. Fred had introduced them to each other three nights earlier at a downtown hotel, where they had agreed to work together and had settled on the money. They went into the truck stop for breakfast, eating quickly, sharing a few muttered phrases. Then they walked back out and went to Hitman Jack's car. Hitman Jack opened the trunk, pulled out an envelope, and handed it to the Colonel.

Young opened the envelope and withdrew three photographs. They looked as if they had been developed by a commercial company—the kind of company that develops pictures people drop off at their corner drugstore.

"What's this?" Young asked.

"The mark," Hitman Jack said. "That's her at a shopping center."

"Looks like she's at the Galleria," Young said.

"I guess. Big shopping center."

"She must have been out there to see her lawyer."

"I don't know. I just followed her there to do a recon."

"So what is this for?"

"I want you to take them to the guy and make sure it's his wife. I don't want to do the wrong person."

Colonel Young was a small man with an aging face. When he stared, the bones in his face stood out. He held the pictures and stared back at Hitman Jack, searching his face.

"Look," Jack said, "you told Fred yourself you never got close enough to her to see her face good. I don't make mistakes. I like everything right. I want things buttoned up. I don't want any fuck-ups. Just take the fucking pictures to the guy today, say, 'Is that her?' And then call me."

"I can't get to the guy today," Young said. "Why does it have to be today?"

"Because I'm going to do it Monday."

"You're going to do it Monday?"

"Yeah. Next Monday night. You told Fred it had to be this week or next. So it's this Monday."

"The guy wants proof."

"What proof?" Jack asked testily.

"He wants it to look like a robbery. He says to take her Rolex watch, and she's got a ring he wants to see, and there's a necklace or something with the kids' pictures inside it. She always wears them. So he says take them and then show them to him for proof."

"I don't like to carry shit."

"Well, that's what the guy wants, or he won't pay."

"All right. So when can you get to him?"

"Tomorrow."

"Then call me up. I'm set to go Monday. I got plane tickets out of here. I can't get a refund on them. It'll fuck me up if I don't hear back. My plan is for Monday, okay? I need confirmation right away."

"He wants it done by next week, the latest."

"Right. So get the pictures to him and call me."

"Okay," Young said. He climbed out of Jack's car with the pictures. Jack drove away. The entire scene had been recorded on video and audio tape.

That afternoon, Linda took the cat to the vet. She had been going to the same vet for years.

"This is a very sick kitty, Linda," he said. "He's going to have to stay. He's very anemic, and he's starting to dehydrate. I'll put him on an I.V. You never know. He might bounce back, but I can't really offer much hope."

"Oh dear."

"If it goes the other way? I think we'll have to put him down."

"Yes. I don't want another cat of mine to have to go through that again."

Linda began pulling her things together to leave.

"It may take several days for me to really know," the vet said. "If it looks bad, of course, I will call you for permission before I do anything final. You may want to come be with him."

Linda stopped and walked back toward him. "No, I don't think so. Not this time. If you think it's necessary, you just go ahead and make the decision."

"Sure," he said. "I understand. But of course I'll call you first."

Linda felt herself flush slightly. She tried to think.

"Look . . . yes, of course. Call. But, uh . . . I also trust your judgment. Whatever you think must be done."

"Yes. Certainly."

She reached out and picked up the cat. She hugged it and kissed it. "Good-bye, Theo," she whispered.

She turned moist eyes to the vet. "Do everything you can for him."

When she got home, the kitchen was raucous with laughter and pot-banging. Her birthday was on Friday. Rezilla and the children were happily and messily baking a cake in the kitchen.

She sat at the long table in the family room area, which was separated from the kitchen proper by a long counter and cabinet. The sound of the children kidding and having fun with Rezilla made her smile. She rose and wandered to the front of the house. She looked down and noticed a collection of porcelain figurines on a coffee table in the library. They were all renderings of characters in the Beatrix Potter stories. She knelt and looked at them, picking them up one by one. There was Peter Rabbit, of course. And Mr. Jeremy Fisher. She rose, walked out into the huge foyer, and climbed the spiral staircase to Kathleen's room.

It was empty, crisp, and silent—every pillow and ruffle perfectly in place. At one end on a table was a huge Victorian doll house. Across from it was a tall glass-front cabinet. She walked to the cabinet and looked in. There they were—the rest of the Beatrix Potter characters. Benjamin Bunny. The Two Bad Mice. Farmer McGregor. How Kathleen loved them. How Linda loved reading the stories to her.

She stopped herself. She tried to think whether she could cry. She often cried, anyway, because of the divorce, because of all that happened. There would be nothing unusual about her crying now. She went back out to the top of the stairs and listened. Faintly in the distance, she could hear the sounds in the kitchen. She returned to the edge of Kathleen's bed and allowed herself to cry for a while.

The next morning, Robert withdrew $2,000 in cash from his checking account. At 12:27 P.M., Colonel Young met Robert outside the King Palace Chinese Restaurant on Fitzhugh Avenue in East Dallas—the part of the city where a large population of Southeast Asian refugees had settled in the previous five years, creating an instant "Little Asia." As a distinguished businessman, retired military officer, and holder of the Bronze Star, Colonel Young was something of a celebrity among the restaurant owners in Little Asia. He was always given a good table and preferential service—things Robert noticed and appreciated.

The Colonel had excellent manners and a gentlemanly mien. Dealing with him was not at all like dealing with the sort of person one might imagine as a hit man. Robert appreciated that, too. Even though he needed the services of the very worst kind of criminal, Robert had no taste at all for having lunch with a person who acted the part. Colonel Young was a mercy in that regard, even if he was irritating in other ways.

Young and Robert were shown to a corner booth. Right after they were seated, two FBI agents entered the restaurant and unobtrusively prevailed upon the maitre d' to give them the adjoining booth.

During the course of the meal, Colonel Young took out the envelope with Hitman Jack's photographs of Linda at the Galleria and spread the pictures on the table. The agents in the next booth managed to see the pictures and heard Young ask, "Is that her?"

They heard Robert say, "You got it."

Robert then slipped his own envelope out of his jacket pocket and handed Colonel Young a $2,000 progress payment toward the full $45,000 price of the murder.

When Robert and Young had finished their meal, they both got into Young's car and drove just around the corner to a school lot, where Young got out of the car and burned the photographs. It was a minor blow for the FBI agents, who had hoped eventually to retrieve the photographs with Robert's fingerprints on them.

The children were in and out of the house all day Thursday. Linda spent a good deal of the day sitting on the edge of her bed, fully clothed, staring out the window through a glaze of tears.

In Duncan, Oklahoma, her parents sat quietly in the large timbered and vaulted living room of their home, staring out through the picture window. Virginia's eyes were dry and worried, John's eyes rimmed and wet. They were uncertain whether they could speak in their own home. They exchanged one brief phone call with Linda in which they wished her a happy birthday and then said things like, "Is it hot down there?" and "Are you ready for our trip?"

Thursday night at 10:25, Young called Hitman Jack and said Robert had identified the photographs and had given him a $2,000 down payment for the hit.

Linda celebrated her birthday with Zsa and the children at lunchtime on Friday. Afterward, Stephen and Kathleen ran down the block to play with the Lehner children. On the days when Robert was to pick them up, both children were always a little manic about getting in some play time with their friends before he arrived. When they were with Robert, they spent most of their time locked inside the dark house on Pagewood, waiting for the inevitable long evenings on the town. Robert loved to dress the children lavishly and then show them off at dinner. He usually drove them back to Pagewood and dropped them, to be put into bed by his servants, while he stayed out longer.

Around 2:00 P.M., Rezilla and Linda began rounding up the children and getting them ready to go with Robert. Robert would come to pick up the children at four o'clock. Rezilla knew without being asked to have the children ready and waiting for the usual drill.

At a few minutes before four, the children were standing in the foyer by the door with their little suitcases in one hand and stuffed animals in the other, dressed to the nines because Robert would probably park them in his office for several hours before dinner.

Little Kathleen could sit on her suitcase and lose herself in a trilling secret conversation with a favorite teddy bear. With her huge round eyes and long silky hair, she looked a little like a plush toy herself. But Stephen was a little man. He was always grim and tense before his father picked them up, steeling himself for the long dark week ahead. He stood rigidly by his suitcase, watching his sister play with the bear.

Robert's normal practice was to park around the corner and wait for four o'clock to arrive, then race down the block in his long black funeral Cadillac and come to a grinding halt in the driveway in front of Caruth. Then, visible only as a dark outline inside the deeply tinted windows of the car, he would sit in the driveway and talk on his portable telephone for fifteen or twenty minutes while Linda, Rezilla, and the children stood waiting inside in the foyer.

When he honked his horn, Linda would shoo the children through the door. Once they were locked inside the car and Robert was making his loud dirt-spewing exit, Linda would step outside and wave to them. Stephen always kept waving until the car had carried him out of sight. On one occasion, Linda had rushed down the walk toward the street, only to see Stephen still staring backward toward the house almost half a block away. She never walked out to the street again.

This time Robert pulled into the driveway slowly and quietly, right on time. He tapped the horn lightly as soon as he came to a stop. Rezilla opened the door, and Linda pushed the children out. When the children were in the car, she stepped out onto the porch herself.

Robert backed out of the driveway with uncharacteristic caution and backed out into the street to turn around. Then he pulled forward slowly.

Linda was waving to the children, who were waving back. The children kept waving, and Linda kept waving. But something was wrong. Robert stopped the Cadillac in the middle of the street. His window was rolled down. She was looking only at the children, but she turned and looked at Robert.

He was staring at her. Something in his face caught her heart. His face was not cruel, as it had almost always been in these last two terrible years. There was a slack quality about his eyes and mouth. Almost like sadness.

"He is saying good-bye to me," she thought. "He is taking his last look at me alive."

Her hand dropped. She stared back at Robert. All of a sudden it occurred to her that she would never see Robert again as a free man, if things went the right way.

"It is good-bye," she thought. "One way or the other."

She turned and went back into the house. "If one thing goes wrong," she thought, "I will never see my babies again."

Rezilla was standing in the foyer with a broom in one hand and a dustpan in the other. John had installed the wrong kind of bulbs in the overhead lights, and the bulbs had been blowing up all week long, showering the floor with glass.

"What a mess," Linda said. "Daddy put those bulbs in all over the house, didn't he?"

Zsa saw her face and was shocked. "Oh, Linda, it's going to be all right. It's not so bad."

Linda looked at her closely.

"They haven't all blown up," Zsa said. "The ones he put in back are all right."

Linda went up to her bedroom and locked the door. She picked up a picture on her dresser. It was of Robert, at a cast party for the USO Show the summer after Oklahoma University, when she and Robert were fresh young lovers. She sank backward on her bed with the picture in both hands.

The phone rang. She lifted herself up, blew her nose quickly with some Kleenex from a silver box on the end table. It was Miriam, calling to wish her a happy birthday.

"What have you been doing, Linda?"

"Oh, lying here on my bed, boo-hooing over all my troubles."

"Oh, Linda, I'm so sorry."

"Yes. So am I. I guess you can tell."

"How are the children?"

"They're wonderful. Zsa had them bake a birthday cake for me, which we ate most of at lunch. Just what I need."

"Are you looking forward to our trip?"

"Oh yes, Miriam, very much. I think it will be so nice in Colorado when we get there. I can't wait."

"Mama said Daddy wants to drive the motor home down there on Tuesday so you all can get it loaded up, and then he's going to drive you all the way back up here and pick me up."

"Yes."

"Well, that doesn't really make sense, Linda. It almost makes more sense for me to fly down there and meet you all. . . "

"No, no, I don't think we should change the plans. You know how Daddy is about last-minute changes. They're going to stop at the shopping center in Denton on the way down and buy stuff for the trip. You don't want to have to do that."

"Well, it's not really last-minute. . . "

"No, Miriam, this is how I want to do it, too. It's more convenient. The children will do better this way. "

"All right. That's fine. They're coming down Tuesday?"

"Yes."

"What time? Do you know?"

"Yes," Linda said reflexively. "At four o'clock."

"Oh," Miriam said, faintly amused. "Daddy has given you an exact hour of arrival?"

"Yes. Approximately. Four o'clock."

"Ha. You sound a little better."

"I am better. I always feel better when you call."

"Good night, then. Take good care of yourself."

"I will. You, too."

Stephen called at 7:00 P.M.—the hour appointed by the court. He put Kathleen on to say good night. Then he came back on and reported on their day so far. They were still dressed in the clothes Rezilla had put on them, still waiting to be taken to dinner. He asked his mother three times if everything was all right at home, and then he said good night and hung up.

Linda walked through the house, making sure all the lights were turned out. She smiled to herself. It occurred to her that her fear of being alone in a darkened house was not strong enough to overcome her lifetime of frugal habits.

On Saturday morning, Linda drove to North Park Mall, a short distance from her home, to shop for the sting. Joe Masterson had told her emphatically that she could not bring any clothing or personal items that might enable anyone to deduce that she had prepared in any way for her disappearance.

She had been pondering this problem off and on ever since the last meeting at Ike's office. The problem was Rezilla. Rezilla was uncannily efficient and had an almost photographic memory for objects in the house. If Linda accidentally left an item of clothing, even underwear, at her parents' home after a trip to visit them, Rezilla would come to her a week later and say, "Linda, there's a pair of panties missing from your drawer," or, "Linda, I can't find your green blouse with the white collar and the lace on the pockets."

That meant Linda had to buy everything she would need during her disappearance. She had been making a mental list all week. She walked from store to store, buying underwear, blouses, shorts, skirts, a toothbrush, toothpaste, replacement make-up, shampoo, a comb and brush, a pair of sneakers, and other small items. When she got home, she went to the little office area in the large hall at the top of the spiral staircase and retrieved several file boxes Ike had given her for just this purpose.

The problem was transporting all of her sting items out to the car on Monday. She was to show up at Ike's office to keep a phony appointment at 4:00 P.M. Monday. It was at that point that Ike would pass her into FBI custody, her disappearance would begin, and the sting would be launched.

Obviously she couldn't walk past Rezilla carrying a suitcase, or Rezilla would know something very strange was going on. In fact, Joe didn't want her to get anywhere near a suitcase in the next week, in case Colonel Young was watching the house with optical instruments.

The solution—something Ike had dreamed up—was the stack of empty file boxes. They were red boxes with a cross-hatched pattern on the top and green metal reinforcements at the corners; a type made especially for lawyers and law firms. She could pack all of her things in three file boxes and then carry everything out to the car that way. It would look as if she had been doing her homework, getting ready for the imminent trial date in her divorce case.

In the silence of the huge empty house, she packed and repacked her things in the file boxes, trying to make everything fit. She had bought books to read during the sting, but when she finished packing she decided she wanted to read something that evening. She didn't want to unpack the boxes in order to get one of her new books. She remembered a book she had started and then laid aside somewhere up in the semi-finished area of the attic where she kept her wicker furniture. She walked up the steep staircase to the attic door, which was kept locked but with a key in the lock, in case very young children were ever in the house. Some of the attic was unfloored and potentially dangerous.

She turned the key and pushed open the door. Her heart immediately began pumping like a piston, her skin began to tingle in waves, and a scream formed like a ball deep in her throat, forcing its way upward slowly. There on the floor of the attic, barely visible in the darkness, was the form of a man, flat on his back, spread-eagled and motionless.

"Oh!" she shouted. "Oh! Oh!"

It was the inflatable plastic scarecrow she had used as a decoration in front of the house the previous Halloween. At some point she had carried it up there and just heaved it in through the door. And there it lay, with its oversized corpse-white straw-man head and googly eyes staring up at her.

By the time she got all the way back downstairs to the library, her breathing was almost normal again.

At 7:00 P.M., Stephen called. He said that he and Kathleen were about to get into the Cadillac with Robert to go meet Robert's date for dinner at the Mansion on Turtle Creek. Stephen asked four times how she was doing, whether she was all right, and whether his grandparents would be waiting at the house with the motor home when Robert brought him back next Wednesday. Linda spoke to Stephen and Kathleen for a total of ten minutes. Then she heard Robert in the background telling them they had talked long enough, and she said good-bye, rather than get them in trouble.

Robert had been busy with work and had seen little of the children since picking them up. He had two full-time servants at Pagewood—a housekeeper and a handyman/driver. Except for their public dinners with their father, the children had been with the servants since Friday evening.

"Well, you've been with me almost two days now," Robert said in the car on the way to the Mansion. "I have no idea what's new in your wonderful little lives. How 'bout it, Bubber? What's been going on, back at the ranch?"

"What do you mean?" Stephen asked primly.

"What's new? Anything going on at home?"

Kathleen leaned forward: "The kitty is sick. Mama had to take him to the vet. The vet said he was a very sick kitty."

"Oh, what a shame," Robert said. "We'll all just have to pray for the kitty, won't we?"

Kathleen smiled and sat back quietly, as she always did when her father was sarcastic.

"Have your grandparents been with you?"

"Yes," Stephen said. "They left."

"They did? Well I'm sure they'll be back soon."

"Yes," Stephen said. "We're all going on a trip to Colorado. To Silverton. To ride a train. Grandpa and Grandma are going to come down in the motor home and pick us up."

"And when will that be, pray tell?"

"I don't know. After you take us home, I would think."

"And who else has been around the house?"

"No one. You always ask too many questions."

"Just keeping tabs on you, Bubber. So is your mother there all alone?"

"Far as I know. Just Zsa. Only she's not there 'cause it's the weekend."

"Ah, yes. Zsa goes home on the weekend, doesn't she?"

"Yes."

"Good for Zsa. Well, here we are at the Mansion. I expect you both to behave."

"We will," Stephen said.

On Sunday, Linda spent most of the day sitting by herself in the family room, either on the sofa, where she tried to read, or at the table, where she sat with her head in her hands, trying to hold herself together.

In mid-afternoon, she called her veterinarian at home.

"I know you think I'm a terrible old spoiled Park Cities witch for bothering you on a Sunday at home. . . "

"No I don't, Linda. I should have called you yesterday, and I got busy and didn't. Theo is a little bit better."

"Oh really! Oh that's so good! That's the only good news I've had in days."

"Poor thing! Listen, Linda, I don't want you to get your hopes up. Theo is having a bit of a rally. I was just down there not half an hour ago, and he looked better. His color was better, and his white cell count has been getting just barely a little better in the last day or two. But you know, we do see this sometimes, and it doesn't mean a thing. They just crater anyway. He's very sick."

"I know. I so appreciate your care of him."

"I will call, of course, if things take a turn for the worse and a decision has to be made."

"Yes. But I trust your judgment."

"I appreciate that, Linda."

On Monday, Linda woke up at dawn, paralyzed with fear, thinking of everything that might go wrong. She lay in bed, shivering, for an hour. Then Rezilla's voice came on the intercom.

"Linda, are you still in bed? Do you need to wake up this morning? Do you have anything to do?"

"No, Zsa. I'll be right down."

When she got to the kitchen, Rezilla asked her what Stephen had been saying in his nightly phone calls. Linda relayed all of the news Stephen had given her since last Friday evening. Then, while Rezilla told her a story of something that had happened on the bus from her neighborhood in the South Oak Cliff region of Dallas far across the Trinity River on the other side of the city, Linda lapsed into a half-listening trance.

"My life is completely and totally in the hands of God and these FBI agents," she thought. "And I just met them. They showed me identification, but I couldn't see it, because I was crying. I don't really know who they are. They could work for Robert, for all I know."

In her mind's eye she saw Robert looming over her, an enormous ogre standing on a mountain of money, hurling bloody thunderbolts down on her head while a crowd of well-dressed diners from the Mansion looked on and politely applauded.

"Linda, what is the matter with you?" Rezilla asked. "I know something is the matter with you. What is it?"

Under ordinary circumstances, Linda would have answered honestly. But this time she stared back at Rezilla, helpless and tongue-tied.

"Nothing," she said. "I'm just tired. I stayed up late last night working on the case. I have to go back up there right now and finish something."

"You going to see Ike today?"

"Yes. I have an appointment at four o'clock."

She climbed back up the enormous spiral staircase, rising smoothly on her dancer's legs, lifting the trail of her robe in one fist. She went to the little writing desk at the head of the stairs, sat down, and wrote out a will. When she finished it, she folded it like a letter and slipped it into one of the filing boxes with her clothing for the sting.

Then she went to her dressing table, took out a plastic storage bag, and dropped into it her gold lady's Rolex watch, a diamond ring, and two large shrimp shell earrings. Finally she removed from the drawer of her dressing table the flat round dollar-sized monogrammed locket that she always wore. Inside were newborn baby pictures of both Stephen and Kathleen. On the outside were tiny teeth marks where Stephen had chewed the locket.

Linda held the locket up by the chain and smiled when she remembered at what a tiny age Kathleen had begun laughing and reaching for this and other jewelry. The little boy wanted to eat the jewelry. The little girl wanted to wear it.

She had asked Joe if the locket had to be included, and he had insisted.

"I don't care what happens to any of the rest of that stuff," she said to him, "but I want that locket back."

"We'll see that you get it all back. Hitman Jack doesn't like to carry stuff. He will dump it as soon as it has been shown to Robert for proof."

"Dump it?"

"Yes. Linda, you do remember that Hitman Jack is our guy?"

"Oh yes."

"He won't dump your locket. He will have special instructions on the locket. He won't really dump anything. He will bring it all to the FBI operations center."

She took a nap later in the morning, then ate a late lunch. After lunch, she got dressed, then went downstairs and sat in the library for a while, thinking that she might read. But she just sat instead, staring at the Beatrix Potter figurines. "Stephen will call for me at seven," she thought. "Zsa will be gone. There will be no answer."

Ever since the court had fixed the 7:00 P.M. calling time, Linda had never missed a call. She was always sitting by the phone fifteen minutes ahead of time, in case Stephen called early, although Robert never allowed him to call a minute early. If someone else happened to call, she always told whomever it was that she would have to hang up and call back later in order to keep the line clear.

In the way that children know everything, Stephen knew all of this, even though Linda had never said a word to him about the phone calls. The calls were always managed as if they were casual, almost incidental.

The children had enough intensity and tension in their lives. She liked, whenever possible, to pretend that things were normal. Sometimes they talked to each other during the calls. Sometimes she read to him and Kathleen on the phone. Often she sang songs from the Disney scores to them, and they sang duets together over the telephone.

But Stephen knew. He knew that the calls were not casual. He knew she would never miss a call.

At three o'clock, it was time to take the file boxes out and put them in the trunk of the Cadillac. Zsa offered to help, but Linda insisted on doing it herself, lest a box fall open and Zsa see the actual contents.

At 3:30, it was time to go. All of a sudden, her breath began to come short. There was something she was forgetting. Something Joe had told her to do when she left. She could not remember. She knew there was something. But she could not be late. From here on out, it would all be military precision and razor's edge timing.

Rezilla was ironing in the back room.

"I'll be going now," Linda said.

"What do you have to do tomorrow morning?" Rezilla asked.

"It's . . . uh, it's the same thing. Preparing. The court date is a week from today."

"Okay then. I'll wake you up when I come in."

"Good. Thanks, Zsa. I won't get back until late this evening, so you just lock up and don't wait for me. Go home early if you can. I'll be real late."

"All right then."

Linda wanted to walk over and hug Rezilla and tell her she loved her, but she was afraid she might lose her composure.

Rezilla watched her walk out into the garage. She tried to walk confidently through the garage to the car, but her eyes flitted everywhere and her body cringed reflexively, waiting for a bullet or a blow. She got into the car and pushed the remote to open the door behind her. She backed out and drove away from Caruth.

At the Galleria, she opened the trunk of her car and removed the plastic bag containing her jewelry, which she slipped into her purse. She left the file boxes full of her effects in the trunk of the Cadillac, as Joe had instructed her to do, and she went to Ike's office. When the receptionist ushered her into Ike's office at exactly 4:15, Joe Masterson was standing inside smiling at her with hands crossed at his waist.

"All ready for Operation Linda?" he asked.

Ike was standing behind his desk, looking just the least bit befuddled.

"I'm all ready," she said. She handed Joe the bag with her jewelry.

Rezilla was hurrying with the last of her work, taking advantage of the boss's early departure to try to catch an early bus home. She finished up by wiping the sinks in the kitchen, then turned on the lights in the back corridor and the family room, using the dimmer to put them on low so that there would be just enough light to help Linda get in safely from the back. Linda was a stickler about leaving the lights on and wasting electricity, but Rezilla hated for her to have to enter the house in total darkness. Rezilla set the alarm system, locked the door behind her, and hurried off to the bus stop.

Linda, Ike, and Joe walked out of Ike's law firm through a back door. They took a freight elevator down to the ground level. When they got to Linda's car, Joe said that he would drive. He asked Ike to follow in his own car. But then, just as Ike was about to walk away, Joe said, "Linda, did you mess up your bed before you left?"

That was what she had forgotten.

"No. No, I'm sorry. I knew I forgot something. Is it essential?"

Joe paused. "Yes, I'm afraid it is. When Rezilla comes in tomorrow, we want her to think you spent the night there. Your parents arrive at four in the afternoon. We don't want anybody getting excited much before that, because our colleague at the University Park police station won't be in place until after four to take the report. The bed needs to be messed up, so Rezilla will figure maybe you just got up real early and left to do something."

"I would never do that."

"I know, Linda, but . . . believe me. The bed has got to be messed up."

Ike stood nearby, waiting for Joe to sort it out.

"Is Rezilla gone by now?" Joe asked.

Linda looked at her watch. It was 4:30. "Yes, I'm sure she is, I'm sure she caught the early bus."

"Okay," Joe said, "Here's what we do."

It was agreed that Linda would drive her own car back to Caruth. Ike and Joe would follow in Ike's car. They would park a few blocks away while Linda went back in and messed up her bed to make it look slept in. Then Linda would drive back to Ike's car. Joe would get into Linda's car with her and drive it to their destination. Ike would follow in his own car.

By the time Linda got back to Caruth, she was so nervous she could barely breathe. She pulled up behind the house but did not drive the car into the garage. She walked past the garage to the door that opened directly into the back sun room. She pushed open the door hurriedly, turned off the alarm, and rushed up the back staircase to her room. She went into the bedroom, pulled back the covers on her bed, and punched the pillow a few times with her fists. Then she hurried back down the stairs. On her way out, she noticed that the lights in the family room and the back corridor had been left on dim. She flipped them off, let herself out, and drove back to join Ike and Joe.

CHAPTER FIVE

S he scooted over, and Joe slipped into her car behind the driver's wheel. He drove smoothly and quickly toward downtown. "You all right, Linda?"

His smile loosened something at the center of her chest.

"Yes. No. I mean, I think I'm going to be all right."

"You will be."

They drove into the West End—an area of turn-of-the-century brick warehouses at one end of downtown Dallas. Some of the old warehouses had been converted into nightclubs and bars. Joe made several sharp turns down narrow streets and alleys through the warehouse district, then turned down a steep driveway underneath one of the warehouses. He pulled a remote control device from his briefcase and pushed a button. A heavy iron gate lifted up slowly in front of them. Joe drove Linda's car down the steep ramp and came out in a dimly lit parking area underneath the building. Ike followed them in. Joe stopped Linda's car in the center aisle, turned around, and pointed the remote device back at the gate to close it behind Ike.

While Joe maneuvered the car into a parking place, Linda's eyes adjusted. She looked around behind her and on all sides. Large men were moving about in the gloom, some of them dressed in business suits, others dressed as workmen. Some of them looked like bums. Several of them were carrying shotguns, machine guns, large pistols, and other weapons. One scurvy-looking man walked by with a shotgun that he placed in the trunk of the car parked next to Linda's. He saw Linda getting out, smiled politely at her, and dipped his head.

"Where are we?" she asked Joe in a small voice.

"Not important," he said.

"Are all of these men here for me?"

"Nope. This is a regional operations center. You and I are just one little operation."

Walking toward them purposefully was a short, squat, burly young man with a black goatee, a punk buzz haircut, and a single earring. He was dressed in a burgundy tank top and skin tight black bicycle shorts. He looked like a cross between a sumo wrestler and a tattoo artist. He had a large black revolver hanging beneath one hairy armpit.

"Linda, this is Agent Mike Fiori," Joe said.

The wrestler extended his hand politely. "Nice to meet you, Mrs. Edelman. Everything all right so far?"

"So far," she whispered.

"Mike is going to follow you and Ike to the edge of town and make sure you're not being followed. Then you'll be on your own."

Ike was standing nearby, listening intently.

"On our own?" Ike said.

"Yes," Joe said. "You'll be all right. You'll be on your own, but . . . you'll be all right. There will be eyes on you."

Linda handed her keys to Agent Fiori. "What's going to happen to my Cadillac?" she asked.

"Nothing," Joe said. "It will be in excellent hands. Right here."

Joe took the keys from Agent Fiori and opened the trunk. He and Ike transferred the file boxes and ushered Linda into Ike's car. He walked around as Ike was sliding into the driver's seat and patted him on the arm. "Obey the traffic laws, okay?"

"Yes, Officer," Ike said.

Ike eased the car out of the space and maneuvered it over to the gated entry ramp. The gate lifted up with a smooth whirring noise. Ike drove up onto the street and turned toward the freeway. He looked in the mirror and saw the agent following in a small green car.

It was almost 5:00 P.M. The Texas sun, even in late afternoon, painted a ferocious glare over the glass walls of the downtown buildings. They had to push their way through heavy rush-hour traffic for several blocks, then drove up a long curving freeway ramp only to drop into a massive stop-and-go traffic jam.

"Is he behind us?" she asked.

Ike looked up in the mirror. "Yes. Right behind us."

It took forty-five minutes to get from downtown to the beltway on the outer fringe of Dallas proper; as soon as they were well into the suburban community of Mesquite, new logjams formed, and the cars and huge trucks on the freeway ground to a halt again. By the time they began to hit a few stretches of open road toward East Texas, it was seven o'clock.

The phone rang. It rang in the empty family room. It rang upstairs, next to Linda's bed. It rang in the back room, the library, at the desk at the top of the stairs, in the guest room. All over the empty expanse of Caruth, just as the first filmy shadows of evening were beginning to march through the house, the telephone rang. And rang. And rang.

Stephen sensed his father towering over him and turned.

"Mother is not answering," he said.

"She must be out."

"She's never out. She's always there when I call! She's just not answering! Something is wrong! I want to go home."

"You cannot go back to Caruth tonight, Stephen, you know that."

Stephen slammed the receiver in its cradle and whirled to confront his father. "Something is wrong, I said! She's never not home!"

"You cannot go home, Stephen," Robert said. "That's it. End of discussion." He turned and began walking away, down the long carpeted corridor where Snubby Ellis once had threatened him with a gun.

"Wait, Daddy," Stephen shouted. "Wait! Just let me call Mrs. Lehner! Maybe something happened to Mother. If anything bad happened at the house, Mrs. Lehner would know about it."

Robert stopped walking but did not turn. He kept his back to Stephen for a long moment while he thought. Ordinarily the children's phone calls from Pagewood were strictly limited to the seven o'clock calls the court said Robert had to allow them to make. He turned back slowly and smiled.

"Of course, Stephen, if that will make you feel better. Do you need me to look the number up for you?"

But Stephen had already snatched up the phone and was dialing before Robert finished speaking. "I know it by heart," he said breathlessly.

Ike and Linda drove for an hour without speaking, finally reaching the dark pine forests that cover Deep East Texas. Ike took an exit off the freeway and followed a narrow blacktop state road into the woods. He came to a tiny crossroads settlement—a gas station, convenience store, and abandoned barn, all beneath the pale buzzing glow of a light designed less to illuminate than to kill bugs.

"We're almost there," Ike said. "There's nothing at the house to eat. I completely forgot. We need to buy some things."

They went into the store and picked up several armloads of emergency groceries. The woman behind the counter gave Linda a very long look, turned away from her coolly, and then said to Ike, "Well, hello, Mr. Vanden Eykel. Out for the weekend?"

Ike looked her in the face for a long flustered moment, turned back and looked at Linda. He saw the back of a hunter standing at the magazine rack. He turned back to the woman behind the counter, still speechless. He always stopped here at the beginning of a weekend, but he was always surrounded by the excited whirl of his own children and his own wife, all of them popping things down on the counter for him to buy.

"Yes," he said. "Well, actually just for the night."

The woman stared at him.

"Just for a while," he said.

She stared.

"Going back," he said "Just the night, for a. . . "

She stared.

"Yes," he said. "We'd like to buy these things, please."

Ike and Linda carried two bags of groceries out to Ike's car, climbed in, and beat a hasty retreat.

When the hunter came to the counter with a candy bar, the woman was still staring out through the screened door, watching Ike drive off. She turned back to her customer, shook her head, and clicked her tongue.

"You never know," she said.

Gerry Hubbell stared at her and said nothing while she rang up his candy bar. Then he left. He followed Ike to the dirt turnoff to the long rough road through the woods to Ike's lake house. At the turnoff, Gerry switched off his headlights and followed from a long distance, so that he could barely see Ike's red brake lights glowing and extinguishing in the distance through the trees—off and on, off and on, like red eyes opening and closing.

"Mrs. Lehner, this is Stephen Edelman. I am very sorry to disturb you so late."

"Oh, hi, honey. It's not too late. It's just seven o'clock. What can I do for you, Stephen? Where are you? Aren't you at Pagewood?"

"Yes, ma'am."

"What is it, Stephen. What can I do for you?"

"Mrs. Lehner, I called my mom at seven exactly, like the court said for me to, and she didn't answer."

"I see."

Merriellen Lehner immediately picked up the telephone set and began stretching the long cord. She walked out into the living room and stooped to try to get a view out of the side window. There were two houses between her house and Linda's, but she might see something, if there were fire or police lights or something else going on.

"Well, honey, did you let it ring? Maybe your mom is just in the tub or something."

"She wouldn't be in the tub at seven when I call. She's always there when I call, Mrs. Lehner."

Merriellen had sat with Linda too many times, watching her hover by the phone, waiting for Stephen's call. She knew he was right, but she also heard a rising note of panic in Stephen's voice. She knew how fragile both Stephen and Kathleen had become in recent months, as their parents' divorce had grown uglier. She had seen Stephen curled in a ball on the floor in his room, shaking from head to toe, and sucking his thumb.

"Stephen, I'm sure she just got going and lost track of time. She was probably in the tub or out working with the flowers. Why don't you call her back in a bit?"

"Okay. If I can."

"Oh, Stephen, by the way. Did your father allow you to call here? To call me?"

"Yes ma'am."

"I see. Well, wait a while and try her again. Will he let you do that?"

Stephen dropped the phone to his leg and turned to his father, who was standing behind him. "She says for me to wait and then call mom back. Will you let me do that?"

"Of course, Stephen, if you're worried about your mother," Robert said loudly.

Merriellen heard him over the phone and winced. "Stephen," she said, "ask if you can call me back if you still don't get her."

Robert gave his permission for this as well—a remarkable concession. Merriellen hung up the phone carefully, then raced to the front of the house, out the front door, and down the sidewalk to Linda's house. By the time she got there, she could hear all of the phones ringing inside. She walked from window to window, stepping into muddy flower beds in her white tennis shoes, and gouging her legs on rose thorns. The house was empty and motionless. The phones inside continued to ring, and with each ring she could feel the little boy's heart knotting tighter. She raced back to her own house.

Her own phone was ringing.

"Mrs. Lehner, she's not there." He was half-screaming into the phone. "She's not home! Something's happened to my mother! Someone has hurt her! She's always there when I call!"

She heard Robert in the background say, "Stephen, calm down! Get a grip on yourself!"

"Stephen!" she said. "Listen! I think she's just visiting a friend."

"No."

"Yes! Stephen, listen to me! I think something happened, and she had to go up to Oklahoma, to Duncan, at the last minute and visit a friend. I think that's what happened."

"She would have called."

"She will call, honey. As soon as she gets there. But she's still on her way. I think it was an emergency."

Stephen didn't respond. She could hear him breathing. Her nurse's ear told her that the rate of his breathing was coming down slightly. He was calming.

"Stephen, honey, I'll find out, and I will call you."

There was another long silence at the other end. Finally a tiny mouse-like voice said, "Do you promise?"

"Yes, honey. Yes, Stephen. Your mommy is okay. I will find out where she is, and I will call you. But she's just visiting a friend who needed help. She is perfectly fine. She is all right. I will call you."

The moment she got off the phone, Merriellen raced back into the kitchen, looked up a number written on the back of her telephone book, picked up the phone again, and called Rezilla. It was 8:00.

"Rezilla, this is Merriellen Lehner. I'm very concerned. Linda was not at home to take Stephen's seven o'clock call."

Rezilla said nothing for a moment. Then in a near-whisper she said, "That man has got her. He's doing something to her."

"Rezilla, don't say that! Please! Do you know where she is? Where did she go?"

"She had an appointment with the lawyer this afternoon.

"Did she say she'd be late?"

"Yes."

"Could that be it?"

"No. Not if she missed that child's telephone call. He's got her, Miz Lehner. That's the only way she would miss little Stephen's telephone call. If that lawyer tried to keep her late to miss that call, she would walk out on him. To miss his call, she'd have to be kidnapped or dead."

"Oh, please don't! Don't even . . . Rezilla, I'm going to call Ike's office and see if anyone is there."

She told Rezilla the story she had made up to comfort Stephen, about the friend in Oklahoma with a sudden emergency. Then she hung up and looked up Ike Vanden Eykel's office phone number.

She got Ike's answering service. She told the service it was an emergency and she absolutely had to hear back from Mr. Vanden Eykel immediately.

While she waited, she went upstairs to her sewing room.

Three months earlier, Merriellen Lehner had taken Maggie, the third of her four children, to Baltimore for rare open-heart surgery. While she had waited for the child to recover, she had calmed her own nerves by sitting on the floor of her hospital room cutting out sewing patterns. But as soon as she came home with the recovered little girl, life had started up full-tilt again and there was no time to sew the clothes she had cut out in the hospital.

While she waited for Ike to call back, she oiled up her sewing machine, sorted through the jumbled stack of pinned and taped fabric, and began sewing a dress.

Ike started talking as he drove down the narrow red-dirt lane through the pine woods toward his lake house, telling Linda where the neighbors' houses were, what was in his house, how to work the lights, and so on. She barely heard him. The moment they had turned off onto the dirt road and plunged into the woods, it had occurred to her to wonder why everyone thought leaving her alone in an extremely isolated place was the best strategy.

Ike stopped the car. She couldn't see much of the house in the headlights. It looked new. He got out, opened up the door, and turned on some lights. She followed him inside. Then they both decided to go back outside to get the groceries and the file boxes full of her things.

Linda stepped out through the open door first. She inhaled sharply and threw a fist in front of her mouth. A man was standing by Ike's car, staring at her.

"Hi, Linda," the man said.

She didn't recognize the voice at first. The man's face was half hidden in shadow. He stepped forward.

"It's Gerry Hubbell," he said. "I'm sorry. I didn't mean to frighten you."

Ike had come to the door and was standing just behind Linda. "Mr. Hubbell," he said, looking almost as disconcerted as Linda. "What are you doing here?"

"Just checking on you. May I come in?"

"Of course."

Rezilla's phone rang.

"Hi, Zsa. This is Stephen. Do you know where my mommy is?"

Rezilla swallowed and sat down on the chair by her wall phone. Robert would never allow Stephen to call her under normal circumstances. She repeated a version of the story Merriellen had already given Stephen, that his mother had been called to visit a friend in Oklahoma.

"You're going to be all right, honey. Your mama's just fine. You're going to think this is all silly come tomorrow."

Stephen said Kathleen was "having trouble." Rezilla asked to speak to her.

"My mommy's not home, Zsa," the little girl said when she came to the phone. "Stephen called our house and she wasn't there. I'm scared."

Rezilla did what she could to calm both children. As soon as they were off the phone, she called Merriellen Lehner.

"He let them call me at my home," she said. "He would never do that. He's covering it up. Something is wrong. You need to call up to Oklahoma. Do you have either her sister's number or her parents'?"

"Yes, both. I'll call. I will call you back."

Merriellen hesitated to disturb Linda's parents. She decided to call Miriam first, in Oklahoma City. There was no answer. She waited a moment, then picked up the phone and called John and Virginia in Duncan.

Virginia took the call.

"This is Merriellen Lehner. Linda's neighbor?"

"Oh yes, Merriellen. How are you?"

Virginia's heart sank. Merriellen would not be calling unless she knew something. No one was supposed to know yet. It was not supposed to start until 4:00 P.M. tomorrow.

"Mrs. DeSilva, I am so sorry to bother you so late at night."

"That's quite all right, Merriellen. We were just sitting up. I was reading, and John's in there watching television."

"Well, I just called, because I got sort of concerned. Stephen called me up, all in a snit, pretty upset actually, because he called his mother at seven this evening and there was no answer. I went over there and checked, and the house was empty. There's no sign of trouble or anything, but you know how she is, she never misses those calls, and I worried."

Virginia said nothing. She listened in absolute dread of questions.

"I wondered if you knew where she was?" Merriellen said.

"Well, no, not really. I do know she had an appointment with Ike, her lawyer, late today, and they had a lot to go over together. She could be working late with him, I suppose."

Merriellen looked at her watch. "This is pretty late, though," she said. "It's getting on toward nine."

"Yes, that is late," Virginia said.

There was a long pause in the conversation.

"They had a lot to go over," Virginia said.

Merriellen was uncertain what to do or say. She was perplexed by Virginia's lack of urgency. It was absolutely incredible that Linda would stay out this late and miss Stephen's call. It was totally unlike anything

Linda would ever do. But Linda's mother was calm about it. Merriellen's only choice was to try to make Virginia feel more alarmed by the situation, and she didn't feel right about doing that.

"I talked to Rezilla," Merriellen said.

Virginia said nothing.

"She said Robert had allowed the children to call her, too. I think that's quite unusual. Very unusual, in fact. He's been so mean about the phone calls. He barely lets them call Linda, even when the court order says he has to."

Virginia said nothing.

"I called Miriam," Merriellen said, "but there was no answer. I wonder if they could be together."

"No," Virginia said, "Miriam is out with one of her teacher friends this evening."

Another long silence ensued.

"Well, maybe Linda will come back in a little while," Merriellen said. "But if she's not back in the morning, do you want me to call?"

After a barely perceptible pause, Virginia said, "Oh yes. Please. Thank you. We would want to know, naturally."

"All right. And I'll call Miriam back or wait and call her in the morning. If Linda still is not home."

Merriellen put down the phone. She walked back out through the front door and down the walk to Linda's house again. She stood out on the sidewalk staring at the huge silent mansion for a long time. Virginia's reaction had been very odd, she thought. She went back to her own house, climbed the stairs to the sewing room, and settled in with her patterns and needles again.

John was standing behind Virginia when she finished talking on the telephone. He pointed with his finger toward the front door. Together they walked out on to the lawn, where Virginia recounted the conversation she had just had with Linda's neighbor. John asked her to repeat parts of it until he was satisfied he had heard it word for word.

"This is not good, Virginia."

She looked into his face. There was alarm on her own face.

"No," she said. "It's not. What's going to happen?"

John stared out toward the dimly lit street for a full minute.

"John?" she said.

"Hmm." He turned back toward her. "Well, Merriellen knows. She knows. And she called Rezilla."

"Yes. And it turned out the children had called Zsa, too, looking for their mother. But what does Merriellen know, John? She knows what? About the FBI?"

"No, no. Not that. Just that something is wrong. He let the children call Rezilla, too?"

"Yes. That's what Merriellen said."

John's hand flew up to his mouth and his lip barely quivered for an instant. "Oh. The poor little things. He let them call Rezilla. That pig. That only means one thing."

"Yes," she said. "He thinks she's dead."

John took Virginia in his arms and held her in silence on the lawn. Where their faces touched, tears mingled.

"All right," John said, pushing away. "Merriellen was playing it cool, because she didn't want to get you all stirred up. She probably wonders why you were so all-fired calm and collected."

"Well, John, what can I do? I feel like, if I say one single thing, I'll get caught. I'll say the wrong thing. I don't know anything to do but try not to say anything at all."

He thought that over for a moment. Then he sighed and shrugged. "Come morning, that phone's gonna come right off the wall. When they all see she's really gone. They'll get Miriam all stirred up."

"Oh, poor Miriam," Virginia said. "Do you think we should try to call Joe Masterson?"

"Yeah. I thought of that. But what's he going to do? Call everybody up and tell them not to call us up?"

"We could just not answer the phone."

"Virginia," he said. "They . . . do you realize what the people who care about Linda are going to do when they decide for sure that he's got her? If we didn't answer that phone, they would send the police here looking to see what happened to us."

"Oh," she sighed. "All of a sudden, this is a mess."

"It will be all right. We just have to play it by ear. Look, let's just go back in the house, grab a couple hours sleep, and then head out of here about four in the morning, before things really bust loose. At least if we're on the road, we won't have to answer the phone or the front door, either."

Ike took Linda through the lake house, showing her every light switch and lock. Gerry Hubbell followed, saying almost nothing.

Ike pointed toward the huge picture window on the wall of the living room. It was a glistening plate of black.

"The lake's out there," he said. "If you're sitting up at dawn by any small chance. . . "

"Ha," Linda snorted. "No chance about it. I will be."

"Well, then you'll see the lake appear about twenty yards straight out there. We're on a little cove. You might see fishermen, Linda. Especially on the weekend, they're often out there."

Both Linda and Ike turned to look at Gerry Hubbell. "Will there be anybody else out there?" Ike asked.

"She'll be okay," he said quietly.

Ike went to the master bedroom at the back of the house. Linda followed him, mainly because it made her uncomfortable for some reason to be alone in the living room with Gerry. When she got to the back, she saw Ike standing on a small footstool, reaching back into a high blanket shelf in the closet. She realized he didn't know she was behind him.

Ike's hand came back out of a pile of blankets, holding something. The object glinted in the overhead light. Linda froze in her tracks. It was a small pistol.

Ike stepped off the stool and turned, pointing the pistol at Linda.

"Oh," he said suddenly, dropping the gun to his side, "I didn't see you back there."

They stared at each other awkwardly.

"You carry a gun?" she said.

"He does now," Gerry Hubbell said behind her.

She whirled. He was standing in the hall.

"Until this is over," Ike said. "They got me a special permit." He shoved the gun in his waistband and ushered Linda back out to the front of the house. He and Gerry took standing positions in the kitchen while Linda seated herself on a tall stool at the counter that divided the kitchen from the living room.

"Do I get a gun?" she asked.

"Not necessary," Gerry said.

"Do you have one I could have?"

"No."

She turned to Ike. "Ike, do you have another one I could have?"

"No, I'm sorry, Linda. I just have this one."

"Mrs. Edelman," Gerry said, "believe me, you will not need a gun. Now I've got to go."

"So do I," Ike said.

Linda jumped off the stool and walked toward them. "You're not really both going to leave me out here, alone in this house. Why can't you stay? Why can't we sit up and talk? We'll have a slumber party. Whatever. I don't want to be left here alone all night in this house."

Gerry forced a smile. "My wife wouldn't think too well of my spending the night here," he said.

Linda turned to Ike.

Ike shrugged and held his palms out. "Mine either," he said, grinning sheepishly.

"You're going to leave me here alone? I cannot believe it."

"You'll be fine," Gerry said.

He turned, walked out of the house, and drove away.

"Are you really going, Ike?"

"I have to."

She looked at the bulge in his waistband. "Don't shoot yourself with that thing."

"Linda," Ike said, watching the taillights of Gerry's car disappear. "I want you to do something for me. I don't want you to answer the telephone or talk to anyone unless it is me. Not to anyone. Not Joe, not Gerry, not anyone. They are supposed to call me first if they need to reach you. That's the deal."

"Why are you telling me this?"

He turned back and took her by the shoulders. "Just listen to me, Linda. When I call, I will let the phone ring three times, then I will hang up. I will wait thirty seconds. Then I will dial again. Pick it up when it starts ringing again. Do not say one word. Pick it up and wait. If you hear my voice, it's okay. If you hear anyone else's voice, even theirs. . . "

"Joe's or Gerry's?"

"Anyone! Do not speak. Just hang up. Do you have it?"

"Yes. I think so."

"Please repeat it."

"Three rings. It stops ringing. Wait thirty seconds. It rings again. Pick it up when it rings again, stay quiet, talk if I hear your voice."

"Promise me. You will not pick it up otherwise."

"I promise."

"Three rings. Thirty seconds."

She came forward and took his hand. "What's going to happen, Ike?"

He shook his head. "I don't know, Linda. I don't know."

Ike pulled the gun from his waistband, went out to his car, and drove away.

Linda watched through the door while Ike's car disappeared into the woods. She locked the door. She walked through the house slowly, stopping at some of the windows to try the locks, passing others. She opened the kitchen cabinets to look at the food she and Ike had bought, then walked away, leaving the cabinet doors hanging open.

For a while she sat on a stool at the counter. She moved to a sofa in the living room and stared at the glistening black expanse of the plate-glass window.

She sat for a long while, remembering. The scenes of her marriage to Robert passed before her, sometimes so vividly that she heard sounds and smelled odors she had never before remembered.

How like dreaming life is, she thought. As in dreams, there is a seam in life where the universe changes abruptly—so totally and instantly that one fails to notice the change. Somewhere in the course of her life such a seam had been passed, and now Linda wanted to sort back through all of the scenes to see if she could find it.

In the gray light half an hour before dawn the lake appeared outside the window, just where Ike had said it would. There were fishermen, but they went away.

At dawn, the telephone rang. At the first ring, she struck for it with her hand but then pulled up short. She had to count the rings. One. Two. Three. She began to reach again. Four! And then it stopped ringing. Thirty seconds later, it began ringing again.

She bit her finger and drew in her breath. Wrong! It was the wrong signal! Ike had said three! He had been so adamant. So precise. The phone kept ringing. She started to pick it up, then stopped herself.

Two minutes later it rang again. One. Two. Three. Four! It stopped. After thirty seconds, it began to ring again. The ringing drilled into her ears and made her head throb.

Maybe he had forgotten. That must be it. Ike must have forgotten the signal himself. It was too off, too much of a coincidence that someone would call this way, letting it ring four times each time . . .

It rang again. One. Two. Three. Four!

Ike would never forget something like that. He was too compulsively organized about things he considered urgent. That was how Ike handled emergency and battle. She had seen it in the divorce. He was the opposite of her first lawyer. Ike's response to crisis was to draw down and pull in tight, to become ever more focused and vigilant, ever more wedded to the plan.

Again. Four rings!

Something already had gone wrong. There was something haywire.

Linda walked to the counter between the kitchen and the living room. The phone kept ringing. She went to the refrigerator and poured herself a glass of orange juice. She carried the glass and put it down on the counter. She sat on a stool and lifted the glass to her mouth. But her hand was shaking violently, and the orange juice flew all over her face and neck in little splats. The phone kept ringing. She dropped the glass on the counter, where it shattered. The shards made a glassy blue island in a bubbly puddle of orange. She began to cry and then to weep. The phone continued to ring.

Half an hour after dawn, when the first Westmoreland bus came by, Rezilla was waiting. The bus was almost full of people, all but two or three of them black, many of them wearing the white dresses and denim work clothes that were the uniforms of domestic service. Dallas was an odd town, racially. The 1960s had passed the city over, like a tornado skipping over a low place. Now, twenty years too late, the spirit of the sixties seemed to be waking up in black Dallas.

It was a long bus ride. The bus system in Dallas was designed to be convenient for the whites, inconvenient for blacks. Feeder lines from all of the black neighborhoods led into downtown, where passengers were dumped out and forced to transfer onto a few express lines heading north on the maid runs.

Rezilla opened the front door of Caruth at 6:45 A.M. She turned on the lights in the foyer and front hallway, then walked back to the kitchen. She looked around. She noticed that the lights in the back corridor and family room had been turned off, after she had put them on dim just before leaving the house the night before. She went to the intercom and held down the talk button.

"Linda, are you there? Linda, I need to come up and see if you are all right. Are you there?"

She took her finger off the button and stepped away from the intercom. She took a moment to regulate her breathing and to calm the shaking in her hands. Then she climbed the stairs and knocked at Linda's door. She pushed the door open slowly. It made a soft scraping sound as it passed over the deep carpeting. Behind heavy drapes, the room was dark.

"Linda?"

Rezilla turned on the light. The room was empty. She walked to the bed. She reached out with her hand and felt the bed. The covers had been pulled back a foot or so at the top and the pillows had been deliberately mussed. They were punched-in, as if someone had hit them with a fist, instead of being flattened as they would be if someone had slept on them. The bottom of the bed was still perfectly smooth—drum-tight as it had been when she herself had made it up the day before.

She sat down on the end of the bed and made a quick inventory of what she had learned. Linda had not slept in the bed, she knew. Someone had deliberately disturbed the bed to try to make it look as if Linda had slept in it. Rezilla knew someone had entered the house after she had left the night before, because someone had turned off the lights in the family room and back hall.

Someone had taken Linda. It had happened at some point after Rezilla had left the house the night before. It could have happened just minutes ago, just before she arrived. Or moments ago. Whoever it was could still be in the house.

She rose, walked to the head of the bed, picked up the phone, and dialed Merriellen Lehner. Before the first ring expired, Merriellen threw down her sewing and snatched up her cordless telephone sitting next to her on the floor of her sewing room, where she had spent an entire sleepless night and had completed three dresses.

She exploded from the front of her house and ran down the sidewalk in her big flouncy yellow Mexican housedress to Linda's house. She ripped open the door and raced up the spiral staircase to Linda's bedroom, where she found Rezilla with her hand still resting on the telephone.

"She's gone," Rezilla said. "He's got her."

Merriellen stood in the doorway. "To do what?"

"He's torturing her."

Merriellen shook her head. "If he's got her, or if he has paid somebody to get her, then they're going to kill her. That's how Robert is."

"Oh, good Lord, Miz Lehner. What are we going to do?"

"When is he supposed to bring the children back?"

"Tomorrow. The grandparents are coming down today to be ready to take them on a trip to Colorado to ride on a train."

"Oh, good God," Merriellen said. "I have got to call them."

She raced back down the stairs, out the door, and back to her house, where she had all of the phone numbers. She called Duncan, Oklahoma.

She allowed the phone to ring for a long time. She redialed and let it ring again. She knew they had to be at home. She had just talked to them the night before. But there was no answer. She could not imagine where they could be at this hour. Then a flash of fear made her shiver. Linda gone. John and Virginia not answering the phone.

She called Miriam in Oklahoma City. Miriam answered after three rings, in a very sleepy voice. Even though Merriellen knew Miriam well, Merriellen had to explain twice who she was before Miriam could get up to speed.

"Rezilla believes that Linda did not spend the night at the house?" Miriam asked.

"Correct. We have been worried since yesterday evening, because Stephen called here and at Rezilla's house looking for his mother. She missed the seven o'clock phone call."

Neither woman spoke for a long while. Then Miriam said, "Merriellen, do you think it's Robert?"

"Miriam, I am just trying to understand how Linda could not come home."

"You said she went to see Ike?"

"Yes."

"Did you call Ike?"

"Yes. I got his service last night. He hasn't called back."

They agreed that Miriam would try to reach her parents or neighbors of her parents. Merriellen was to try again to get in touch with Ike.

Merriellen called Ike's office. As she dialed, she looked up at the big round clock on her kitchen wall and saw that it was only 7:30. Ike answered the phone himself on the first ring.

"Ike Vanden Eykel."

Merriellen explained who she was and what was going on. The moment she began to explain, Ike's skin started crawling. This was half a day ahead of schedule. This was all wrong.

Ike remembered who Merriellen was. He had met her once when he had gone to Caruth to look the house over and to have Linda sign some things. He remembered her as a live wire, something of a fireball. Now she was talking to the children at Pagewood. Robert would be grilling them after every conversation.

Ike pulled his desk drawer open as he spoke and looked at the gun. At that moment, he believed there was absolutely no way to tell what was going to happen next.

He told Merriellen he and Linda had made their meeting fairly brief and that Linda had walked out of the office saying she was on her way home. He said he assumed she had parked across the way in the parking garage.

"I think her parents are headed down here today," Ike said. "You might wait until they get in. They might be able to shed some light on something."

Merriellen held the receiver away from her face and stared at it for a moment. Wait until her parents get in? They might be able to shed some light?

"Her parents are not answering their telephone, Mr. Vanden Eykel. Rezilla and I are afraid that Robert has either kidnapped her or hired someone to do it for him and that they plan to kill her. I think that this situation is quite urgent. Extremely urgent."

Ike made a silent fist-slamming motion at the desk, then held his fist to his own forehead and grimaced. His mind was flying, trying to find the right way to play it. The woman would think he was nuts if he didn't show some kind of alarm.

"Well, I agree that this could look very bad, unless there's some other explanation. But if something has actually happened, we don't want to do anything to tip off Robert. He would be the main suspect. He still has the children, I believe."

"Yes. He brings them back tomorrow."

"Look, let me start notifying the authorities from here so I can control that. I would appreciate it if you would keep this under your hat, meanwhile, and tell Rezilla to do the same, until we know exactly what's going on with those children. And if the rest of the family gets wind of this, tell them to please stay away. If we get a big scene going there at Caruth, it may just spur Robert to do something worse."

Merriellen agreed reluctantly. When she hung up, the phrase "keep this under your hat" reverberated. What did the man think this was? A problem with cockroaches? What did he intend to do about the fact that Linda was at this very moment gone, might still be alive but might be moments from being murdered?

Ike pushed back from his desk, cursing silently in his teeth. He reached for the phone and called Joe Masterson, who was at his desk and answered on the first ring.

"Masterson."

Ike told him what was going on. Joe weighed it for a moment, then said, "It's bad, but it's manageable. We'll have to get you over there to calm those women down. Can you do that?"

Ike didn't answer. He tried to think if he could calm them down. He had no idea.

Miriam listened to the distant ringing of her parents' unanswered telephone. She remembered Linda had said on the telephone last Friday that John and Virginia had fixed an exact time for their arrival in Dallas. Four o'clock. Linda had said it twice. Miriam remembered it, because it had seemed funny for them to have arranged a precise time that way.

The trip from John and Virginia's front door in Duncan to the front door of Caruth took exactly three hours. Miriam looked at her watch. It was not yet 8:00 A.M. on Tuesday, July 21, 1987. It was far too early for them to have left already, given their planned time of arrival.

Miriam hung up the telephone slowly. In a daze, she walked through her house to the back door. She stepped outside. She had planted her small backyard as a beautiful and perfectly kept grotto of roses, shrubs, and bedding plants. In the morning, even in July, it was always cool and quiet out here. The breeze brought her the rich scent of damask roses, the nutty smell of grass still wet with dew, and the clean breath of an ancient prairie breeze. Both of her hands were shaking.

Linda was gone. Missing. Her parents were not at home. Missing. She did not know where Stephen and Kathleen might be. Something terrible had come into life. A darkness had come over her house. Her breath was short and trembling, and for a moment she felt as if she might fall. Then she turned, walked back into the kitchen to the wall phone, and started dialing.

She began calling relatives to see if anyone knew of a change in John and Virginia's plans or of some other factor that might explain where they were. She called the home of Virginia's sister Jeanne, who lived on the other side of Oklahoma City from Miriam. Jeanne was not at home, but her husband, Bill, said that he did not think Jeanne and Virginia had spoken in the last few days. Miriam did her best to keep the call with Bill low-key.

The moment she hung up, Bill rushed to a writing desk in the living room and dug out a phone number. He called the church where his wife was attending a morning aerobics class and demanded that she be called to the phone.

"You better get home right away and call Miriam," he said. "Sounds like Linda's husband has done something to her, and I don't know, but John and Virginia may be in trouble, too."

Jeanne threw on her warm-up suit and drove as fast as she could to her pleasant ranch-style home on a curving street in northwest Oklahoma City. When she came into the house, she saw that her husband was even more distraught than he had revealed on the telephone. She asked him a rapid-fire series of questions.

Jeanne went to the telephone and dialed her older sister, Ruth, who lived in Duncan. Straining as hard as she could to keep her own voice casual and calm, she told Ruth that there had been some confusion about the plans for John and Virginia's trip to Colorado with Linda. Miriam, she said, wanted to make sure they had not misunderstood what vehicle they were to take. Would Ruth be so kind, Jeanne asked, as to ask her son, Sam, to go on over at some point this morning and look in John and Virginia's driveway to see if the motor home was still there?

Her sister Ruth got off the phone, sat at her kitchen table for a moment, and decided Jeanne's request was very odd, that something must be wrong, that it must involve Linda, which meant that it must involve Robert, which meant that it could be something terrible. Sam was not going to be reachable in the next hour or so, so Ruth got into her own car and drove quickly to John and Virginia's house. By 9:00 she was back at her own house and had reported to Jeanne that the motor home was gone but that their car was still in the garage. Jeanne thanked her and said that she was thinking about going down to Dallas with Miriam to get things sorted out and might be gone for a day or so.

Twenty minutes later, Ruth's son, Sam Johnson, returned her call to his beeper. As soon as he heard what was going on, he hung up and called the Duncan police to report John and Virginia missing.

Substantial people like John and Virginia DeSilva did not suddenly disappear very often in Duncan, Oklahoma. The Duncan police took a description of the motor home, looked through their own records, and found the auto license tag number. They relayed all of their information to the Oklahoma State Highway Patrol with a request that the patrol put out an all points bulletin looking for the motor home. Just as the bulletin came on line in the Oklahoma highway patrol computer system, John drove over the bridge crossing the Red River into Texas.

Miriam called Southwest Airlines. The soonest she could get to Dallas was 1:00 P.M. She hung up. Her phone rang. It was Jeanne. Jeanne told her the motor home was gone.

Miriam sighed with relief. "Oh, then they did leave. I think Merriellen said she had talked to them last night. Maybe they got worried and left early."

Miriam said she was thinking of driving down. If her parents were on their way, then they were going to walk in on a terrible scene at the house. There might be police and reporters: Who knew what might be going on? She said she might try to get there ahead of her parents.

"Well, I'll go with you," Jeanne said. "You can't drive it alone."

Miriam hung up. Her phone rang. It was Merriellen.

"I just spoke to Ike," Merriellen said. "He said he saw Linda yesterday afternoon and that she was fine when she left his office. He said he's worried about doing something that might make Robert not bring the kids back."

"Like what?" Miriam asked.

"I don't know exactly."

"Then Ike thinks Robert has done something to her?"

Merriellen paused. "Everyone does."

"I'm coming down by car with my Aunt Jeanne. We're leaving immediately. I have to drive over and pick her up."

"I am supposed to tell you that Ike is going to take care of notifying the authorities, and there's no need for you or anybody else to come."

Miriam was stunned. "No need to come? My sister is missing. What do you think, Merriellen?"

"I think he's crazy. I don't . . . I don't understand him. Of course you should come down. But he asked me to tell you not to."

"Merriellen, dear, I appreciate your position in this. But my sister is missing. My parents are on their way down there, about to walk in on goodness knows what. And I don't know Ike. I may have met him once or twice, but I don't really know him. He's Linda's new lawyer, that's all I really know about him. This is family for me. I'm coming. And so is Jeanne."

"Good."

Merriellen flung down the phone. It was a few minutes after nine o'clock. She was still in her Mexican housedress. She ran her hand up half-consciously through her normally meticulous dark brown hair and

Linda backstage at the Minskoff Theater in New York, taking a break from the play *Irene*, where she appeared with Debbie Reynolds and Jane Powell.

Linda in her theater days, with Rock Hudson . . .

Beverly Sills . . .

and John Davidson.

Linda DeSilva.

Robert and Linda.

Robert Edelman in the Caruth master bedroom, shortly before Linda filed for divorce.

A portrait of Linda and the children taken as a Father's Day gift for Robert.

Linda and her children, ready for Park Cities' Fourth of July celebration.

Linda's sister Miriam.

Grandma, Grandpa, Stephen, and Kathleen—Christmas at Caruth, 1985.

Stephen and Kathleen in front of the house on Caruth.

Linda and her family visit Disneyland in the summer of 1987, unaware of the danger that has followed them there.

Rezilla, Stephen, and Kathleen— Walt Disney World, 1986.

Linda and her sister
Miriam after a tearful
homecoming.

Linda and her lawyer
Ike Vanden Eykel.

A tearful reunion with Rezilla.

found it hanging down limp and oily on her forehead. While she thought about Ike, she reached over and picked up a huge purple and white polka-dotted hair-bow that belonged to her daughter and pushed it back into her hair. Taken together, the housedress and the bizarre bow created an effect something like Lily Tomlin's little-girl-in-a-rocking-chair character. Merriellen, who normally never left an eyelash out of place, didn't notice. She was thinking about Linda's car and the visit to Ike's office.

At that very moment, Ike was standing in his office, dialing the number at his lake house for the twelfth time that morning. One. Two. Three. He hung up. He re-dialed. No answer.

"Answer the damned phone, Linda!" he shouted.

Another lawyer, walking down the corridor outside Ike's office, dipped his face in smiling and said, "Go get 'em, Tiger. Hope it's billable!"

"Hey!" Ike shouted angrily. "Hey! Shut the damned door! Come back here and shut that damned door, will you?" He jabbed ferociously at his intercom. His secretary was not in yet. He jabbed at another button to reach the receptionist. "Will you please get down here right now and shut this office door and keep it shut!"

"Yes, Mr. Vanden Eykel," the receptionist said. She looked up just as the lawyer Ike had just yelled at was passing. The lawyer looked back down the hall at Ike's door, then looked at the receptionist and shrugged, with a question in his eyes.

"Do not ask me," she said, getting up in a huff to go shut Ike's door.

As soon as Miriam had hung up on Merriellen, Miriam's phone rang again. It was Rezilla.

"Miriam, I just tried to call your folks in Duncan, and there was no answer."

"No, Rezilla, they've left already for Dallas. I think they must be worried. Have you heard from the children?"

"They called me last night at home, but they haven't called today. Your folks are on their way here already?"

"Yes. We checked. The motor home is gone."

"Miriam, you know that they are going to walk in on a scene here, if Linda isn't back. Ike's been calling here, trying to get us all to calm down, but I don't know . . . I don't know. . . ."

Miriam could hear Rezilla choking back tears.

"Rezilla, I am leaving this minute to come down there with my Aunt Jeanne. We intend to try to beat Daddy there. You know how slow he drives in that thing, I'm sure we can do it."

"Please come as fast as you can, Miriam. We are all praying to the Lord and doing everything we can."

"I will pray, too, Rezilla."

Merriellen called her mother, who lived only a few blocks away. Her mother listened in silence while Merriellen explained what was going on. "I need you to come stay with the children," Merriellen said.

"What are you going to do, Merriellen?"

"I am going to look for her."

"Robert is a dangerous man."

"I know that, Mother. I have to try to find her. She might still be alive."

"Why aren't the police involved?"

"I don't know. They may be. Ike is supposed to call them. I don't understand what is going on. Please come now."

As soon as her mother had arrived and was installed with the children, Merriellen rushed out the door and drove off down the street. Her mother watched her disappear.

"She must have no idea how she is dressed," her mother thought to herself.

Merriellen pushed the car to go faster, driving too fast through University Park, breaking out onto the North Dallas Tollway at a dead run. The tail end of rush-hour traffic was still moving toward downtown Dallas on the other side, but her side of the road was fairly clear. She snaked her way in and out of a clump of cars near the entrance ramp and then floored it. In a few minutes, she was back off the tollway and moving up into the parking garage at the Galleria.

The part of the garage where Linda would have parked served the retail stores in the attached shopping mall and provided visitor parking for the nearest office tower. At 9:15 in the morning, it was almost entirely deserted.

She looped around and around the floors, looking for Linda's car. In the gray distance she saw a few people walking toward the elevators. Once or twice, people heard her car approaching and turned to look at her.

How had she become involved in this? Her own husband was the perfect father and head of a family. They had suffered medical crises with the children, but their lives otherwise had been blessedly free of discord and trauma.

Now, all of a sudden, creeping around alone in a gloomy parking garage, it struck her that this situation might well have to do with murder. It was a thought that kept coming home and then fading—too terrible to hold in sharp focus for long. Robert was perfectly capable of it. If anything, Merriellen had worried in recent months, as Ike began winning victories and inflicting legal wounds on Robert, that Robert would snap. And that he would snap in a physically violent way.

She had seen Linda after some of the beatings. It made her heart freeze to see the bruises and the swelling. She had seen Robert racing his stupid black Cadillac down Caruth Street, screaming at them all with his eyes bulging out, practically frothing at the mouth. He was a horrible man.

Her own husband would talk to anyone. He had always maintained outwardly civil relations with Robert. But he had warned Merriellen early on, practically as soon as the Edelmans had moved onto the block, that she should steer clear of them. Then when the divorce began, it was clear to everyone on the street that the Edelman house was trouble.

She remembered seeing little Stephen that day, curled in a ball in his mother's arms and wailing, terrified she would be taken from him and his sister, petrified of going to live with his father.

She remembered the time Stephen came over to her house and lay curled in a ball on the kitchen floor while the other children played around him. She felt his forehead, talked to him, and figured out that he was nauseous and suffering stomach cramps from severe constipation. It was during one of the periods when Robert was occupying Caruth and Linda was at the Howard Johnson.

Linda had told her that Stephen was unable to defecate while he stayed with Robert. He would wait until Linda had returned and his father was gone.

On this stretch, Robert had been in the house with the children for twelve days. Merriellen questioned Stephen and determined that he had not had a bowel movement in that entire time.

She called Linda at the motel and got her on the phone with Stephen. Linda pleaded with Stephen to use the bathroom in Merriellen's house. Just as Stephen was beginning to agree, Robert appeared in Merriellen's kitchen door.

"Who is he talking to, Goddamnit Merriellen?" Robert said.

"His mother! Please, Robert, don't interrupt."

Robert stalked into the kitchen, grabbed the little boy's free hand, snatched the phone from him with the other, and smashed the phone against the counter.

"Nice trick, Bubber," he said through clenched teeth. "Now let's go home and have a little talk."

He dragged the boy out of the kitchen and across the lawn. Stephen—limp, sallow, and speechless—stumbled to keep up.

In the car, prowling the parking garage that morning, she wondered how anyone could turn her back on children, once having seen them in that condition. How could she have turned her back on Linda, who was such a fine mother in spite of it all, such a trooper, such a good friend, so smart and so undeserving of this fate? She could not have. No way.

And yet, she thought, as she wheeled the car around on the top floor of the garage and began heading back down the ramps to the exit, this situation probably had to do with murder. From all that Rezilla had been able to put together, the killer or killers must have seized Linda here, in this very building, then taken her home for some reason or gone there themselves with her keys, turned off the lights, and mussed the bed.

They must have been here. They could be here now. Who knew? They might know who Merriellen was. If they had been watching the house, they would know that Merriellen was the neighbor and Linda's most frequent visitor. They could have been watching her just now, while she scoured the garage with her eyes.

Just as she reached the exit and broke out into the bright Texas sunlight, she looked up in the rearview mirror and caught a glimpse of herself—no makeup, the yellow housedress, her daughter's polka-dot bow sticking out of the top of her head like Minnie Mouse.

"Pretty good disguise, anyway," she thought.

Rezilla went through the kitchen and the family room, yanking open drawers, flying with strong fingers, spilling pencils and Scotch tape and old Post-it notes, moving quickly, drawer to drawer, cabinet to cabinet, thrashing, stooping, reaching on her tiptoes. Finally her finger touched a leathery surface on a high book shelf. Her hand sprang open like a trap and clutched the object, which she snatched down and held before her eyes.

This was it! Linda's telephone directory. Rezilla went to the small writing table that held the telephone in the family room. She moved the phone over to the long breakfast table and sat down. She opened the book to the A's and put her finger on the first name on the list. She began calling each and every person in the thick book, making the calls short and to the point.

"This is Rezilla Williams, Linda Edelman's housekeeper. Mrs. Edelman is missing, and I need to know if you have seen her in the last twenty-four hours. We don't know what's wrong, and I'm sorry, but I have to go so I can keep making calls. Please call here if you think of anything. Thank you very much."

On her way back to Caruth, Merriellen stopped at several stores where Linda shopped. She made inquiries and handed out phone numbers both for Caruth and her own house. By the time she got back to Caruth, Rezilla had reached the L's.

"Let me take over for a while," Merriellen said. "You take a break. Get yourself something to eat or lie down."

Merriellen called a doctor, a distant cousin, then came to Janet Lesser's name.

"Rezilla, have you called Janet yet?"

"No, I didn't get to her."

"Oh boy."

Linda was the common link between Merriellen and Janet. It was not that they disliked each other, but Merriellen, with her down-home no-nonsense approach to things, and Janet, always cool, always distant, always almost barely haughty in her reserve, were not each other's types. Merriellen wondered how she was going to react.

"What do you mean, missing?" Janet asked.

Merriellen quickly recited what already had become a rote speech, describing the basic set of facts.

"Well, Merriellen, you need to call Ike."

Merriellen explained all of that.

"You need to call her sister, up in Oklahoma City."

Merriellen explained all of the calls that had been made, described the visit to the parking garage, the search of the stores. After Merriellen stopped talking, Janet was silent for a long time.

"Oh my God," Janet said flatly. "That monster has killed her."

"Janet! We do not know that she is dead, yet."

"Oh my God."

Merriellen heard Janet's voice break on the other end. A torrent of sobs followed. "I can't . . . I can't believe . . . I can't believe he has done this."

Merriellen waited for Janet to regain her composure. Then she said, "Can you come help us?"

"I am on my way."

As soon as she had hung up on Janet, Merriellen called Ike again.

"Ike, have you notified the authorities yet?"

"I'm working through a private detective on that first, Merriellen. This is a guy I've used a lot in the past, and I really have a lot of confidence in him. I think we need to be discreet about all this for as long as we can."

Linda watched the small green boat draw nearer. The boat was a few hundred feet away when Linda saw that the man in it was Gerry Hubbell. She smiled and waved. He nodded. He increased the speed, then cut off the engine sixty feet out, reached back, and lifted up the prop. The boat slid up smoothly onto the grassy shore. He stepped over the seats and sprang out onto the lawn gracefully.

"You all right?" he said. He was wearing tennis shoes, khaki shorts, and a loose blue polo shirt.

"Yes," Linda said. "I guess. I'm tired."

"Didn't sleep?"

She laughed. "No. I did not sleep. And you scared me to death."

"I did?"

"With the boat."

"The boat?"

"There were some other men out here right at dawn in a boat. They left. Were they FBI?"

"Linda, let's button up here for a little while, lock it up and then I'm going to take you for a boat ride."

John and Virginia stopped for breakfast in Sherman, Texas, and took as long as they possibly could. Then they dawdled on down the highway as slowly as possible. Even at that, they reached the shopping center in Denton an hour before most of the stores were to open.

"Half an hour away from Linda's house," Virginia said heavily, surveying the sprawling deserted parking lot with a baleful eye. There were huge shopping centers on both sides of the freeway.

"How much do we have to buy?" John asked.

"Oh, just a few things. Nothing, really. It won't take us twenty minutes."

John looked at his watch. "We'll have to stretch that out to about six hours," he said. "We're not supposed to be there before four."

"I know when we are supposed to arrive," she said.

From the moment they had driven out onto the interstate highway toward Dallas, Miriam and Jeanne had kept up an unbroken stream of anxious conversation. Miriam filled Jeanne in on some of the details of Linda's divorce process, especially Ike's increasing pace of victories over Robert and his lawyers.

"Miriam," Jeanne said, "I know this is none of my business, really, but, especially under the circumstances, a body can't help wondering. . ."

"I do not know the answer," Miriam said.

"I was going to ask why. . ."

"She stayed with Robert. I don't know. But look at our family. Look at our whole family, Jeanne. You know the answer. People just don't get. . ."

"Divorced, I know. Still, he must have been such a. . ."

"Horrible man. But I don't think . . . I don't think Robert was horrible all the time. It was really only in the last few years. . ."

"When the real estate market in Dallas collapsed. . ."

"Yes, Jeanne, that had to be part of it. Money was so important to Robert. It was his whole source of self-respect. You know, when he was at OU with us, Robert could barely pass a normal course. I don't know why. I do believe he's smart."

"Clever."

"Maybe. But the one thing Robert has been able to do and do well is make money. And all of a sudden, he was losing all of it."

But even the prospect of going down the tubes financially could not have been enough to propel Robert into this kind of thing. They agreed it had to be a combination of things—an array of forces closing in on him. Certainly the divorce was a big piece of it.

Before Ike, the divorce had been set up as an absolute steam-roller—just the sort of operation the male-dominated, macho cowboy legal machinery of Dallas was designed to carry out. The divorce would strip Linda first and then crush her.

But Ike had turned all of that around. All of a sudden, all bets were off. Ike was the steamroller, and Robert was looking at a very tough pro-cess in the property settlement. In just a few weeks from now, if things had stayed on schedule, Ike would have been ramming through all of Robert's books like a fighter jet through clouds.

Immediately after getting the initial unsigned consent order set aside, Ike had informed Robert's lawyer that he wanted to get the divorce issues "bifurcated." That meant he wanted to have the issue of custody of the children tried separately from the issues of the property settlement. It was, in part, a response to Dr. Meyer's stern warning that something had to be done to spare the children more turmoil, and soon.

Linda and Ike had been braced for a battle royal with Robert over this question. But Robert had astonished them both by agreeing immedi-ately. It was very uncharacteristic.

By getting the custody issue bifurcated from the property issue, Ike had stripped Robert of the one source of leverage that could have any effect on Linda. Robert must have seen that, and yet he had agreed. It was, at the time, Robert's one great gesture toward reason and decency.

Linda explained to Miriam what she thought it meant. Mainly, she said, it meant that the custody issue would be settled by fall.

"But when will you be divorced from him?" Miriam asked.

"Oh, I have no idea. The property has to be settled first, and that could take years."

"Oh, Linda."

"But I don't care, Miriam. Once the children are safe from him, I don't care if the divorce takes forever."

"How long does Ike say it will take?"

"Another year, at least."

Now, of course, it was clear why Robert had agreed: he was already planning to kill her. There would be no custody issue. There would be no property issue. There would be no Linda.

Miriam and Jeanne talked and talked, trying out one hypothesis after another. It was about 11:00 A.M. when they reached Denton.

"Jeanne, I think I remember Linda saying my folks were going to stop here in the shopping center and pick up some things. Let's get off and drive over by the Dillard's store. I know I can spot that motor home. It's the size of a whale."

At the precise moment when Jeanne and Miriam were exiting to go to the parking lot in front of the Dillard's store, John and Virginia were leaving the Dillard's parking lot, driving under the freeway to the shopping area on the other side, where they had decided to eat lunch at Luby's Cafeteria.

Linda walked around making sure all the doors were locked. Gerry followed her, watching. She stepped outside and locked the door on the lake side with Ike's key. Then she followed Gerry back down to the water. He pushed the fiberglass dinghy part of the way back out into the water and then steadied it for her while she climbed in over the bow. Gerry sloshed into the lake in his sneakers, then stepped into the boat. Standing in the stern, he lifted up a long wooden oar and stuck the blade into the muddy bottom. With one smooth push he launched the boat off the shore and sent it gliding out into deeper water.

Linda was sitting on the small plank seat in the bow, with her face toward Gerry in the stern. She was wearing shorts, sneakers, and a light shirt.

His build was deceptive, she thought. In a business suit, with his short white-gray hair and piercing blue eyes, he had looked like a middle-aged advertising executive. Here on the lake, pulling on the starter cord of the outboard motor—his neck, arms, and back rippling with trained muscles—he looked more like a middleweight prizefighter.

The motor caught. He adjusted the throttle, and the exhaust cleared from blue to white and then to an almost invisible wavy gas. Gerry steered the boat around and headed it out toward the middle of the lake.

Linda had been happy to get out of the house. Now suddenly she felt very tired. She had sat up, wide awake, the entire night, sifting back through her life with Robert, panicking at every bump and whistle in the night. Now she was exhausted. She dropped her face into her hands, rubbed her eyes, and yawned. When she looked up, she saw that they were moving straight out toward the center of the lake.

It was a huge, meandering, man-made body of water. Barely visible in the distance, a covey of sails was beginning to move out of a cove. Probably a sailing club coming out on the lake for a morning regatta, she thought. People from other parts of the country were always surprised to find so much sailing activity in Texas—another example of how Texans refused to be dictated to by their natural circumstances.

Her eye met Gerry's. He was staring straight at her. She put her face back down in her hands. She did not know if she could ask Gerry about the phone signal; Ike had told her the phone signal was to be a secret code between him and her, excluding Gerry, Joe, and everyone else. And then Ike had drawn his gun and left.

"Where are we going, Gerry?" she called over the motor noise.

"Little ride," he shouted back.

She eyed him carefully. "You never say much."

"I do sometimes. Not with you, though."

He smiled.

"Why not with me?"

"You weren't supposed to hear my voice too much. We didn't want you to be too familiar with it."

"Why not?"

"I'm the hit man."

CHAPTER SIX

M erriellen descended from her bedroom to her long bright kitchen. Her mother was sitting at the heavy oak table, watching the children draw with crayons.

The phone rang. It was Ike.

"What are you all planning to do over there?"

"What do you mean?"

"Are you thinking about filing a police report?"

"Yes. We are. Rezilla and I are headed down to the University Park police station right now."

"Well, you know, you're not really supposed to do that yet."

"Why not, Ike? Who says?"

"I mean you're supposed to wait twenty-four hours before you do that. They don't officially accept them before that."

"Is that right?"

"Yeah. And I'm still kind of antsy about those kids."

"But what about Linda?"

"Yes, I know, it's really a tough call. Why not do this? Why not hold off on the police report for just a few more hours, let me see what my private detective has to say?"

They had barely hung up when Janet Lesser exploded into Linda's house through the front door. She strode forcefully into the center of the family room. All of the breeding, delicate features, and focused manner that could make her seem so elegant in serene moments could also make her look sharp and tough when she was truly angry.

She stopped in the kitchen, put her hands on her hips, pitched her face forward, and screamed at Zsa: "Robert has killed her!"

"Please don't say that, Janet," Rezilla said, rushing over to her. Rezilla caught Janet by the shoulder and pulled her to her. Janet's face was wet with tears. "I don't think that's what he did," Rezilla said. "I think he's got her some place, and they're torturing her, trying to get her to sign something about his money."

Merriellen came into the room. "Janet!"

Janet stared at her and then slumped into a chair and buried her face in her hands. "Oh my God. I just can't believe this has happened. What do the police say?"

Merriellen looked at Rezilla, then at Janet. "I just hung up from Ike. He doesn't want us to file a report until the kids are home safely."

Suddenly Janet was sitting up, alert and at attention.

"Let me understand this," she said crisply. "Am I to understand that you have not yet filed a police report?"

Merriellen and Rezilla looked at each other.

"No report has been filed?" Janet asked again, her voice rising.

Merriellen came forward, shaking her head and holding out her hands defensively. "I just talked to Ike, and he said the police will not accept a missing persons report until the person has been missing twenty-four hours."

"I should think the University Park police would accept a missing persons report," Janet said archly, "when we damned well came and gave it to them. Or I would know the reason why."

Merriellen joined Janet at the table. Janet was staring at her, staring at Rezilla, back and forth, waiting for a response.

Rezilla came over. "Mr. Vanden Eykel told Merriellen he's afraid if we do something to stir up Robert, then Robert might not bring those children home tomorrow morning."

"What?" She stared at them. "What?" Janet, however delicately, was spitting her words. "Robert is the murderer in this situation. Or torturer or whatever. And Ike Vanden Eykel thinks we should tiptoe around and not do anything to tick off Robert Edelman, because then Robert Edelman might not obey the custody order that Mr. Vanden Eykel is so proud of?"

"Come on," Janet said, getting up out of her chair and pleading with her arms. She leaned forward from the waist and held her pursed fingertips up to them, imploring. "Come on, people, let's start getting real here. I mean, what on earth is going on in this house?"

Speaking to the floor and gesturing skyward with her fingers, she prowled the floor. "Rezilla is conducting a phone bank from the kitchen. Merriellen, bless her heart, is driving around town casing the parking structures. It is time to go down to the University Park police station and file a report! Immediately! And to hell with Ike Vanden Eykel! Our beloved friend, Linda, is either dead or about to die! And we have got to pull out all the stops!"

Merriellen and Rezilla both nodded yes, both terrifically relieved to have been brought to this conclusion, and both began busying themselves, preparing to leave to file the report.

"Are you coming?" Merriellen said to Janet.

"Well, won't you need someone here, while you're gone?" Janet said.

Rezilla put down her purse. "I can stay."

"Well, you really need to go," Janet said. "You're the one who can speak for the house."

"I'll stay and man the phones," Merriellen said.

"All right," Janet said. "Although, as the neighbor . . ."

Merriellen looked at her quizzically.

"I just thought, as her neighbor, you might carry more . . ." Janet faltered again.

Merriellen waited.

"Well, you know how it is with my family, Merriellen, everybody thinks we own the place, and I wouldn't want to do anything that might prejudice them down there at the police station in any way where Linda's case. . ."

"Fine," Merriellen said quickly, getting up and slapping her palms on the table, "I'll go. I'll just have to hope they've never heard of my family down at the police station."

They started for the door.

"Wait," Janet said. "Do you know what Linda's license tag number was?"

"It's in the drawer in the writing table over there, on a green pad," Merriellen said. "Rezilla found it upstairs in her desk."

Merriellen and Rezilla went down the alley together to Merriellen's back door. They walked into Merriellen's kitchen to get the keys to her car. Merriellen's mother was standing at the telephone, with the receiver pressed to her shoulder.

"Ike Vanden Eykel!" she whispered hoarsely.

"Oh," Merriellen said. "Again? I just got off the phone with him. I'm just not going to talk to him right now. I know he'll be mad at me if I have to tell him we're going ahead and filing the report."

While Merriellen gathered up her purse and keys, Ike's excited voice could be heard leaking out into the kitchen from the receiver: ". . .know they're there. . ."

"No, they've left already," Merriellen's mother said.

". . .tell them to stop . . . at least take this number. . . . Tell her to call. . . "

She scribbled a note and handed it to Rezilla as she followed Merriellen out the door.

In the car, Rezilla squinted at the scribbled note. "He wants us to call somebody named Masterson," she said. " 'Joe Masterson,' it looks like."

Miriam and Jeanne left Denton at noon, having failed to find the motor home anywhere. With half an hour's drive left to Caruth, they reasoned that John and Virginia had gotten ahead of them on the freeway, even at John's cautious pace, and that John and Virginia would be waiting for them when they arrived at Linda's house.

Shortly after Miriam and Jeanne pulled out onto the freeway, John and Virginia finished their lunch and drove the motor home back over to the side where Miriam and Jeanne had been looking for them. They parked the motor home and turned on the television set, settling in to kill a few more hours.

As soon as Merriellen and Rezilla were out the door, Janet went to work. She reasoned that Linda had been taken in her own car from the parking garage at the Galleria. Merriellen had told Janet that Ike had fixed the time of Linda's departure from his office at just after 4:00 P.M. Whoever had taken her would have known, from Robert, that the first attempted contact with Linda would be at 7:00 P.M. when Stephen would try to call. Certainly Robert would know that Stephen would have a very bad reaction to the unanswered call and that things might start happening at that point, as indeed they had.

Linda would be in limbo, then, for three hours or less, from the time she left Ike's office until Stephen's unanswered phone call. Janet could not imagine that her kidnappers would have kept possession of her car for more than two hours.

Janet rummaged through drawers in the writing desk in the family room and found a map of the Dallas/Fort Worth region. She took it to the long table in the center of the family room and spread it out. Working from the mileage scale at the corner of the map, she roughed out a circle encompassing everything within a two-hour drive from the Galleria.

For the last four years, since her own protracted and difficult divorce, Janet had been making a good living for herself as a broker of commercial real estate. The career was thrust on her by necessity, but she had found, to her surprise, that she liked being in business. It made her feel good to close deals and make clients happy. It also made her feel good to take competitors—especially competitors who reminded her of her ex-husband—and beat them at their own game. She gobbled up information, data, gossip, anything she could get her hands on that might give her an edge. Among other things, Janet had come to know the map of Dallas/Fort Worth like the back of her hand.

She sat at the map and drew red circles wherever there was a shopping center, hotel, airport, convention center—any place that might have a large parking lot where the kidnappers might have dumped Linda's car. Then she pulled out phone books and began writing phone numbers next to each circle. When she had finished, she began calling each of the numbers, asking for the security office, telling whoever answered that she was looking for the automobile of a possible murder victim. She provided the person at the other end with a description of the car and the license tag number. Finally, she provided both Linda's and Merriellen's phone numbers for callbacks.

Calling all of the red circles she had made took an hour. When she had finished that task, Janet called a former college roommate, now living in Florida. A bit of trouble with a gold-digging surfer-hunk had caused her old friend to need the services of a private detective at one point recently. Janet remembered that her friend had made a concerted search for a detective and had come up with a person who was supposed to be of high caliber. But she could not remember whether the detective was in Florida or Dallas.

He was in Dallas, her friend said. He was a former FBI agent and a respected, competent practitioner of his craft. Not cheap, however. Janet took his number.

Joe Masterson called Ike.

"Those women are going to get somebody killed, Ike."

"Joe, I don't know what to do. Now they're not answering my calls."

"No, they're not answering your calls. You know where they are?"

"No."

"They're on their way to the University Park P.D. to file a missing person. My guy is not there to take it."

"Can you get him there?"

"No."

"Can you reach anybody?"

"No."

"What are you going to do?"

"Plan C, my friend. Nothing to do but Plan C. We'll have to hope whoever they get at the University Park P.D. has got half a brain in his head and files some kind of a report. Based on that, I can go to the house this afternoon with somebody from the University Park P.D. and do a pretext interview."

"I'm sorry?"

"Pretext interview. The pretext is that Linda is missing and they have filed a report on it. They would expect some kind of follow-up. So I go do that. That gives me an opportunity to inject myself directly into the scene, and, I hope, get some control over it. I mean, these women are wild, Ike. They've been on the case only a few hours, and they're already pulling our story apart at the seams."

"Where is Linda?"

"She's okay. You talk to her this morning?"

"No. Not yet. I've been tied up. So, when do you go to Caruth and do this pretext interview? After the grandparents arrive?"

"Yes. Probably."

"So some of the people in the house will know the story you're telling them is a phony, and some won't."

"Can't be helped, my man. We have to play this thing as it flies."

"Do you think anybody else is tipped off yet? Anybody else in her family or in the press or anything?"

"Shouldn't be. The first time the word goes out big-time that she's missing is tomorrow when we put it on the law enforcement computers. Before that, nobody else should really be aware."

In a rambling former-hotel-turned-government-office a few miles from the capitol building in Oklahoma City, a young woman sat at a computer terminal. She was an employee of a new division of the Oklahoma attorney general's office set up to deal with prosecutions for failure to pay court-ordered child support. She was dipping in and out of the recorded traffic on the state law enforcement computer network, trolling for names from a list of people whom the division was especially eager to find. While scrolling through a long series of activity reports, she came across the A.P.B. for John and Virginia DeSilva of Duncan.

"Wow," she muttered. "That's Joe's aunt and uncle." She picked up a phone and called the Duncan Police Department. After a brief conversation, she hung up the phone and walked down a long winding corridor, out through an open breezeway, and into an office in what had once been a poolside retail shop.

Some people considered chasing down delinquent fathers and locking them up a dirty job. For Joe Pearsall, still in his early thirties, it was a relief. For several years, as a local assistant district attorney in Oklahoma City, he had specialized in prosecuting child abuse cases. In that work, he had been exposed to horrors that might never allow him an unbroken night's sleep again in his life.

After several years of intense work on that beat, he finally admitted to himself that he needed a break. But he still carried a profound anger for adults who betrayed their responsibilities to children. This new job with the state attorney general, running down scumbag fathers who didn't pay their child support, seemed like an excellent compromise between his feelings and his nerves.

"Joe," she said, peeking into his cubicle, "did you hear about your aunt and uncle in Duncan? There's an A.P.B. out on them."

Before she had even finished relaying the details, he was on the phone to his parents, Bill and Jeanne Pearsall.

"Dad, what's going on with Uncle John and Aunt Virginia?"

His father explained what he could.

"Is Mother there? Can I speak to her?"

"She's not here, son."

"Where is she?"

"She's on her way down to Dallas with Miriam. They went down to help find Linda. They left this morning."

Joe let the receiver fall on his desk. "You are kidding me," he muttered to himself, staring off into the distance. "You have got to be kidding me."

Linda watched Gerry steering with the motor handle in the stern of the boat. He was smiling at her, but it was not a cold smile. It was a nice smile. For the last several minutes, since telling her he was the hit man, he had been silent.

At first, after he had said it, she had been too frightened to speak. Then she decided that she would have to determine what he had meant, in order to know what to do next. Once having made the decision to talk to him, it was easy for Linda to assume the role of a confidant person. All she had to do was act.

"What do you mean you're the hit man, Gerry?"

She smiled politely when she asked it.

"I'm the undercover guy. Hitman Jack."

She watched him for a while longer.

"Why are you out here? If you're Hitman Jack, why aren't you back in Dallas, meeting with Colonel Young, getting evidence?"

He shrugged. He twisted the handle on the motor, and the boat slumped down in the water and slowed.

Linda twisted around and looked ahead. They were pulling into a little marina with gas pumps. There were fishermen on a dock lowering bait buckets into a boat. Relief flooded into her heart, and tears sprang to her eyes. When she turned back around, Gerry searched her face quizzically with his eyes.

The boat bumped up against the dock. Gerry stood up and tied the stern to a piling. He climbed up on the dock, came forward, and asked Linda to hand him a loop of the anchor rope in the bow. When he had secured the boat, he gave her his hand and helped her up. They walked into a little shop in a cedar-shake shed at the foot of the dock and ordered coffee.

Sitting at a round table with a green checkered oilcloth in the back, they stirred their coffees silently for a long while.

"That part starts Wednesday," he said.

"What?"

"The part where we try to get a meeting with Young and also see what we can get Robert to do for us. We have to wait until Wednesday, when your kids are home. We don't press until the kids are back."

"Oh." She shook her head, to show that she understood. Her eyes were still rimmed with red.

"Joe will go to Robert and inform him that your car has been found. It will already be on the computer, and Robert will already know."

"How?"

"Young has connections."

"In the Dallas police department?"

Gerry shrugged. "We will formally notify Robert on Wednesday afternoon that you've been missing since Tuesday morning. We will tell him there has been a search, that your car has been found with evidence of foul play, and he's our number one suspect."

"You will tell him that?"

"Sure. I think Joe already went over this with you."

"Then I forgot."

"We will tell Robert he's a suspect, because he would be. Even he knows he would be. It would seem weird if he wasn't."

Gerry looked intently at her for a moment. He looked around. The place was empty, except for the cook-waitress, who was behind the counter washing pots.

"Linda, what did you think? I was the guy?"

"The guy?"

"The guy. The bad guy."

"I didn't know." Her lip trembled. "I don't know anything, Gerry."

She held herself steady and spoke quietly. "I don't know where I am, you know. I don't really know where my children are. My husband is try-ing to kill me. I don't know where my parents are. I don't know who you are, really. Why are you out here? Are you my guard?"

"I am one of your guards, for now."

He smiled—an open, warm smile. "My wife and I also happen to have a place out here. Joe and I just about fell off our chairs when Ike said he had a place out here. Joe's been to my place out here a few times. We use it on the weekends. This deal is pretty convenient for me. That's why I'm here, Linda. Because I'm on my weekend. At my weekend place."

She lifted her face tentatively. She picked up a paper napkin and daubed at her cheeks. "Something bad has been happening at Ike's house," she said.

Gerry tensed. "What?"

"The phone. Ike told me not to answer unless it was his signal. He was going to let it ring three times, then hang up and call back. Somebody's been ringing, but it rings four times. Then they hang up."

"And call back?"

"Yes."

"It's probably Ike," Gerry said.

"Why would he do his own signal wrong?"

"He's not. It's . . ." Gerry leaned forward and doodled with his finger tip on the tablecloth. "You've got the Dallas phone system over here. It's digital. It's all computer-driven. You've got the local boondocks phone system over here. It's predigital. If you went down and looked at the switches in Dallas, they'd look like a bunch of computer boards. If you looked at the switches out here, they'd be big old racks with a bunch of funky old mousetrap switches on them going clickety-clack.

"The ring doesn't translate directly from one system to the other. The ring you hear on your end in Dallas is not the ring out here. And the number of rings is not necessarily one for one."

"So he could be hearing three. . . "

"And you hear four. But it's the same call. It's Ike. He's probably halfway nuts about now."

"He told me only to answer his call."

"Yeah." Gerry sat back and sipped the dregs of his coffee. "He's worried about you. He feels responsible. He's a good guy, isn't he?"

"Yes."

"But I'll tell you something. We are, too. Joe, me, the other FBI people. And don't ever forget about Fred Zabitosky. Here's a guy who's a national hero, and he has a tough time putting together a living, believe me. He could use some money. He doesn't know you from Adam. But he risked his life to save you, Linda, and he's continuing to risk it now."

"I will never forget him. Whoever he is."

"He's a hero, that's who he is." Gerry paid for the coffees. "Listen," he said, "I have a jeep parked up here, and I need to take you and rent you a little car."

"I don't need one."

"Well, we want you to have one anyway. Let's go."

In the jeep on the way to the nearby town where they would rent a car, Joe said, "You watch TV?"

"Not much. It's too violent. I don't like the children to see much of it. They have enough ugliness in real life to contend with."

"Well, you're not missing much," he said.

He drove for a while in silence.

"Everything on TV is gray," he said. "People are gray. Events are gray. Everybody's sort of the same, sort of good, sort of bad, sort of both mixed together.

"Real life's not like that. Not in situations like this. In situations like this, there are people who really are the bad guys. And there are people who really are the good guys. There is a difference, in situations like this. It's black and white. It's not gray.

"The good guys are on your side, Linda."

"I feel as if you and Joe are my guardian angels."

He smiled. "Listen. The way this thing has gone? I would say you've had somebody looking over you a long time before Joe and I came on the scene. And right now, from what Joe's been telling me, you've got a hell of a team of friends and family working back there to find you, too. I just hope we can keep them on the ranch."

Officer Frank Clifford of the University Park police department was not a happy camper. In his mid-forties, with a round protuberant gut, a graying butch haircut, and slightly bucked teeth, he could be mistaken for an aging redneck Howdy Doody. In fact he was a middle-aged cop who was sick of his job.

He had just been chewed out by his superior for having caused the Mexican lawn crew of the governor of Texas to be an hour late the day before in arriving for work at the governor's huge estate on Turtle Creek in Highland Park. Officer Clifford did not deny to his superior that he had stopped the crew, in their battered Chevrolet Suburban pulling a rickety wagon full of lawn mowers and weedeaters, or that he had stopped them because they were obviously Mexican.

Of course he had pulled them over for being Mexican. In the old days, it had been more or less official policy in the Park Cities that you pulled people over for the offense of driving on Park Cities thoroughfares while being of the wrong ethnicity. You practically got the departmental citation for pulling over lots of black and Mexican motorists and doing it on Turtle Creek Boulevard at high noon so the citizens, when they passed by in their Rolls Royces and their big gray Benzes, could see their tax dollars at work.

Now it was all changing. The Park Cities were going soft. You practically had to catch a minority person in the act of committing a crime in order to pull him over and have a little chit-chat with him about where he was coming from and where he was headed.

It griped Officer Clifford to no end to have to go in and sit there and have some idiot twenty-six-year-old lieutenant give him a lecture about people's "civil rights." What these young people on the force today did not seem to understand was that the wealthy people who lived in the Park Cities had chosen to live there because it was a place where people didn't have any civil rights.

The most the lieutenant ever needed to do was give a little speech about, "Don't go being mean to no Meskins if you can hep it," and then Officer Clifford could have nodded and said, "Oh yes sir, I will be a kinder and gentler peace officer from here on out," and then everybody would have gone on about their business and been buddies forever. But instead, this brat lieutenant had treated Officer Clifford like he was a criminal and like he was supposed to go down and plant the governor's damn tulip bulbs himself.

And now this. A good-looking, dressed up, rich Park Cities lady and her neighbor's colored maid, telling him how, goodness gracious, the lady next door didn't come home last night.

Because of the lecture he had to sit through on the Mexican deal, Officer Clifford was late getting out on patrol. Another younger officer had started interviewing these two females when they first came in, but he had been called out on a traffic accident all of a sudden. That meant that Frank Clifford drew the black bean, as they say in Texas. He had to come sit here and listen to the rest of the two ladies' long tale of woe and complete any report that might be filed, which was likely to keep him here in the department until lunchtime, which could mean the ultimate disaster—having to eat lunch in the commissary with all of the young hotshots.

Before he had come to work in University Park twenty-six years ago from his home in a small town in East Texas, Frank Clifford had never seen so many people who could not even manage to get their butts home at night. The poor old Mexicans he harassed all the time were model citizens next to the drunks in the Benzes that he wasn't supposed to do anything about. And now here was another earthshaking case of a rich lady going through a divorce who missed her curfew, and he had to sit here and hear all about it because of the Mexicans.

"Did you understand what Mrs. Williams was saying about the lights?" Merriellen asked him again.

"Who's Mrs. Williams?"

Merriellen nodded toward Rezilla, sitting two feet away on a folding metal chair.

"Oh, her." He turned to Rezilla. "Yeah, you turned the lights off, and then when you come back in the morning, well, lordy, they'd turned their selves back on. Do you figure it was a ghost?" He grinned at her through his enormous front teeth.

"I turned the lights on, not off," Rezilla said evenly. "When I came back in the morning, they were off."

Officer Clifford put his feet up on his metal desk, lifted his nose in the air, and looked at Rezilla through slitted eyes. "That's right," he said quietly. "They were off. Was there something else?"

Merriellen's face flushed slightly. "Officer, why have you not written down anything we have said so far?"

He put his feet down and leaned far out across the desk toward the two women, clasping his pawlike hands together and wiggling the thick fingers. "Well now, ladies, let me ask you something. I know you feel like that your friend, Mrs. Ellerman. . . "

"Edelman," Rezilla said.

Officer Clifford paused and looked hard at her. "I know you feel like your friend Mrs. Ellerman. . . "

"Edelman," Rezilla said. "You said it, 'Ellerman.' That's wrong. It's not Ellerman. It's Edelman. The lady's name is Edelman. Linda Edelman."

He rested on his elbows on the desk but wagged one index finger back and forth in front of Rezilla. "Darlin'. . . "

"Officer," Merriellen said, "please do not address Mrs. Williams that way."

He sat up straight, brushed at the buttons on his shirt, and then folded his hands primly on the desk. "Has it occurred to either one of you fine ladies that your friend, Mrs. Edelman, might have stayed out all night because she's got bit by the lovebug? Or because she maybe went to a friend's residence and partied a little bit too hearty and needed to sleep it off? Have you ever heard of any cases where residents of this community did actually behave in such a manner and it was not a federal case?"

Merriellen was so angry that she forced herself not to speak for a full thirty seconds while she regained her composure.

Finally she said, "Do you intend to take a missing persons report from us?"

"I'm listening."

Merriellen reached into the manila folder she had brought. "I have written out a physical description of Linda," she said, removing a sheaf of paper. "I would appreciate it if you would copy it. And here is a photograph of Linda. Can you copy that?"

"No," he said.

"Why?"

"We're not equipped."

"Can you photocopy the description?"

"I don't need it, ma'am. We really don't take missing person reports here. We're not equipped. What you need to do is call the Dallas P.D."

Merriellen and Rezilla stared at him, dumbfounded. Rezilla rose first.

"We might just as well go, Mrs. Lehner."

Officer Clifford shrugged noncommittally.

Merriellen snatched up her papers and her photograph and hurried toward the door, muttering about, "What in the hell I pay my taxes for. . ."

As soon as they got back to the family room at Caruth, Merriellen called the Dallas police department's 911 emergency number and asked how to proceed with a missing person report. The 911 operator provided her with a phone number. When she called that number, she reached Investigator Patricia Canton, who took all of the information Merriellen had put together, including a detailed description of Linda.

University Park and Highland Park are distinct communities with a common border, completely surrounded on their external borders by the city of Dallas. By special agreement, Dallas provides Park Cities residents with certain services. It's a cozy deal for the Park Cities residents, who don't pay Dallas city taxes. The arrangement reflects the fact that many Park Cities residents have more influence in Dallas than the people who live in Dallas itself.

Half an hour after her call, a Dallas police department patrol car pulled up in front of Caruth and picked up the photograph Merriellen had found. The officer told Merriellen he had been informed on his way to the house that the investigations unit wanted to know if there was any way anyone at the house could come up with the serial number of Linda's car, as opposed to the license plate or registration number.

He said Investigator Canton needed the actual manufacturer's serial number, and that it might possibly be found on sales or loan information somewhere in the house. If anyone came up with the number, the officer asked that the person give Investigator Canton a call. He then took the photo and drove off.

The doorbell rang. They all looked at each other in shock.

"Oh my God," Merriellen said, "it's going to be Miriam."

When the door pulled open, Miriam and Jeanne first saw Rezilla leaning around the edge of the door, then saw Janet and Merriellen standing back in the shadowed foyer. They saw that all three of the women in the house were crying.

"No!" Miriam shrieked. "No! NO! NO!"

Jeanne tried to snatch at Miriam's shoulder to catch her, but Miriam plunged into the house ahead of her and grabbed Merriellen by the shoulders. "No!" she said, shaking her. Merriellen only stared back at her and cried. Miriam went to Rezilla, whom she grabbed with both hands in the same way, sobbing out, "No, Zsa, no, Zsa, no!"

The longer she looked at the faces around her, the weaker Miriam felt. Her knees began to turn to jelly beneath her, and she started to sink toward the floor. Jeanne stepped forward forcefully, grabbing her by one arm and the other elbow. She half-lifted and half-shoved Miriam into the house.

"Where can she sit?" she said crisply. "She needs water."

Merriellen and Janet bustled to get Miriam into the family room. Rezilla rushed to the sink for water. They all sat at the long table, watching Miriam swallow her water.

"I am Jeanne Pearsall, Miriam's aunt," Jeanne said quietly.

They all nodded toward her.

"Hello, Jeanne," Janet said. "I'm Janet Lesser. This is Merriellen Lehner. We're glad you could come help."

Miriam put her glass down and arranged herself in her chair. She blew her nose and brushed at her hair. Then she faced the women.

"Is my sister dead?"

There was a long silence.

"We have no idea," Janet said.

Jeanne exhaled audibly, and Miriam clutched her hand around the glass, fighting for composure.

Merriellen explained that she had been in the process of filing a missing person report with the Dallas police when Jeanne and Miriam had arrived. She explained that Ike had opposed the idea but that they had decided to do it anyway.

"You were right to go ahead and do that, Merriellen," Miriam said very quietly and evenly. "I can't imagine what Mr. Vanden Eykel is thinking."

They all nodded silently and watched her.

"I need to know two things from you," she said. "Where are the children?"

They told her the children were still with Robert, as far as they knew.

"Are my parents here?" she asked.

"No, Miriam," Rezilla said. "We haven't seen anything of your parents or heard from them so far today."

Miriam and Jeanne exchanged grim looks.

"What is all this?" Jeanne said, looking around at the stacks of lists, maps, and phone logs on the long table.

"We're trying to find her," Merriellen said.

Miriam nodded to them through tears. "Please . . . please go ahead. I'll be all right. I'll help you. Just a minute."

Merriellen, Janet, and Rezilla sized up the newcomers for a moment and then decided to take Miriam at her word and get back to work.

"Why did the Dallas police department want the manufacturer's serial number?" Merriellen asked.

"I don't know," Janet said.

The women decided to go ahead and try to get the information the investigator wanted. They rifled through the drawers in the writing table in the kitchen and in the desk at the top of the stairs. By then, Miriam had joined them and seemed to be in good possession of herself, although her face was completely drained of color. "There's another bunch of stuff, I think, up in the attic in a drawer over in the area where Linda has her wicker," Miriam said.

Miriam and Janet started up the spiral staircase together to go look in the attic.

When Miriam started up the stairs, Jeanne took a look around the cavernous downstairs of the huge house. Normally light and airy, every room was now darkened by heavy floor drapes drawn tight.

"Wait a minute," she said. "I think I'll go with you."

The three women went to the attic door and found it locked. They did not look down and notice that the key was in the lock.

Janet went to the head of the spiral staircase and called down: "Rezilla! Rezilla, do you know how to unlock this door?"

Merriellen came out of the family room and heard her. She went back in and asked Rezilla, who told her the key was in the door.

"The key is in the door," Merriellen cried.

"What?"

"The key . . . oh, wait a minute." Merriellen hurried up the stairs to show them the key. She brushed past them in the narrow corridor and worked the key herself.

"Come on up. I'll show you," she said. "You have to be kind of careful. It's only half finished up there."

The four women crowded together in a bunch on the steep narrow staircase.

"Would you please turn on a light?" Janet said irritably.

Merriellen fumbled around. She was just beginning to be able to see, in the scant half-light from above. She ran her hand around on the wall.

It did not occur to her to look for the switch back outside the door, in the corridor.

"I can't find it. It must be at the top."

The breathing of the four women as they climbed the stairs fell together like the harmonic wheezing of a leaky pipe organ. With each step higher, the group moved more tensely, more slowly.

They stood together at the top of the stairs, allowing their eyes to adjust. Then, in almost perfect unison, they began screaming at the tops of their lungs, clutching for each other and stamping their feet. Three yards away from them was the dark figure of a man, flat on his back with his arms and legs spread wide. When the women stamped on the loose flooring of the attic landing, the body bounced in the air and writhed, as if clawing to get up, which made them scream and stamp harder.

Then suddenly they were motionless. Now their breathing was more like four wood saws, pushing and pulling.

Janet spoke first.

"What in the living hell is that thing?"

Jeanne was speechless. Miriam was nodding her head no.

Merriellen took a step forward. Then another. Then she reached forward with one toe and gave the figure a little kick. It jumped and wiggled in the air, and all of the women gasped.

After a moment, Merriellen said, "It's her inflatable guy."

Janet said, "Her inflatable what?"

"Her inflatable scarecrow guy."

Miriam clasped one hand to her heart. "Oh my goodness! That is what it is."

Jeanne was looking around at the other women and surveying the rest of the attic.

"Her inflatable what?" Janet snapped.

"Her scarecrow doll. It's a scarecrow. Like in the Wizard."

"The what?"

"*The Wizard of Oz.* It's the scarecrow guy. She had it in her little scene that she made for the front of the house. At Halloween."

The other women were now breathing quietly. Jeanne had turned her face away to hide a smile she could not quite suppress.

"She keeps it up here inflated?" Janet said angrily.

Merriellen found a switch and flooded the attic with light. "Come on," she said. "There's a file cabinet over here by the exercycle. Let's look in there."

The searched the file drawers but came up with nothing.

Miriam and Jeanne went back down the narrow staircase to the second floor, leaving Merriellen and Janet in the attic. At the bottom of the stairs, Miriam turned to Jeanne and said, "I deeply appreciate your coming here and staying with me for a while. I'm real scared."

"Are you worried about your folks?" Jeanne asked.

Miriam began to cry softly. "I'm terribly worried about them. They should have been here ahead of us. It's been eight hours or more since they must have left Duncan. I can't imagine where they are. We know Ruth went and looked this morning and saw the motor home was gone. I just . . . I can't imagine."

Jeanne took her by the arm and put her face close to hers. "Miriam, you have got to be strong. That is the only way to get through this. It is the only way you can help Linda or those children."

Miriam nodded silently, with her eyes squeezed shut.

Up in the attic, Janet spied a telephone on a little end table next to the exercycle. "Didn't Linda buy that car at Lone Star Cadillac?" she asked.

"Yes," Merriellen said.

"From that real cute salesman Robert was so jealous of? The one who was in the bachelor auction for the 500? The one Sparkle Masoud went out with?"

"Yes."

"What was his name?"

"Brian. Brian Thomas."

Janet called information and got the number for the dealership. She called and asked for the salesman. The operator put her on hold. The salesman answered.

"Mr. Thomas, this is Janet Lesser. My brother, Jeff, has purchased cars from you in the past, I believe."

"Yes he has, Miz Lesser, and so has your brother-in-law and about a half a dozen other members of your family. How may I help you?"

"I am very close friends with Linda Edelman, and I happen to need to find out the serial number of the car you sold to her last year."

There was a pause at the other end.

"Is that a fact?" he said. "Well, you know, Miz Lesser, I know you and your family real well, and we've done a lot of business together in the last few years, but what you're asking . . . that's really supposed to be considered confidential-type. . . "

"Mr. Thomas, Linda has been missing for almost twenty-four hours, and we are trying desperately to find her. I need this information to give to the Dallas police department. I would be more than happy to provide you with the name and number. . . "

"She's missing?"

"Yes."

"Linda Edelman?"

"Yes."

"How long?"

"Almost twenty-four hours."

"Oh man!" he said. "That bastard must have killed her!"

Five minutes later, the salesman called back with the serial number. Joe Masterson called Ike.

"You have got to get those women under control. They're running around playing private detective. They've got the Dallas P.D. in on it now. I thought I asked you an hour ago to have that woman, whatever her name is, the neighbor. . . "

"Merriellen Lehner."

"Why didn't she call me back?"

"I don't know, Joe. What happened? I thought you said they filed a report with the University Park P.D. What happened there?"

"I don't know. We're checking it out. Whoever they talked to brushed them off. Now I've got to get that straightened out so we can still get in there pretty quick, like in about an hour, and do a pretext interview."

"Can you come in with the Dallas P.D.?"

"No, we still can't trust Dallas on this. I'll have to wait until my guy at University Park gets his situation lined up. We haven't even sent the word back to the Colonel yet that the job's been done, and these women are pulling the story apart limb from limb already. At this rate, Edelman's bound to catch a whiff of something on the bait. Then who knows what happens."

"I'm sorry."

The phone rang in the family room, and Rezilla answered it.

"Edelman residence."

"May I speak to Jeanne Pearsall, please."

"I'm sorry, you have the wrong number."

Rezilla hung up.

Miriam looked up quizzically.

"Wrong number," Rezilla shrugged. "Somebody named Pearsall."

"Oh, Zsa," she said, flapping a hand, "that's my Aunt Jeanne."

The phone rang again instantly. Rezilla picked it up and heard an angry male voice on the other end, high pitched with the first notes of panic. She shoved the phone to Miriam, who took the call and brought Jeanne to the phone.

Joe Pearsall's voice boomed from the telephone: "Mother, what are you doing down there?"

Jeanne held the telephone away from her ear.

"Why on earth," he shouted, "would you deliberately put yourself in a situation like that?"

"Joe, I can't talk to you unless you talk quieter."

"Is Linda missing?"

"Yes, Joe."

"Do people think Robert killed her?"

"Yes, Joe."

"Well, what are you doing there, Mother?"

"We're trying to help find her, Joe."

Jeanne heard the receiver at the other end bump against the hard surface of Joe's desk. Even though she could not see him, she knew the gesture well. He had just banged the phone down and was sitting, staring into space with his hands gripping the sides of the desk as if he had just pitched over the steepest peak of a roller coaster.

Then she heard him scrabbling to get the telephone back to his mouth.

"Mother, this is a murder case. You are a senior citizen. . . "

"I am not!"

"You are, too!"

"I am not!"

Neither one of them spoke for a long time.

"I am coming down there," Joe said. "I am coming down and get you."

"Don't do it, Joe. I won't go. I will not leave Miriam alone here, and not you, or Bill, or anybody else is going to make me. And Joe?"

"What, Mother?"

"I can't keep this phone line tied up like this. We're expecting a lot of leads to start coming in about now."

For several minutes after he had hung up, Joe Pearsall sat at his desk in silence, gripping the sides.

The minute Jeanne hung up, the front doorbell at Caruth rang. John and Virginia had arrived. The women in the kitchen looked at each other for a long silent moment. Without speaking a word, they decided with their eyes that the normal move at this point would be for Rezilla to go to the door.

Rezilla walked to the front of the house and pulled the door open.

For John and Virginia, all of a sudden, this was show time. It had been one thing to carry the secret around all week within themselves, to spend this long grueling day in faceless shopping centers and traffic on the freeway, not telling, not knowing. But now, all at once, with a great and dangerous secret in their hearts, they had to face the others, who did not know.

Rezilla, believing that she would be the first to tell them Linda was missing, burst into tears on seeing them.

It occurred to Virginia that things had been happening all morning, events transpiring, and that she did not know where the situation stood. Rezilla's tears suddenly frightened her. What if the plot had gone awry already? She felt her knees weakening beneath her.

Miriam stepped forward and ushered her parents into the house. She managed to maintain an outward general composure, but her lip was trembling slightly as she told them.

"Linda has been missing since last night. Her bed was messed up a little, but Zsa does not believe she slept in it."

As she spoke, Miriam monitored her parents' faces closely, ready to spring forward and help them if the shock proved too much. But the instant she began to tell them the story, John and Virginia realized that the script was still in order. They decided nothing had gone terribly wrong yet. Miriam noticed that her mother seemed to grow calmer as she heard more of this terrible news—a strange and confusing response.

They were all standing inside the large foyer when the doorbell rang again. Rezilla opened it. It was Ike.

Ike looked in and saw what might be bedlam. People were crying, milling, talking all at once. He stepped in quickly to introduce himself to the ones he did not know already, in order to get things under control.

Miriam shook hands with him. She noticed that Ike had stepped past her parents without stopping to say hello to them, which seemed out of character for Ike—almost rude.

The phone rang and Janet went to the back of the house to answer it. While everyone talked, the crowd at the front of the house began drifting under its own weight toward the family room. Even though Joe Masterson had told him exactly whom he would find in the house, Ike was taken aback by the scene that met his eyes. Without a word of conscious decision-making, and with no experience at all between them at this sort of thing, the five women in the house had converted the family room into an impressive and effective operations center.

Spread in the center of the long table was Janet's map, with the concentric distance circle drawn in magic marker around the Galleria area. Arranged at various points along the table were phone lists, Linda's personal directory, a description of Linda, pictures of her, lists of pertinent information and data about the car, bank deposit slips, and so on. At one end of the table was the telephone, and next to it were careful logs of all calls made and all calls received. There was also a note pad carrying information gleaned from the calls and a running rough draft report on the information gathered so far.

Janet was on the telephone.

"Busy, busy," Ike said, trying a small smile.

Merriellen looked at him with an expression of confusion. Jeanne and Rezilla were impassive.

"We're trying to do what we can," Miriam said nicely.

Janet slammed the phone down. "Of course we're busy. We're trying to keep Linda from being murdered. Why wouldn't we be busy?"

Embarrassed by Janet's sharp speech, Miriam said: "We're all a little upset."

Janet shook her head and rose to her feet. "No, no. Wrong. In my personal case, that is not true. I am not a little upset. I am a lot upset. I consider the kidnapping and possible murder of one of my very dearest friends to be extremely upsetting."

Ike nodded, stepped more or less to center stage, and began to speak. He explained that a full-scale police investigation was now underway and that, in fact, investigators with the University Park police department and the FBI were coming to the house in half an hour to conduct interviews with everyone.

John and Virginia sat still as stone, watching Ike's every expression. If Ike stuck to the script, too, then it meant Linda probably was all right.

Everyone else in the room was staring back and forth from Ike to John and Virginia, wondering first what Ike knew, then wondering what effect his words would have on John and Virginia.

"The police have been notified," Ike said, "and the FBI has taken jurisdiction of the case."

John and Virginia began to breathe more easily. He was sticking to the script. John exhaled, took off his glasses, and rubbed his eyes. Virginia nodded impassively.

Miriam, who had been watching her parents' faces during Ike's speech, was even more confused by their reaction. The grimmer the news got, the better they seemed to feel about it.

"Mother, do you understand? Do you understand what Ike has said?"

"Yes," she said flatly. "It's terrible."

John stared back and forth at the two of them, then nodded and said, "Terrible. This is terrible. She's just . . . just gone, that's all. I hope they can find her."

Janet watched the entire exchange with a keen, unblinking eye. When Ike paused, Janet walked over to Virginia and knelt down at her side. Quietly and calmly, she described for Virginia all of the things she, Merriellen, Miriam, Jeanne, and Rezilla had been doing to try to find Linda.

If anything, Janet's description of their efforts only made Virginia uneasy. Virginia tried to react enthusiastically and gratefully to the efforts of the women, but Janet's sharp eye saw that Virginia was somehow made more nervous by what Janet was telling her than by what Ike had just told her. Janet decided there was either something odd about the way Linda's parents had taken the news of their daughter's probable murder, or else there was just something odd about them.

Ike looked at his watch. "Now look, folks," he said, "I need to tell you a little something about a couple of visitors we are about to have."

The doorbell rang. Rezilla went to get it. It was Joe Masterson, accompanied by an extremely contrite Officer Frank Clifford.

Rezilla dipped back into the library. "It's a policeman and a man from the FBI," she said.

Ike muttered under his breath.

Janet and Miriam both heard it and looked up sharply at him. Ike shrugged and walked out to meet the police.

Officer Clifford reintroduced himself to Merriellen and Rezilla with much bowing and scraping. He had been informed by his lieutenant only thirty minutes earlier that Mrs. Edelman was indeed considered missing, that the case was being taken very seriously, that the FBI was in on it already, and that so far Officer Clifford had handled his end of it even worse than he had handled the governor's lawn crew. With his face bathed in a film of sweat, Officer Clifford introduced Joe all around, introducing him to Janet twice. Ike made a great show of shaking Joe's hand and saying he was glad to meet him.

Miriam felt queasy suddenly. Ike's muttered reaction to the appearance of the police; the little speech he had been trying to make, obviously to prepare them for this meeting; his studied formality on meeting the FBI agent: all of it was spinning together in Miriam's mind. With only split seconds to figure it out, she was on the verge of deciding it meant that Linda was already dead, that Ike knew about it, and that these men had come to notify the next of kin.

Joe, meanwhile, was studying Miriam and Rezilla closely, trying to decide if they had already figured anything out. Merriellen and Janet were less likely to spot holes, but Miriam and Rezilla were family. Where Merriellen and Janet would be unlikely to pick the story apart on anything less than a factual basis, Rezilla and Miriam would be feeling every word said in their bones and weighing every facial expression in their hearts.

He watched Miriam in particular. Miriam felt him watching her and decided it meant somehow that he knew something terrible.

Everyone took seats in the library. Officer Clifford began questioning all of the family members and Rezilla. Joe sat behind a small tea table with his lap desk before him and his half-moon glasses at the tip of his nose, nodding thoughtfully and taking an occasional note.

Both John and Virginia had decided by now that the sting was still on, which meant that Linda probably was alive. Both of them became more relaxed as the interview progressed.

"Well, I think that about wraps it up," Officer Clifford said, lifting his note pad and preparing to fold it up.

"I would like to say a few words," Joe Masterson said. He took off his glasses, carefully placed them on the floor with his lap desk, and then stood up. On his feet in the center of the room, rocking easily from foot to foot as he spoke, he was a commanding presence.

"The bureau has been asked to lend some of its expertise in searches in this matter, due to the type of person who is the obvious main suspect, his access to cash, and the obvious fact that a person of this type would be capable of quickly transporting a victim across state lines.

"I am confident that we will find out what has happened here and do it fairly quickly. There is an aspect of the case that bothers me, however, and that is the children. As you know, they are still with the father. We don't want to do anything that might prompt him not to bring the children back as scheduled tomorrow morning."

"Like what?" Janet interrupted.

All eyes turned to her.

"I'm sorry," she said. "I'm afraid I can't quite get what's going on here. If he is the main suspect, then why don't you go arrest him?"

"We don't even know what to arrest him for until we find out what happened to Mrs. Edelman," Joe said.

John turned to Janet and said, "They have to build their case."

Janet shook her head. "No, no, I'm sorry, that just doesn't . . . I still don't get it. Why are we worried mainly about building a case? Why aren't we worried mainly about saving Linda's life? She might still be alive. Why wouldn't you go arrest Robert and search his office and his house and shake it out of him. . . "

"Please, Janet," Virginia said sharply. "Agent Masterson and the other policeman are doing everything they can, I'm sure. I think they are the ones who have the experience here. We have to trust them."

Janet gazed at Virginia, uncomprehending. Then she turned and gazed at Joe Masterson. She shrugged. "All right. The last thing I want to do is interfere. I'll go."

She turned to leave.

"Just a minute," Joe said. He said it in an even voice, not loudly, but there was something in his tone that would stop a charging lion in its tracks.

She froze and turned back around slowly.

"I do not want a word of this situation breathed outside this house," Joe said. "If Linda is still alive, and if you breach security on this situation in a way that tips Robert, you may very well cause her death."

When Linda had completed the paperwork for her rental car, Gerry led her back to Ike's lake house. The house looked different by day, smaller and cheerier than it had the night before. It was mid-afternoon.

"You're leaving me alone again," Linda said, standing on the gravel drive and leaning into the window of Gerry's car.

"Afraid so. You'll be all right. There are eyes on you."

She watched his car disappear into the trees. Before she went inside, she searched the woods intently with her eyes but saw nothing.

Over the course of the next two hours, Merriellen went home and came back three times to mention things she had forgotten to say, or to see if she could help with dinner, or to make sure John and Virginia didn't need anything. Rezilla stayed until after 6:00 P.M., causing herself to miss the last rush-hour express bus from downtown to South Oak Cliff, which meant that when she did leave, she faced an hour or so standing around on the deserted downtown streets waiting for a local.

"I'm so worried about you all," she said at the door.

"Just go on, Rezilla," Miriam said. "You have your own family to think of."

All but one of Rezilla's children were grown and had families and homes of their own. One adult daughter, who was retarded, lived with Rezilla and depended on her for care.

Rezilla stared back in at them. "No," she said, bustling back in through the door. "I'm staying the night. I'm staying until I see those children home."

"But Rezilla, what about your daughter?"

"I will call my son's wife and tell her she's got to go over there and pick her up. I am not leaving here until little Stephen and Kathleen are loose from that man."

They pushed the command-post items to the end of the table in the family room and sat down together for a light meal. Few words were spoken. Virginia looked across the table and saw that Miriam, who was looking down at her plate, was crying silently. Virginia looked at John. He saw it, too. She asked him with her eyes what they could do. With a barely perceptible tick of his head, he signaled to her that they could do nothing.

At 7:00 P.M., they waited for Stephen's call. It did not come.

Everyone went to bed before 9:30. John and Virginia took the guest room, where they were accustomed to sleeping. Rezilla slept in Kathleen's bed. Miriam and Jeanne took Linda's bed.

In the silence of their bed, Virginia whispered to John, "I cannot stand for Miriam not to know Linda's alive. It's breaking my heart."

"Be careful," John whispered even more quietly. "We don't know how much they can hear. There's nothing we can do. You know what the FBI man said. We cannot tell her."

"Oh, John."

"I know. I know."

They stared at each other in the dark.

Miriam and Jeanne shared Linda and Robert's king-sized poster bed. Miriam was in bed first. She lay on her pillow, staring at the ceiling. Jeanne started back through Linda's huge dressing room to the enormous bathroom—the one Robert had designed, with the glass shower stall in the middle and matching toilets and sinks against the walls on opposite sides—but she stopped midway across the dressing room.

Miriam became aware that Jeanne was standing in the middle of the dressing room for some time, without moving. Miriam got up out of bed and walked to the dressing room door. She peeked in. Jeanne was staring up at the ceiling.

"Jeanne, what is it?"

"You told me in the car on the way down here that Robert used to sneak into this room through a trap door and steal things from Linda."

"Yes."

"Is that the trap door?"

"Well, I don't know, Jeanne." Miriam stepped into the dressing room and turned on the light. Above Jeanne's head was the rectangular outline of a drop-down staircase to the unfinished portion of the attic. Leading to the trap door was a ladder, permanently attached to the wall.

"I guess that must be it," Miriam said. "She told me she found some insulation on the floor right around here."

Jeanne shook her head. "This house is so spooky. Did you tell me there's another staircase down to the back room somewhere up here?"

"No."

Jeanne turned. "I saw a little bathroom off the hall out there, didn't I?"

"Yes, there is one at the top of the stairs."

"I think I'll use that. Would you mind shutting this door? Can you lock it?"

"I'll shut it. I don't think I can lock it."

⚜   ⚜   ⚜

At 10:00 P.M., Fred Zabitosky called Colonel Young at his home in Greenville, a small city an hour east of Dallas.

"The job's done," he said.

"It's done?"

"Yeah. I talked to Jack. It's done. You need to take care of me and Jack, too."

Young reminded Zabitosky that there was to be a waiting period between the murder and the payoff, in order to give the client time to make sure the hit had really been made and that the woman was dead.

"Yeah, well, the clock starts now, because the job's done," Zabitosky said.

Zabitosky hung up. The man sitting next to him swung around to a computer terminal. They were in a small room, packed with electronic equipment, in the same warehouse building where the transfer of Linda's car had taken place the day before. The man at the terminal quickly entered a report: it notified all departments in Texas and Oklahoma that Linda's car had been found that evening, parked at a rest stop near Durant, Oklahoma, just across the border from Texas. The report said there were signs of foul play, including blood in the car. No body was found, and a search was underway.

By the end of that day, every household up and down Caruth became aware that Linda was missing and that the Edelman children were with their father and due to return at eight o'clock the next morning. Virtually everyone on the block assumed Robert had caused Linda's kidnapping and possibly her death as well.

The next morning at 6:30, Joe Masterson called Ike Vanden Eykel at home. "We've got to push up the schedule a little on this, Ike. I'm fairly worried about what all these women back at the house are cooking up. The neighbor and the other one, Janet, they're really pushing. They'd make great FBI agents. I'd like to have them on my side some day.

"We went ahead last night and put a report out on the wire that Linda's car's been found up in Oklahoma and there's blood on it."

"Already?" Ike said.

"Yeah. It needed to be out there. It'll get to Robert pretty quick, and I'm going to need to go see him today, so we need to have it out there."

"I see. Who tells the people back at the house this news?"

"That's why I was calling you, Ike."

Normally, on a summer morning, several children in the neighborhood were already out on their bicycles or kicking a soccer ball up and down the carefully tended front lawns by 7:30. Usually by then there were women in their front gardens or sharing coffee in their side yards, perhaps still seeing off husbands or welcoming maids.

But on the morning of July 22, 1987, Caruth Street was utterly deserted and silent as a tomb. Children were held inside their houses. A majority of the husbands who otherwise would have already left for the office by then were still at home, standing behind curtains at the front windows with their wives.

By 7:00 A.M., Merriellen had already visited the group in Linda's house three times. They all had decided that Merriellen and Jeanne should stay out of view, in case Robert, for some reason, tried to enter the house. By 7:20, Merriellen had persuaded the woman who occupied the house between her own and Linda's to allow her to take over the shuttered bay window that faced both the street and Linda's front door. Merriellen arranged the shutters, which were inside the glass, so that she could see out but could not be seen.

By 7:35, several other women on the street had heard that Merriellen was in the woman's bay window watching. They came to the woman's back door and asked if they could stand in the bay window, too.

At 7:40, the woman sped off in her car and returned ten minutes later with a box of doughnut holes, which she served with coffee to the tightly packed group in the bay window.

Inside Caruth, John and Virginia sat on the love seat in the library, staring silently at the far wall. Miriam waited in the library door, out of view of the front door when it opened. Jeanne was in the living room, watching Caruth Street from the front window. Rezilla stood just behind the front door, in the small rectangular foyer, between the front door and the large hall and reception area surrounding the grand staircase.

Rezilla had the hardest job. The day before, Joe had explained that the critical interface with Robert would be between the time when he pulled up in the driveway and when the children were actually safe inside the house with the door closed behind them.

Robert could not afford to do anything but turn the children over until he was officially notified that Linda was missing. To fail to turn them over would be a dead giveaway that Robert already knew something had happened to her. Robert would know that.

If, however, in the process of the transfer of the children, he could claim that he saw something or even sensed somehow that things were not right at Caruth, then he could keep the children and argue that he had simply guessed something was amiss in the house and did not want to leave the children until he was assured of their safety. Once he had been officially notified of Linda's disappearance, then he would have every right to keep the children.

If, while Robert was still present and the door to the house open, he could look inside and in any way reasonably construe that something was wrong, then he might be able to use that as his excuse for snatching the kids back. Once he did that, it might be difficult to retrieve them.

Ike told them all: "Once Robert gets the children back in his possession, and we have to go forward and say their mother is missing and presumed dead, then it will be very difficult for us to pry those kids loose from him. The court will say, 'If the mother's gone, the kids belong with the father.' Then, if Robert wants to make a break for it and go to Europe or the islands or wherever, or if something goes wrong with the case and they can't pin it on him, he's got the kids, and we're out of luck."

This moment, about to happen, was the key. If they could get the children away from him and shut the door on him, then the children were home to stay. But if anything went wrong, they could lose them forever.

CHAPTER SEVEN

The intense prayerful silence of the house spread out over the lawn and up and down the length of the street. All along Caruth, dozens of eyes peered through slitted curtains in the front windows of the houses.

They were all prepared for Robert to be late. He was always ten to fifteen minutes late. When he did arrive, he always made the children sit in the car while he smoked and finished his phone call. When he did let them get out of the car, he always watched carefully and insisted they not run to the door. The children always walked slowly and painfully down the long walkway, cringing beneath his eyes on their backs. Linda always waited in the foyer, and when they were safely on the porch, Zsa always pulled open the door. They always exploded forward and into Linda's arms, singing, "Mommy, Mommy, Mommy."

But Robert was uncharacteristically punctual this day. At exactly 8:00 A.M., his long black Cadillac with black-tinted windows nosed around the corner and came purring down Caruth toward the house. The car pulled up to the curb and came to a careful stop at the end of the walk. The doors flew open immediately, and Kathleen and Stephen leapt out.

Stephen raced to the door, with Kathleen running and stumbling along behind. As soon as the children got out of the car, Jeanne could see from her post in the living room that they were already searching for their mother.

Rezilla waited until they had climbed the last step up to the small half-round porch. Then she pulled the door open and held out her hands at the level of the children's heads. They raced past her outstretched hands, skating and sliding into the main hallway, both searching the place where their mother usually waited for them, out of Robert's view.

When they saw Miriam in Linda's place, they immediately pushed by her into the library, still looking for their mother. Instead, they saw their grandparents on the love seat.

Rezilla, with her face still poked out through the open door, mumbled, "It's okay, babies, you're okay now, it's all right."

Robert began to ease the car away from the curb.

"They're in," Merriellen shouted in the bay window next door.

A small cheer went up.

Then, almost back out into the traffic lane, Robert jammed his foot on the brake and brought the Cadillac to a lurching stop. He had heard something. He rolled down both front windows of the Cadillac.

Rezilla watched through the door while Robert looked slowly up and down the block.

He leaned over to examine the back of the DeSilvas' motor home, apparently noting something about the license plates.

He looked up and caught Rezilla watching him. In his high whining drawl, he shouted: "Everything all right in there, Rezilla?"

She smiled and nodded. "Oh yessir, Mr. Edelman," she called out. "Everything's fine. How are you doing today?"

The tinted window of the Cadillac slid upward, closing Robert's unsmiling face from view. The car lurched forward into the street and then, speeding up quickly, disappeared from view.

Rezilla slammed the door and slid the bolt home.

Stephen and Kathleen moved from adult to adult, pleading, "Where's Mommy? Where is my mommy?"

Virginia came forward, knelt, and took Stephen by the shoulders.

"Your mother had to go take care of her kitty. He's still at the vet and very sick."

Stephen looked around quickly at the faces of the adults. "No," he said breathlessly. "She would be here. She wasn't here when I called. She's always here when we come home."

Kathleen was crying in quiet little sobs. "Where is she, Stephen?" she said.

Virginia led them into the living room. "She needs to take care of the poor kitty," she said.

Stephen scoured his grandparents with his eyes, looking behind and around them. He whirled and searched Miriam, bending and twisting to see behind her, too. He gazed into the living room at Jeanne. He whirled and looked at Rezilla. Then he lifted both clenched fists in the air; his face turned purple and crumpled, and he shrieked: "WHERE IS MY MOMMY?"

Miriam rushed up and knelt in front of him. "Stephen, you must listen to me. Your mother is all right."

"No she isn't," he shouted. "She is not! If she was all right, she would be here! She is always here! Something bad has happened! Robert did something bad to my mommy."

"Why do you say that, child?" Rezilla asked, kneeling at his other side.

"Because she's not here, Zsa," he said. He slumped to his knees and then sat with his legs splayed on the floor. "Oh, she's not here! She's not here! I knew something was wrong! She's always here! I knew something bad was going to happen."

Kathleen had been forgotten in a corner of the foyer. She crept forward tentatively, like a little creature afraid of the light. She knelt next to Stephen. She was crying softly. She reached forward with one hand and brushed Stephen's hair.

John and Virginia exchanged ghastly looks. John nodded toward the children, who were both crying now in each other's arms on the floor, and said to Miriam and Jeanne, "Get them upstairs. Out of the hallway."

Jeanne rushed down and picked up Kathleen.

Miriam took Stephen's hand, lifted him to his feet, and led him upstairs. "Everything is going to be all right," she said softly.

Stephen looked up at her and said, half in a wail, "No, no, no, Miriam, you're telling a lie. She would be here, if she was all right."

Merriellen appeared from the back of the house.

"What are you going to do with them?" she asked.

John shook his head. "I don't know."

"Well, you have to do something," Merriellen said. "Those children are in very bad shape. They can't just be left like that."

Rezilla said, "They have an appointment this morning at ten o'clock with Dr. Meyers, the psychiatrist the court appointed. I just didn't think about it, what with Linda missing and all, but maybe it would be good for them to go ahead anyway and show up."

"Maybe," Virginia said. "I think I should check with Ike."

"With Ike?" Merriellen asked, surprised. "What does Ike have to do with it now? We have the children back. I thought that was all he cared about."

"Well, I'd just like to check with him, anyway. But I hate to tie up this phone. Might I use your phone, Merriellen?"

Merriellen shrugged. "Certainly."

Virginia hiked down the alley at a determined pace. She let herself into the back of Merriellen's house and barely nodded hello to Merriellen's mother. She snatched the phone off the wall and dialed Ike's office number from memory.

Ike answered his phone.

"I hear they're in!" Ike said.

"The children? Yes. But how did you. . . "

"Joe called me. They knew about it."

"Ike, the children are very bad. Stephen is extremely bad. I am very worried about this."

She took the receiver away from her ear and leaned her head against the wall for a moment, fighting back tears. She put it back to her mouth, and her lips were quivering.

Merriellen's mother watched her from the far end of the kitchen.

"I cannot stand it, Ike," Virginia whispered. "I cannot stand for the children to be torn up like this. I just don't know if I can stand all this."

"You've got to stand it, Virginia."

"I have never done anything like this before."

"None of us has."

"But I can't stop worrying about what this is doing to those children."

"No. I know. I can't either. I know. I agree, Virginia. We've got to do something."

"They have an appointment at ten with a psychiatrist."

"This morning?"

"Yes."

"Well, let me see. Maybe Joe can work that into the deal somehow."

Ike put Virginia on hold, called Joe, and ran it down quickly for him.

Joe pondered what Ike said. He was beginning to feel his blood boil, but he fought it back down. Things were getting a little ragged around the edges, but he told himself that was the sort of thing you have to expect when you're dealing with people stupid enough to commit murder. It's never going to be a neat and tidy situation.

Joe needed for someone to lie to the children and do it effectively. As long as the children were anywhere where Robert could get access to them, it was imperative that they not know that their mother was alive. But he did not want them to be told that she was dead or missing. That seemed unnecessarily cruel.

Some big old responsible adult with a gift for gab needed to get up there and tell the children a very convincing lie—something that would make them think their mother was going to be all right, something that would explain all the excitement but that would also be a lie any adult would see through in a moment. Then if Robert put the pressure on the kids, all he would find out would be that someone had told them a lie—just what he would expect someone to do in real life.

But Joe could not call up the house and instruct everybody there what to tell the children without arousing suspicion among those who were not in on the sting. It would be inappropriate. It would not ring true.

Now they wanted to take the kids to a psychiatrist. What was wrong with people nowadays? They didn't know how to lie to their own kids anymore? They had to pay a psychiatrist to do it?

Joe pounded a silent fist on his desk. Whatever they had been telling the kids, it was not working. The kids saw through the whole thing, somehow. At least, they knew that their mother was in danger, and they assumed their father was behind it. And Ike was telling him it was eating the kids alive.

"All right," Joe said into the telephone at last, "call Rezilla. I don't want the mother giving instructions to the psychiatrist, because she's in on the deal, and something might slip. It's better if the call is from some-body who's cold, who's not in the know. Tell Rezilla to go ahead and call the shrink and tell him she's sending the kids. Then you call the shrink, too, and smooth him out a little. Maybe he can calm them down."

"What does Rezilla tell the psychiatrist?"

"What she knows."

"What does the psychiatrist tell the kids?"

"He tells them what you tell him to tell them."

"What do I tell him to tell them?"

"You better tell him . . . tell him the mother is missing, but we're looking for her. You see, the problem now, Ike, is, we put it out on the wire last night that her car was found in Oklahoma with blood on it."

"That could be in the press any minute."

"I doubt it, but it could."

"Yeah, well, I don't think I can conceal that, then, from Dr. Meyers. I mean, why would I?"

"About the car?"

"Yeah."

"Why not?"

"I would know."

"Would you? I guess you would. You would have just heard about it maybe."

"So why would I conceal it from him?"

Joe thought for a moment. "Well, Rezilla doesn't know yet, because we haven't done a next-of-kin notification at the house yet about the car. So, don't say anything to her about it, because you really shouldn't know ahead of her. But I guess you better call the psychiatrist and set him straight. He won't figure out exactly who knew what when, or care, really. I guess you would tell him what you know, so do that, but tell him not to tell the kids about the car."

"Yeah, they'd really suffer over that."

"Well, Ike, I don't want that. I am jimmying and fixing and screwing with this deal right now, changing everything around at the last minute, and I've got a guy out there undercover who could get hurt, but I am doing it because I do not want those children to be caused unnecessary pain."

"I appreciate that, Joe. I appreciate what you're doing."

"Tell him that you are trying to convince the kids their mother is off making an emergency visit to a friend, and maybe he can do a better job of it than they have been able to do so far. Tell him to try to get the kids calmed down if at all possible. It's very important to get the kids to chill out, but, obviously, you can't tell him why. And Ike, make sure the grandfather goes along for this and keeps his ears open. I won't have any ears there. I want to know what's said, in case Edelman gets to this shrink and puts the arm on him."

Dan Meyers was sitting at his desk in his little log-cabin office building when he received both calls, first from Rezilla, asking that he tell the children their mother was missing and being searched for by the authorities, and now from Ike Vanden Eykel, who was on the phone telling him Linda's car had just been found, covered with blood, and that he wanted Dr. Meyers to tell the children their mother was off visiting a friend.

For a man who had been sitting, not five minutes earlier, quietly reading an academic article in the peace of his own office, this was quite a little piece of work all of a sudden. While Mr. Vanden Eykel talked, Dr. Meyers was quickly reviewing his options. As the children's court-appointed psychiatrist, it was not really his job to inform the children of their mother's probable murder. That was properly a family chore.

But he also knew this family. The father was out of the question— cruel, abusive, with a terrible temper. He had probably killed the woman himself or paid someone else to do it.

The children, especially the boy, were at extreme risk emotionally and psychologically. Since he had met Stephen a year ago, the boy had become even skinnier and more anorexic looking. He was sick almost all the time with sinus infections, digestive flus, and the like. He had reverted to sucking his thumb—in fact he curled up in a fetal position on the floor at the least provocation or opportunity, sucking his thumb and whimpering to himself.

And yet he was a trooper. He and his mother seemed to have that in common. They could pick themselves up and do the show. Dr. Meyers had come to admire Stephen.

Kathleen was a very different case. She was a pretty little girl with a beautiful voice, both when she spoke and when her proud mother asked her to perform songs from Disney movies for the doctor. She was poised

and confidant far beyond her five years of age, in a stagey, almost laugh-
ably adult way. And she was a survivor. Whenever the explosive trauma of
her parents' battles came too close, Kathleen always found a way to put
herself at a safe distance. She tended to speak of her parents as naughty
people about whom she was deeply concerned.

Dr. Meyers asked Ike a few questions about who else was present at
the house with the children. He did not know the grandparents. He
made a quick calculation and came to the conclusion that he, Dr. Meyers, was the only dispassionate responsible adult he knew of whom he
could trust to handle this moment without damaging the children.

"All right, Mr. Vanden Eykel. You want me to tell the children their
mother is absent from the home. They already know that."

"Well, I want you to try to tell them something that will calm them
down."

"Yes, you want me to lie to them. You need to understand that these
children have been very severely victimized and damaged by a lot of
adults who had their own agendas that were more important to them
than the children's feelings. I'm not just telling you this to lecture you or
to try to make you feel sorry for them. The point is that they are both
very smart little kids, and they are extremely skeptical of what adults tell
them. Lying to them may only backfire.

"I will see them. But what I say or do not say to them will depend on
my judgment, as a physician, of what will serve their health and their
mental well-being."

Ike was silent for a moment.

"Mr. Vanden Eykel, is there something else going on I need to know
about?"

"No, no, I don't think so. That sounds fine. You'll see them, then?"

"Yes. I assume so. I have an appointment with them in an hour."

"My only thought on the car and the signs of foul play is that they
have not found Linda yet, and it's still possible. . . "

"Oh, yes, certainly, the business about the car being found and the
blood and so on. I think that's probably not necessary."

"Right. Agreed. I just wanted you to know the score."

"She's presumed dead."

"Yes. I think so."

"The father is the suspect?"

"Yes."

"Does the family know the car has been found?"

"I believe so. I think the FBI is telling them now."

As soon as Ike hung up, he called Caruth and told John to be prepared to be the one to drive the children to see Dr. Meyers.

     ❋   ❋   ❋

Linda was lying on her back on top of the neatly made-up king-sized bed in the guest bedroom of the lake house, with her hands at her sides, balled into fists, and her eyes squeezed shut. She was trying to force herself not to look at her watch. Suddenly she realized she had been holding her breath for too long. She gasped for air, flung her watch before her eyes, sat up, and pounded on the bed with her fists at her sides.

The phone rang. She leapt to her feet and raced to the kitchen. One. Two. Three. Four rings.

It stopped. She waited. It had barely begun to ring again when she ripped the receiver from the wall.

"Are my children home?" Linda almost screamed into the phone.

Ike held the receiver away from his ear and winced.

"Yes. Dropped them off at eight o'clock sharp."

"Where are my parents?"

"They're fine. They're at Caruth."

"Oh . . . I've been so . . . no one told me. He wants to kill them, too. This is all so . . . Ike, this is ridiculous, I know, but I remembered last night that I dropped my poor kitty off at the vet with leukemia, about to die, and I don't even know if he's had to put him to sleep."

"I will find out." He jotted down the name and number of the vet.

"Are Kathleen and Stephen all right?" she asked.

"Yes. They're going to see Dr. Meyers."

"Dr. Meyers? Oh, that's right. They have an appointment. Well, I don't think they should have to do that today. Why don't you just tell Rezilla to call and cancel it."

"I think they need to keep the appointment, Linda."

Linda said nothing. Then finally she said in a soft, falling, weary voice, "They are not all right. That's why you want them to go. Is it Stephen? What is going on with Kathleen? Oh, Ike. . ."

She gasped for breath.

"Ike, I can't stand this."

"You have got to stand it."

"But for them . . . I can't stand it for my little ones, Ike. I can't stand it."

"Linda! This is a murder plot, for God's sake! I'm sitting here with a loaded gun under my coat, waiting for that son of a bitch to come in through the door any minute and shoot me! Everybody is doing the best they can! If we don't win, he wins! We have got to do this! You have got to stand it!"

After she hung up, she sank to her knees in the corner next to the refrigerator. For a long time she stayed there, sobbing and muttering the names of her children.

After he got off the phone, Ike walked out to his secretary and handed her a note. "Please call this guy. He is the Edelman's vet. Find out if their cat's okay."

"All right," she said. She put the note at one side of her desk and returned to her work.

"No, sorry," Ike said. "You have to do it right now. I'm leaving. Call me in the car as soon as you know."

When Joe Masterson called Caruth, the phone was busy. It was 9:00 A.M. The kids' appointment with Dr. Meyers was at ten. Joe Masterson needed to get to Caruth and do a next-of-kin notification that Linda's car had been found. Officially, it needed to be done before or simultaneously with Ike's call to the psychiatrist.

Joe called Merriellen from his car. He asked her to go over to Linda's house and tell everyone that he was on his way. But Merriellen could not leave her kitchen without fetching her mother from upstairs to watch her youngest child. By the time Merriellen got to Linda's house, Joe was already there, sitting on the love seat in the library with the half-glasses and the lap desk.

John, Virginia, Miriam, Jeanne, Rezilla, and Janet were gathered around him when Merriellen entered. They were all silent, red-eyed, and trembling. John and Virginia sat on the sofa together. Miriam was in a chair, with Jeanne standing behind her. Rezilla sat in another chair. Janet was leaning against the wall next to the fireplace.

From the moment Joe had appeared at the door, they all had assumed it was to notify them Linda had been found dead. The mood was so tense and grief-stricken that even Virginia had decided again that something really had gone wrong with the sting and she was about to be notified of Linda's death.

Joe looked up at the room. "We have found Mrs. Edelman's vehicle. . . "

"Oh God!" Janet sobbed, clutching for the mantle.

Virginia grabbed John's hand. Miriam sat stick-straight in a chair, nervously flicking tears away from both cheeks.

"There were signs of foul play," he said.

"Oh dear," Jeanne said suddenly and only semiconsciously. "Oh dear."

"There was blood and other signs of a struggle. No body has been found as of yet, but a search is continuing. The car was found at a freeway rest stop near Durant, Oklahoma. This is now officially an FBI case."

They all stared at him for a long time without speaking. Janet came away from the wall.

"Mr. Masterson. . . "

"Joe," Virginia interrupted, "she's not dead."

Joe gave Virginia a careful appraising look. He wasn't sure what she meant. "We do not know that she is dead, Mrs. DeSilva. We have not found her."

"Mr. Masterson," Janet said, "what is the status of her husband at this point?"

"We will question him shortly."

"Is he a suspect?"

"Our investigation is continuing, Miss. . . ."

"Lesser."

"Miss Lesser, we are continuing to look at a number of suspects, but I think it's reasonable to assume that he would be one of them."

Rezilla left the room, to make sure the children were not near. The rest of them peppered Joe with questions for the next half hour, except for John and Virginia, who were silent. They had realized, as soon as Joe got into his spiel, that the sting was still on.

Rezilla came back into the room. "The children are ready."

Joe watched intently. He turned slightly and gave John a barely perceptible look.

Lurching up from the sofa, John said, "I'm going to take them."

Miriam said, "What is Dr. Meyers going to tell the children?"

Joe watched. No one answered her. He kept his silence.

"Well, I won't have them lied to, at this point," Miriam said.

"This is pretty rough stuff for kids," Joe muttered.

"I don't care. They already know they're being lied to. That's half of what has them so frightened. I won't have it. I'm going with them to Dr. Meyers' office. And Dr. Meyers is going to tell them the truth."

Joe nodded understandingly. Behind the expression of kind concern on his face, he was mentally gnashing his teeth. "Just what we need," he thought. "More honesty."

Once John and Miriam left with the children, and as soon as Joe Masterson was gone, too, all of the women gathered at the long table in the family room. Janet Lesser said, "I don't think they're telling us everything."

Merriellen was startled but interested. Jeanne came closer to Janet to listen. Rezilla, who had been working on the other side of the counter in the kitchen, dried her hands and came around into the family room to hear what Janet had to say. Only Virginia was impassive, reading a novel at the table, as if not particularly interested in what Janet had to say.

"Why do you say that?" Rezilla asked. "What do you think they're not telling us?"

"I don't know," Janet said. "But something isn't right. Why isn't any of this in the newspaper yet or on TV? Robert's a big-deal real estate developer. Linda is in the society pages. They're maybe not the most famous people in Dallas, but they're prominent. So how can this be going on for so long, and the media haven't gotten onto it?"

Virginia put down her book. "Well, Janet, I would think you would be smart enough to figure that out. They're trying to get more evidence against Robert."

"Yes, Mrs. DeSilva, but that still does not make sense. Linda has not been found. She could be alive! If they put her picture on TV and in the paper, someone might recognize her, and it could save her life! I have even been thinking, I have a friend who is an assistant Dallas County D.A., and I was thinking about taking Linda's picture to him and seeing if he could get it on television."

"No!" Virginia said angrily. "You watch yourself, young lady! This is my daughter! And I do not want you interfering with the authorities. You are not a police detective. You leave this to the people who are supposed to be in charge."

"Who, Mrs. DeSilva? Ike Vanden Eykel? All he cares about is how this affects his divorce case."

"That is not true."

The other women were watching the exchange with riveted fascination.

Merriellen said, "Mrs. DeSilva, I understand how you feel, but we really don't know anything at all about this FBI agent who has been coming here."

"He's the FBI!" Virginia said. "That's all you have to know! And you need to be careful what you say in this house! We don't know what Robert can hear."

All of the other women gazed at Virginia in silence, waiting for her to explain what she meant. But Virginia began reading her book again, as if nothing had been said. The others exchanged embarrassed little glances.

Janet shrugged and walked toward the back corridor. She motioned with her eyes for Merriellen to follow. They walked out to the alley together.

"I think something's not right," Janet said.

"I think you're right," Merriellen said. "I don't know what it is. I can't put my finger on it. But I have been watching John and Virginia very closely. There is something off about them."

"Well," Janet said, with a flip of one hand. "Off? There's nothing off. They're just from Oklahoma. Virginia thinks everything a man tells her is God's law for her to obey."

"I don't know if that's it," Merriellen said. "It's more like something out of sync with them. There are certain things I can't explain. My mother said when Virginia went over there to call Ike, she said something to him about, 'I've never done this before.' "

Janet stared at her. "Who's never?"

"Virginia. She said that to Ike."

"But do what?"

"I don't know. It's like something that she and Ike know about that the rest of us don't."

"Look," Janet said, "can we go use your phone? I called a private investigator a while ago who worked for an old college roommate of mine once, and he said he might be able to find out a few things for us."

Joe Pearsall received a call at his desk in the child support section of the state A.G.'s office in Oklahoma City. The caller was a friend in the dispatch and communications division of the state highway patrol.

"Got something on your deal," the caller said. "Report on the computer last night. Says we found an automobile belonging to a Mrs. Robert Edelman of Dallas at a rest stop on the freeway near the Durant exit. Blood, other signs of violence."

Joe took notes quickly. "Found the car up here? In Oklahoma? Who's we?"

"Highway Patrol. Our guys."

"So it's your case?"

"No. FBI's got it."

"Already? That's quick."

"Yeah. Real quick. Must be real famous people. Friend of yours?"

"My cousin."

"Hey, I'm sorry, guy."

Joe paused a moment, fighting for composure. "It's all right. No body?"

"Nope."

"Big search going on, I guess."

"No, matter of fact I checked that out. I even talked to one of our guys who's right up there on that stretch of road right now. There's no search on the computer, and he says there's not a sign of anything going on up there."

"Well, that's weird."

"Yeah, ain't it? Famous Dallas person like that, missing and signs of foul play, and no search. Is it a kidnapping or what?"

"No, I don't think so. I think it's a hit. It may be a murder-for-hire. Her husband. Bad divorce, lot of money-type deal."

"Kill her down there, haul her up here dead? No search? So the guy's still got the body with him?"

"Or kill her down there, dump the body down there. . . "

"And drive across a state line in the bloodstained vehicle."

"Yeah," Joe said. "It's screwy. It does not add up."

"Must be somethin' you and I don't know, dude."

Stephen sat on the front seat with John, and Kathleen sat in back with Miriam. No one spoke during the short drive to Dr. Meyers's office. Miriam put her hand forward and touched Stephen's shoulder over the seat.

"Are you okay, honey?"

"Mmm-hmm," he said softly. She peeked over the seat and saw him wringing the front of his shirt into a knot with both little hands. Kathleen stared out the side window of the car with a funny, serene smile.

When they arrived, Dr. Meyers came out and met them on the long ranch-style wooden roofed porch that ran along the front and down one side of his building. He was a big, bluff, athletic-looking man with a broad open face and gentle, intelligent eyes. He knelt down into the car window and said hello warmly to the children. When he held the door to his building open, they both trotted inside up to the landing at the top of the staircase, where they took seats in a small waiting area outside the room where they had their sessions.

John was still coming slowly from the car. Miriam caught Dr. Meyers by the elbow and said, "Dr. Meyers, I'm Linda's sister, Miriam."

"How do you do."

"Doctor, how much do you know?"

He told her what Ike had told him.

She said, "I didn't realize Ike knew about the car. I guess the FBI must have told him already before they told us. Anyway, I just don't think the children should be lied to."

Dr. Meyers stood at the bottom of the stairs and thought about it for a while without speaking. "Mr. Vanden Eykel makes the important point that your sister has not been found yet and could still be alive. I do not intend to lie to the children. I have a relationship of trust with them that is important to them at this point, and I am not going to sacrifice that relationship. But we just do not know yet that your sister is dead."

Miriam looked up at him in surprise. "Oh no! She's not dead yet! I mean, we don't know that!"

"Well," he said, turning to go up, "I will tell them their mother is missing. And we shall see what happens."

Miriam and John sat outside in the waiting area with Kathleen while Dr. Meyers spoke to Stephen first. The room where Dr. Meyers did his sessions was a large one, with a thick plank door. He sat with his patients at the far side of the room, away from the door, so that it was rare for any sound from within the room to be audible out in the waiting area. But all three of them heard Stephen's wail, beginning first at a mid-range note and then shrieking up through octaves, wailing and hanging in the air—a banshee song of the pure, searing, uncontrolled, unmitigated grief of a child. They heard a crash when Stephen threw himself on the floor, and then they heard him pounding and kicking the floor and screaming, "She said she would never leave me! She said she would never leave me! She said she would never leave me!"

Then there was silence.

Miriam squeezed Kathleen's hand.

Kathleen looked up at her and said, "Oh, Aunt Miriam, they must have given us to Daddy."

"No, no," she said. "It's not that."

"Oh," Kathleen said, almost in a whisper. "Then it's something else."

Tears were streaming down John's face and his lips were quivering. "Not right," he was whispering to himself. "Not right."

Dr. Meyers was inside telling Stephen that Kathleen needed him to pull himself together. Slowly, painfully, like a little man pulling himself up from muck, Stephen pushed and clambered his way back to his feet. Dr. Meyers helped him blow his nose and wipe his eyes.

He held Stephen's hand and walked him to the door. He opened the door, handed Stephen off to Miriam, and took Kathleen into the room.

"Oh, Dr. Meyers!" Kathleen said breathlessly, her eyes wide and her hands held theatrically folded before her chin. "Daddy has killed Mommy, hasn't he? I heard poor Stephen crying, and I know that Mommy must be dead."

Dr. Meyers exhaled a long slow breath, gave a finger to the little girl to hold, led her to the far side of the room, and explained to her that her mother was, indeed, missing, but that no one had found her yet.

When he finished, Kathleen gazed at him, still smiling. But huge tears began sliding down her cheeks. And then suddenly, as if in a seizure, she hurled herself at him, sobbing and screaming, "Please, no! Please, no! I want my mommy! I want my mommy!"

Stephen heard her, bolted for the door, yanked it open, and raced to his sister. They clutched each other, embracing clumsily and sobbing into each other's necks and hair. Together, the children sank to their knees on the floor.

Miriam and John stood in the open door, gaping and wringing their hands.

Stephen looked up and saw them. "Grandpa?" he said. "What will become of us now?"

John pitched forward, hurried to them, knelt, and took them in his arms. "Your mother is all right!" he shouted. "Everything is going to be all right! Your mother is all right!"

The children continued to sob and wail as if he had said nothing at all to them.

It was time for them to leave. John and Miriam herded the children down the stairs and out into the car. Dr. Meyers came down behind them and leaned into the car to look at the children. Kathleen was staring glassy-eyed out the window.

"What are you thinking about, Kathleen?" Dr. Meyers asked.

She turned halfway toward him, not quite meeting his eye. "Poor Aunt Miriam," she said in her tiniest, most birdlike little voice. "Now she hasn't any sister."

Stephen was curled in a ball on the front seat, sucking his thumb. Tears were pouring from his eyes.

John was at the wheel, ready to go. He looked up at Dr. Meyers with a question in his eyes.

"This is very bad," Dr. Meyers said quietly. "These children are not well. They cannot be allowed to go back into more chaos now. I am calling Mr. Vanden Eykel as soon as you leave."

It occurred suddenly to John that this was not a good moment to open any kind of battle that might alert Robert's lawyers. "What are you going to say to Ike?" John asked.

"I haven't quite decided," Dr. Meyers said, beginning to back away from the car. "Except that these children are in very precarious shape right now and absolutely must be protected from more stress."

As soon as they had pulled out of the driveway, Dr. Meyers called Ike, who listened without speaking while the doctor recounted practically the entire session.

"You think they're real bad," Ike said finally.

"Mr. Vanden Eykel, if it is not possible to find a way to shelter these children from whatever is about to take place in that house, then I think there is a real chance that both of them, especially Stephen, may suffer a serious psychological collapse."

"You mean a nervous breakdown?"

"I mean a collapse. But a very dangerous collapse, with lasting effects."

John had barely pulled into the garage when Kathleen reached forward with all her might, threw the car door open, and raced into the back of the house past the startled adults and into the kitchen, where she hurled herself into Rezilla's arms.

"Oh Zsa!" she shouted, "My mother is dead, and my daddy has killed her!"

Miriam led Stephen in a moment later. He was still sobbing, dragging himself slump-shouldered, almost limping. Virginia, who had been sitting with the others dutifully making calls at the long table, sent her chair crashing behind her and raced to Stephen with open arms. She took him to a rocking chair at one side of the room, where she held him and petted his head.

After a few minutes, Stephen lifted himself from his grandmother's lap and walked slowly, dreamily, as if in trance, out of the room and up the spiral staircase. The adults all looked at each other. Miriam held up a finger to show that she would follow.

She found him sitting quietly on the floor in the center of the large playroom at the top of the stairs. She entered the room carefully and then sat down just to one side of him.

He turned to her. "Aunt Miriam," he said softly, "would you pray with me for my mommy?"

She took his hands in hers. They tipped their foreheads together, and both of them prayed, their faces glistening with tears.

Just as they were finished, Kathleen appeared in the doorway and said, "Aunt Miriam, I would like to speak to my brother."

"Of course, dear."

Kathleen watched while Miriam left the room. Then she went over and knelt by her brother. When Miriam stole a last peek at them, just before she descended the stairs, the two children were whispering intently to each other.

Joe Masterson took notes while he listened to Ike's report. When Ike had finished speaking, Joe said, "Stay right there. Stay off the phone. I'll be back in touch in five minutes."

Ike sat at his desk, staring at his telephone, without moving, almost without breathing, for exactly five minutes. The phone rang and he snatched it up.

"This is Joe. The situation is not great, but it's manageable. I've got to go lay it on Edelman in about an hour. The University Park police are contacting him right now to make the appointment. It's not a great time for complications. But I have concluded that we've got to change it all up again, get the children out of it and take them to their mother."

Ike sucked in a long deep breath, threw his head back and suddenly thought he might actually shed a tear. "Oh, thank God, Joe," he said. "I think this is right."

"Yeah, well, it's not going to be right if it screws up, because right now is when my undercover guy is most exposed, it's when Linda is exposed, and it's when Edelman is most likely to go ballistic on us. If there was any way those kids could tough it out. . . ."

"I just don't think they can. . . ."

"Well, we're not going to risk it for them. But look, Ike. You have got to handle this. And I mean you have got to handle it right, brother. This is going to be extremely tight. We are talking life and death here, and we cannot afford even the smallest mistake."

Joe laid it out step by step, reading from numbered notes on his legal pad. Ike would have to go to Caruth and get the children out. In the last five minutes, Joe had worked out a new cover story: Ike would tell the group at the house that Dr. Meyers had called him and warned him that any additional stress, especially anything involving custody, would be a threat to the children. The FBI could not legally take the children into protective custody without going before a judge, and now was not a good moment for that.

However, during this gray-area period, while Linda was gone but before Robert could acknowledge that he knew about it, it was plausible and would be more or less legal for the grandparents to take the children into their own protective custody. Therefore, Ike was to tell them all at the house that he had decided the best thing for the children was for the grandparents to take the children in the motor home and drive around up in Oklahoma for several days, not stopping anywhere where they could be found or reached, until the situation had cleared.

The children were to be packed and loaded into the motor home with their grandparents as quickly as possible, because there was no telling what moves Robert might have planned. He might have his own plan for grabbing the children—some scheme already primed and coiled for action, as soon as he was officially notified Linda was missing, which was about to happen.

The children were not to be told that they were being taken to their mother until after the motor home was underway. The danger was that if they knew before they left, they might blurt something to the women who would be remaining behind in the house, who were not to know.

But there was one more wrinkle. With the grandparents gone, the FBI would have no one at Caruth who was in on the sting. Joe didn't think that was a good idea. So he decided that Miriam, alone, was to be informed.

He told Ike exactly how to do it. He was to go to Caruth, take Miriam outside, fill her in, and explain to her that she had to keep her mouth shut or Linda and other people might still be killed. Then he was to announce the new cover story—motoring around Oklahoma—to the house. Then he was to get the grandparents and kids loaded into the motor home. When they were ready to go, Ike was to get into the motor home with them and tell them that the Oklahoma story was a cover, that they were really going to go to Linda, but first they were to go to his office and wait for him. Then he was to get out of the motor home, say good-bye to everyone in the house, get in his own car, go meet the motor home at his office, and give John instructions to find the lake house.

Stephen and Kathleen appeared together in the family room, holding hands. The adults all had been discussing them in hushed tones in a knot at the end of the table. They fell silent and turned to look at the two of them, standing in the doorway together, like Hansel and Gretel.

"Yes," Virginia said. "What do you children want?"

"We want to talk to Ike," Stephen said.

"Well, I think Mr. Vanden Eykel's pretty busy," Virginia said, "trying to help your mommy."

"Please, Grandma," Kathleen said. "We think Mr. Vanden Eykel might know how to find our mother."

"Grandma, please!" Stephen said. "Please! We want to talk to Ike."

"If it will comfort them," Miriam said, starting toward the phone.

But John and Virginia were suddenly both concerned about what might be said over the tapped telephone.

"I think we need to keep this line open," John said. "Why don't you all go over to Merriellen's house and call Mr. Vanden Eykel?"

Miriam shrugged. "Fine, I'll take them."

She started to lead them by the hands toward the front door, but Kathleen balked. "I want Rezilla to come, too."

"And Grandma," Stephen said.

"And Grandpa," Kathleen said.

"Well, I'm going, because it's my house," Merriellen said.

The adults obediently congregated at the front door and followed the children out. Once outside on the front lawn, Kathleen asked that they all hold hands while they walked. The adults all linked hands with the children, and together the lot of them walked in a line across the two front yards and into Merriellen's front door.

Up and down the block, people stepped back from curtains at the fronts of their houses, blew noses, and wiped tears from their eyes.

Ike was at the door of his office, ready to leave, when his phone rang. His secretary cradled the phone and said, "Are you gone?"

"Yeah," he whispered. "I've got to go, now."

"It's one of the Edelman children."

He blew out a breath, walked back to his desk, and took the call.

At Merriellen's house, the adults stood in a ring, looking down on

Stephen, who was holding the phone to his mouth. In a manly little voice, he said, "Mr. Vanden Eykel, this is Stephen Edelman. Do you know where my mama is?"

Ike bit back a pained gasp. "Oh, Stephen," he said, "look, I want you to know, and I want you to tell your little sister that everything is going to be all right. I am coming right now to see you, and everything is going to be all right."

Stephen said good-bye. He hung up the phone carefully. Then he turned and took Kathleen by the shoulders. "Ike is coming!" Stephen said, beaming. "And he says everything is going to be all right!"

Kathleen bounced on both feet and shook her fists in the air. She turned to the adults and said sweetly, "My mama is all right."

Together, in a line, all holding hands, they walked back across the two yards to the front door of Caruth.

Robert's secretary took down the name—Officer Frank Clifford, University Park police department.

"And what does the call concern?" she asked.

"It concerns Mr. Edelman," Officer Clifford said.

"Yes, obviously it concerns Mr. Edelman, since you asked to speak to Mr. Edelman, but Mr. Edelman will want to know what business you have with him? Is it about a guard contract on one of his properties?"

"No, Miss," Officer Clifford said. He looked up at his superior, who was sitting next to him staring at him with one finger raised in the air to signify extreme caution. The superior was wearing a headset with phones on his ears and had a small wire microphone in front of his mouth.

"It involves an investigation. . ."

The superior nodded approval.

". . . that has to do with his wife."

The superior nodded yes and then made a quick cutting motion with the finger to signify that Officer Clifford should say no more.

"Just a moment," the secretary said.

There was a long wait.

The secretary came back on.

"Anything that has to do with Mrs. Edelman is something Mr. Edelman would have to hear with his attorney present. His attorney is Mr. Brandon Jeffers. He and Mr. Edelman can meet with you at your office at 2:30 P.M. Would that be satisfactory?"

Officer Clifford looked at his superior. His superior whispered into the microphone, "What about 2:30?"

In the room full of electronics gear in the warehouse building downtown, Joe Masterson, who was also wearing a headset, whispered, "Yeah, that's okay, but no later."

Officer Clifford's superior nodded yes but made a stabbing motion at his watch.

"Tell Mr. Edelman we will expect him at 2:30, and tell him not to be late," Officer Clifford said.

"Oh," she said with a vague suggestion of a snicker, "I will be sure and remind him to be punctual."

As soon as Officer Clifford had broken the connection, his superior said into the microphone, "Who is Jeffers? I thought you said his lawyer was Ken Fuller."

"It is," Masterson said back into his own headset downtown. "Fuller is Edelman's lawyer on the divorce. Hang on, we're checking."

In a book-lined room elsewhere in the warehouse building, Kathy Hagen was flipping through a bar association directory. She muttered her findings into her own microphone.

Masterson said to the University Park officer, "He's a criminal lawyer."

"Criminal?"

"Yup," Masterson smiled to himself. "Bingo."

Ike was in his car, coming down the North Dallas Tollway at seventy miles an hour. He punched the number of long distance information into his phone and got the number of the small store near his lake house. He called and told the woman in the store that some friends of his were coming to visit in a large motor home. He asked if they could park the motor home on her parking lot behind the store for a few days, since it was too big to drive down the narrow dirt road to his house.

"I guess that's okay, Mr. Vanden Eykel," she said, "only we wouldn't want any . . . well, you know."

"Any what?"

"Well, parties, or like that."

"Parties! Parties? No, no, no parties. These are older people who have some young grandchildren with them. They're just visiting. You and I need to have a talk later on about some things."

"Sure, Mr. Vanden Eykel."

Ike punched the number of the lake house into the phone. He rang the code, hung up, then rang again. Linda answered on the first ring.

"Linda," he said, "the children are coming to you."

"What?"

"The FBI has changed the plan. We are sending you the children. They are fine. They will stay with you until it's over. Your parents are bringing them. I don't have time to explain now. You need to get in the rental car at 2:15 and drive down to the store to meet them."

Linda hung the phone up very carefully, as if it were made of eggshells. She stared at it on the wall. At that moment, the wall telephone in the kitchen of Ike's lake house—an instrument she had despised and loathed only hours earlier—was now the most wonderful object her eyes had ever beheld. Slowly, gradually, a warm deep sense of relief began to pour down through her body, followed by joy. Incredible how the universe can change from darkness and terror to light and resolve, all in an instant, as if a switch has been thrown. She felt that she could face anything now.

The dream was changing again. She made a point of noticing, and, in knowing that it was changing, she felt as if she suddenly ruled the dream.

Ike was wending his way through University Park, counting out the steps again. Get Miriam out, clue her in. Announce to the house. Get parents and kids loaded. Clue them in . . .

The phone rang. It was his secretary. She was sobbing.

"Oh my God, he's killed her!" she said.

A terrible, dry, hard, scratchy chill ran down Ike's spine, and his fingertips began to tingle on the wheel.

"What are you talking about?"

"The poor little cat. They've put it to sleep."

Ike held the phone on the seat of the car for a moment, then put it back to his mouth. "Thank you very much," he said.

He pulled up at the front of Caruth, walked to the door, and rang the bell. As soon as he got out of the car, people stepped away from front windows up and down the block and called others to watch.

Miriam answered the door.

"Hello, Ike," she said. "How are you?"

"I'm fine. I need you to step out here with me and take a walk. I need to talk to you alone."

Miriam's heart leapt to her throat. Without even thinking about it, she was instantly certain Ike was about to inform her that Linda had been found dead. Her knees began to go soft beneath her, and her lip began trembling. Merriellen had told her there were people watching from all of the front windows nearby, and Jeanne had even seen them from her post at the front window upstairs. She looked around quickly and shyly.

"Ike, can you come in?" she asked in a whisper.

"No, Miriam. You need to come out."

She began to take a step forward. A vision of her sister as a dead body came crashing down over her. She stopped and put a hand against the pillar.

"I think I need to sit down, Ike."

Ike took her hand. "You have to come out, Miriam, and you have to walk. I have to talk to you out here."

He led her by the hand to the sidewalk. The windows up and down the block were crowded with eyes.

They turned right at the sidewalk, away from Merriellen's house and toward the side street. A breath of summer breeze puffed at the corner of Ike's suit coat, and Miriam caught a glimpse of the gun in his waistband. Ike began talking quickly and quietly.

"Miriam, Linda is alive."

Miriam gasped. She pulled on his hand and stopped.

"Do not stop walking, Miriam," Ike said, "and do not behave as if I am telling you anything unusual. It is very important for you to behave as if this is a fairly casual conversation. Linda is still in great danger, and you could still cause her death by failing to behave exactly the way I tell you to."

They came to the corner, stopped, and turned back the other way. They passed Linda's house and kept walking, Ike speaking quickly and calmly the entire way.

He told her Robert had hired a hit man. He said the FBI was gathering evidence to arrest Robert. He told her that the children were going to go off with the grandparents in the motor home. He did not tell her they were joining Linda. He told her that no one else in the house, not Rezilla, not Jeanne, nor Merriellen nor anyone else could know anything. He told her Robert had probably bugged the house and that anything they said inside might get back to him or his hired assassins.

"The FBI is just now getting ready to inform Robert that Linda is missing, that her car has been found with blood on it, and that he is a suspect. The hit man is just about to ask him to be paid. If, in the next twenty-four hours, Robert or his hit man or hit men find out this is a set-up, they may murder the undercover people and they might even have a last-ditch plan for getting to Linda."

Virginia was at the telephone, answering calls. Back in Oklahoma, Joe Pearsall had informed two close family members of the computer report on the bloody car. They had called other members of their extended Southwestern clan. Shortly after the children returned from the doctor, the telephone began ringing constantly. Each caller was a second cousin or aunt or uncle or distant nephew, each wanting to know the news, wanting to know if he or she should come.

Merriellen had been sitting at the long table, watching Virginia take the calls. She marveled at Virginia's calm, at the certainty with which Virginia told all of her family the situation was under control and that they should not come to help.

Janet came in and slipped into a chair next to Merriellen. She had been at Merriellen's house, using the phone to talk to the private investigator she had hired an hour before.

She leaned toward Merriellen and whispered to her: "Virginia sure thinks things are going well, doesn't she?"

Merriellen looked up. "Yeah," she whispered back. "I don't get it. I think maybe this is how John and Virginia deal with crisis."

Janet cocked her head and considered it for a moment. "Bad technique," she whispered. "Her daughter is out there getting killed, and she's here being stoical. I hope if somebody ever kidnaps me, my friends will not be stoical about it, at least until after they know for sure I'm already dead."

Merriellen made a little gasp and patted her chest with her fingers. "Please. Don't use that word."

Janet gazed back with arched eyebrows.

"Miriam seems normal," Merriellen said.

"Yes, I would say she's about as much of a basket case as we are. If that's normal."

"What has your private eye found out?"

Janet shrugged. "That something's not right. He has access to the computers. He found the report about the car. But he says it just drops off there. There are no reports from searchers, no further advisories, or any of the things he says would be typical."

They both sat silently, watching Virginia talk on the phone. Finally, Merriellen said, "What does that mean?"

Ike and Miriam appeared in the kitchen. Merriellen and Janet were both taken aback by what they saw on Miriam's face. There was a very faint but unmistakable suggestion of a smile at her lips.

"Is there news?" Janet asked.

Virginia muttered something quickly into the telephone, hung up, and looked at Miriam and Ike.

John put down his newspaper down on the sofa at the far side of the room and came forward. "What is it?"

Ike spoke.

"Dr. Meyers has decided that the children are gravely at risk, if they stay here and are subjected to the stress of this period. We think the best thing would be for the grandparents to load them up, right now, in the motor home, and go drive around in Oklahoma for a few days where they can't be found."

John and Virginia realized a major change was being made in the way the whole operation was to run. They both became quiet and tense.

Janet looked at John and Virginia, then at Ike.

"Mr. Vanden Eykel, when you say 'we have decided,' who is the *we*?"

Ike shrugged. "The FBI and I."

"You and Agent Masterson?"

"Yes."

Janet came out from around the long table. "I'm sure we're all concerned about the children, but did it occur to you or to Agent Masterson that Virginia and John might want to be consulted first about this, since it's their daughter who is still missing."

Virginia stood up quickly. "Rezilla!" she said. "Can you help me pack?"

"Yes, Mrs. DeSilva. Come on upstairs."

Jeanne said she would come up and help, too. John went out to get the motor home started up.

At the top of the stairs, Jeanne touched her sister on the back. Virginia turned around.

"Oh, Jeanne," she said. "Are you all right?"

"I'm going to stay, Virginia. I want to help Miriam."

"God bless you, Jeanne."

"Virginia," Jeanne said shyly, her voice beginning to break. She reached out with a trembling hand and touched Virginia's arm. "Are you and John and the children going to be safe where you're going?"

"Yes," she said. "I think we will be well watched over."

Jeanne's eyes were swimming in tears. "Virginia, I feel so awful. I feel . . . I am afraid Linda may be. . . "

"No," Virginia said, urgently. "She's not! She is going to be all right, Jeanne."

"Virginia, you have always been so strong. But I'm afraid you have got to begin preparing yourself. It just doesn't look good, Virginia. I'm afraid if you don't begin to bend to it a little, it may break you when it comes."

"Jeanne," she said. "Jeanne. You have got to have faith! You have got to have faith! She is going to be all right!"

Jeanne dropped her eyes and shook her head. "She may not be, Virginia."

Virginia wheeled and headed to Kathleen's room. "Come help me pack," she said brusquely.

Ike had stayed in the kitchen to see what was going to be said next.

Janet sat back down, shaking her head. "I'm not saying it's a bad idea to get the kids out of here, but I just don't understand why we're all being so obedient every time one of these two men has an idea about what we should do. Mr. Vanden Eykel, let me ask you something. Why isn't any of this on television? Or in the papers? Why aren't we out plastering the town with posters with Linda's picture on them?"

The phone rang. Miriam took her mother's place at the table and picked it up.

Ike said, "The FBI needs some time to get to Robert."

"Oh, that's brilliant," Janet said. "Yes, indeed, let's spend our time worrying about getting a good case on Robert. We wouldn't want to interrupt him or anything, at least not until he's got her good and dead. That might compromise the court case! I marvel at your priorities, counselor."

Miriam put the phone to her shoulder. "Janet! He knows what he's doing!"

Ike whipped around and glared at Miriam, afraid she was on the verge of giving something away. Miriam shrank back, put the phone back to her mouth, and began talking again to the person on the other end. "We're doing the best we can under the circumstances," she said. "The police and the FBI seem to have everything under control. It would be better if you just stayed up there, and we'll let you know just as soon as we hear something."

Janet and Merriellen exchanged glances. Janet whispered to Merriellen, "Another one for the body snatchers."

Joe Masterson picked up his telephone. It was the chief at University Park. He said he had just been informed that Robert's new criminal lawyer was in court and "would not be able to meet with the police that day."

"Yeah, right," Masterson said. "Okay, I'm handling Edelman now."

He hung up and called Ike's office. The office patched him through to Ike's portable telephone. Ike answered it, standing at the end of the long table in the kitchen at Caruth.

"This is Masterson. Where are you?"

"Caruth."

"Don't respond to anything I say. Edelman is on the move. He's trying to put off the meet. I'm going to his office unannounced myself right now. Get those people the hell out of that house and on the road!"

Ike bounded up the stairs to hurry the packing process. He found Virginia, Jeanne, and Rezilla in Kathleen's room. "Throw some p.j.'s and a toothbrush in a backpack or something," he said. "We have got to go right now."

The children were standing together at the top of the stairs.

"What are you doing with us, Ike?" Stephen asked.

"You're going to go on a trip for a few days with your grandparents."

Stephen began shaking his head jerkily. "No no no. No. You said you would help us find our mommy. We don't want to go away!"

Ike turned to Virginia. "Be packed and ready to go in five minutes." He knelt in front of Stephen, took both of his hands in his, and peered into Stephen's face. Stephen's hands were icy. The little boy's eyes were bloodshot; he was trembling; and his lips were an odd color, as if he had stayed too long in a cold swimming pool.

"Stephen and Kathleen, come with me," Ike said. "I want to talk to you."

He led them down the spiral staircase, out the front door, and down the walk to the sidewalk, where they turned right and began walking toward the corner. Curtains parted up and down the block. By now the windows were thick with opera glasses, field binoculars, and even a few small tripod-mounted telescopes.

"Are we going for a walk, Mr. Vanden Eykel?" Kathleen asked.

Ike squeezed both of their hands. He bit hard to force composure on himself. "Children," he said, "I have something very important to tell you."

They stopped walking, dragging back on his big hands with their tiny ones. Stephen and Kathleen stared into his face expectantly.

"Your mother is alive."

Both children went rigid. They stared up at him in totally focused, intent, motionless silence.

"I know where she is. And that is where you are going now. Your grandparents are going to drive you to your mother."

Ike turned, drawing them around by their little hands, and together they marched to the motor home. John clambered down and opened the door for them. Virginia was coming down the walk with two little backpacks, one hanging from each hand, and Rezilla was following with a suitcase for John and Virginia.

"Get up in the motor home," Ike said.

"Grandpa, guess what?" Stephen said excitedly.

"Oh Grandpa, Grandpa . . ." Kathleen said.

"Get in now!" Ike said in something close to a shout.

The children hurried aboard. Ike came up the stairs behind them and herded them toward the back of the motor home, waving his telephone at them like a paddle. Virginia came up behind him. Ike slipped around her, stepped back down to the door, and barred Rezilla's way. He reached down and grabbed the suitcase from her.

"Good-bye, Rezilla," he said.

"Are those children in there?" Rezilla said. "I need to say. . ."

Ike shut the door in her face and locked it. Rezilla paused for a moment, then turned and walked back to the house.

The children were in the back, jabbering to Virginia. She looked at Ike and shook her head to ask what was going on.

"You are taking them to Linda," Ike said.

"What?" John said. "What's going on? Why is it changing? Is something wrong?"

"Nothing is wrong. I don't have time to explain now. Virginia, do you know where my offices are at the Galleria?"

Virginia nodded that she did.

"Go there. Wait for me in the parking garage. I will be ten minutes behind you."

"I can't get this thing into a parking garage," John said.

Ike thought about it. "Oh God," he said. "Go in the entrance that leads to the parking garage. It splits off to a service alley behind the mall. You can make a loop by going down that alley and back along the service road by the freeway. Just keep going in circles. I'll find you."

Ike turned around and found his way back to the children. He sat down next to Stephen. "I have to ask you to do a very hard grown-up job, Stephen."

"Yes, sir."

He explained to him about the cat.

When he had finished listening, Stephen said, "I understand, Mr. Vanden Eykel. My mom's going to be real sad, but she'll understand. I will explain it to her."

Ike's phone rang.

"This is Masterson. Are they out of there?"

"Not yet."

"I'm about two blocks from his office, man. You need to get them away from that house now!"

Virginia came forward down the narrow corridor at the center of the passageway and sat on a banquette in the little dining area, barely a foot or so from where Ike was stooped over just behind the passenger seat in the cab.

As soon as he had turned off the telephone, she said, "Ike, who else knows now?"

"Miriam is in on it. I just told her."

John slumped forward with his forehead against the steering wheel. "Thank the Lord," he whispered to himself. "I just couldn't stand any more of this for her."

"What about Jeanne?" Virginia asked.

"No," Ike said. "She does not know. She is not to know. That's from the FBI. Miriam is the only one in the house who knows."

"I see," Virginia said. She was quiet for a moment. "Oh, Ike," she said suddenly, "I'm sorry. I forgot something. It will just take me a minute."

"What is it? We need to go right now."

She reached up and squeezed his hand. She smiled. "It's personal."

"Oh. Well. Go on. But please hurry. Seconds count now. And Virginia! Not one word! Not to anyone! It could be very dangerous."

Virginia hurried up the walk and let herself into the house. She rushed to the family room. Merriellen and Janet were gone. They had returned to Merriellen's house to make plans away from the family. Miriam and Jeanne were sitting at the table.

Miriam stood up and came to her mother with brilliant tears in her eyes. When her face was inches from her mother's, Miriam mouthed the words, "You knew."

Virginia embraced Miriam and whispered into her hair, "I am so sorry." She released her daughter, then took her sister by the sleeve and tugged for her to follow. Miriam stayed behind in the family room as Virginia led Jeanne through the back corridor and partway up the back stairs.

Midway up the staircase, Virginia turned and stopped. She leaned forward, close to Jeanne's face, and mouthed the words, "Lin . . . da . . . O . . . K . . . Linda okay."

Jeanne said, "What? What are you saying, Virginia?"

Virginia pointed to her own lips, to indicate she was mouthing the words.

"Read your lips?"

Virginia shook her head vigorously in the affirmative.

"Lin . . . da . . . Linda!" Jeanne said excitedly. "Something about Linda."

Virginia put her finger to her lips to shush Jeanne.

"Linda quiet," Jeanne said.

Virginia shook her head no impatiently and stabbed at Jeanne with a finger.

"Me quiet. You want me to be quiet. Oh, I'm sorry. All right."

Virginia took a finger and tried to draw a large O and a large K in the air. Jeanne did not understand. For a moment, as Virginia's finger swooped ever more emphatically in circles and cuts before her face, Jeanne began to fear Virginia was saying that something had happened to Linda's head.

"Oh my Lord," Jeanne said, beginning to feel faint. "Is she dead?"

Virginia began shaking her head no.

"Hey!" a male voice shouted.

Both women jumped almost out of their skins.

It was Ike, at the bottom of the stairs. "We have got to go now, Virginia! NOW!"

A few minutes later, the motor home had labored off down Caruth, under a legion of watchful, well-wishing eyes behind curtains. Ike said his good-byes and drove away, following the motor home to the Galleria.

When they were two blocks away from Caruth, Stephen, who was sitting in his grandmother's lap, looked up from a long silence and said, "Grandma! I feel as if a spell has been lifted from me."

She looked into his face carefully. "What do you mean, Stephen?"

"You know, Grandma. Like in *Sleeping Beauty*, when the spell was broken."

Jeanne and Miriam were alone in the kitchen. They sat across the table, staring silently into each other's eyes.

"Do you think the house is bugged?" Jeanne asked in a whisper.

Miriam nodded yes. "By someone. By Robert, or the FBI, or both of them. Everyone seems to have a way of knowing what happens in this house before we tell anybody."

Jeanne nodded.

Simultaneously, as if inspired by the same thought at the same instant, they both tipped their heads backward and gazed up at the ceiling. Miriam raised one finger slowly, extended her arm over her head, and pointed up at the round wells that held the recessed overhead bulbs.

They both saw the same thing. In every second or third well, the bulb was missing, where John had installed the wrong bulbs—the ones that had blown up. Little clusters of wires protruded where the bulbs had been.

Jeanne and Miriam peered up at the wires and then nodded to each other, certain they had found the listening devices.

Jeanne motioned for Miriam to follow her into the back corridor, where there was a low ceiling and no recessed lighting. When they were safely in the corridor, Jeanne leaned to Miriam's ear and whispered: "Virginia tried to tell me something about Linda. I'm not sure I understood. It was either that Linda is okay or that Virginia already knows Linda is dead. Do you know?"

Miriam winced and pulled away. She pointed to her ear and then pointed around with her finger to indicate that there were ears everywhere. She leaned to Jeanne's ear and whispered, "Afraid to talk."

CHAPTER EIGHT

J oe Masterson pulled into the parking lot behind Cedar Maple Plaza—
the low-rise office complex with the phony nineteenth-century
Parisian look that Robert had built across the street from the Hunt
family's huge Crescent complex, just north of downtown Dallas. He found
a directory inside the door and took the elevator to Robert's office.

The offices were huge and plush. A receptionist sat just inside the
outer door. Joe walked up to her, smiled, reached into the breast pocket
of his dark-gray suit coat, and removed his FBI identification. He
unfolded it and held it in both hands in front of her face, keeping it there
while she gazed at it.

"I am Special Agent Joseph Masterson of the Federal Bureau of
Investigation. I want to see Robert Edelman, please."

She sat up straight. She was somewhere in her mid-twenties. She
looked smart. She nodded and averted her eyes slightly. "Just a moment,
please, Mr. Masterson." She picked up the phone, punched a button, and
said, "Would you tell Mr. Edelman that a Mr. Masterson of the Federal
Bureau of Investigation is here to see him." She paused, listening to the
phone, then turned to Joe and said, "Mr. Edelman will be right with you.
Will you have a seat?"

Joe sat on a fancy chintz sofa and plucked a copy of *Yachting Magazine* off the over-varnished coffee table in front of him. He scanned the
office. Everything in it had the antique-but-obviously-brand-new look
that all of the law firms, banks, and real estate development offices in
Dallas seemed to have now.

The outer door of the office opened, and a man walked in hurriedly from the hallway. He did not look at Joe. The man barely nodded at the receptionist, who said, "Go right in, Mr. Fuller."

Joe realized it was Ken Fuller, Robert's divorce attorney and also one of the tenants in the building.

The secretary's phone rang a moment later. She picked it up, looked at Joe, nodded, and put it down.

"You can go in now, Mr. Masterson."

Joe walked through to another office, where a secretary was sitting. The secretary rose and guided him into the sprawling inner office, where Robert was sitting behind his huge desk. Robert was larger, close up, than Joe had expected him to be. He looked fatter, puffier in the face than he had looked in the surveillance work. He was playing it extremely calm so far. Fuller sat to one side of the desk in a red leather armchair. Fuller was handsome, smooth, in his late fifties or early sixties, vigorous, and very watchful.

Joe presented his identification to Robert. He held it in front of Robert for a long time, but Robert never once looked at it, staring flatly at Joe's face the whole time instead. Not having been invited to sit down, Joe seated himself in a chair across from the desk.

"Mr. Edelman, I am very sorry to inform you that your wife, Linda Edelman, has been missing since Monday evening. A search for her is underway. The FBI was asked to enter the case when her car was found at a rest stop across a state line, in Oklahoma."

Robert stared at Joe's face, his own face a perfectly impassive mask. As Joe continued to speak, Robert's hand drifted slowly to a package of cigarettes on the desk. He slipped one out, sat back comfortably, and lit it. Both Robert and Fuller remained silent.

"A substance was found in the automobile which appeared to be blood," Joe said. "We have not gotten the report back from the lab yet, but I would say it was definitely blood. We don't know whose it is yet."

Robert took his cigarette in the fancy little middle-finger-and-thumb cigarette-holder pose and exhaled a long stream of smoke at Joe, staring at him impassively.

"Has she been found?" he asked.

"No, she has not been found. A search is underway."

The three men sat in silence, staring at each other for a while.

"We have interviewed a number of people, Mr. Edelman, since your wife's disappearance. Everyone we have interviewed has said that you would be the prime suspect in their mind, if anything has happened to your wife."

Robert puffed on the cigarette and looked at Joe, waiting for him to say something interesting.

"I wonder if you could account for your time, from July 17th through July 22nd, Mr. Edelman."

Robert made a tiny shrug, ran his hand over his desk as if brushing away a speck, and then said very quietly, "Well, Mr. Masterson, I was with my children during that period. They were with me."

Ken Fuller turned to Robert and said, "I would advise you not to answer any more questions along this line at this time."

Fuller turned to Joe Masterson. "Mr. Masterson, my client has engaged another lawyer, a criminal lawyer, who is not able to be here at this time because he is in court on another case. I must advise my client not to answer these questions until he has had an opportunity to speak with the person who will serve as his counsel in this matter."

Robert rose slowly and came out from behind the desk. He went over to a small sofa next to the chair where Fuller was seated and sat down. It was a clear signal that he and Fuller were about to discuss some real business and that it was time for Joe to get back out on the beat.

Joe looked down at his shoes, nodding amiably. "Sure. I understand." Then he looked up at Fuller. "Right now, we just want to find Mrs. Edelman."

Robert and Fuller returned his gaze.

"We're trying everything we can to find your wife, Mr. Edelman, I want you to know that."

Robert stubbed out his cigarette in a crystal ashtray on an end table and looked up. He looked bored.

Joe said: "Her divorce attorney, Mr. Vanden Eykel, advised us that she hired a private investigator named Mike Grimes at one point in the divorce. I had hoped Mr. Grimes might be able to help, but he wasn't."

Joe looked straight at Fuller. "Did you ever hire a P.I. in this deal, Mr. Fuller?"

Fuller said, "No, we haven't hired anybody. Mr. Edelman doesn't have enough money to hire an investigator. Private investigators are quite expensive."

Joe nodded his head to show he understood. Finally he rose. Fuller got up and shook his hand. Robert remained seated. Masterson walked up to him and stuck his hand out to shake. Robert extended a handful of limp fingertips, which he allowed Joe to shake.

As Joe left, Fuller said good-bye. Robert looked away and said nothing. Joe caught a glimpse of Robert's jaw working. Beneath all the fat, bored smooth expanse of his face, Robert was angry.

Joe got into his car and drove straight out of the parking lot.

On the other side of the street, parked at the curb with a clear view of the back door of the building, Agent Mike Fiori waited for Robert to leave.

✿   ✿   ✿

Ike had found the motor home easily—it was the only Greyhound-bus-sized vehicle stuck in a long line of cars on the service road in front of the Galleria. He drove ahead and parked his own car in the structure, then came out on foot and found the motor home not ten car lengths from where he had seen it ten minutes earlier. John let him in.

Joe directed John to a spot just to one side of the entrance to the parking garage where he could safely leave the motor home for a few minutes. Then he and John took the elevator up to Ike's office, where Ike drew John a detailed map showing the way to the store near the lake house. Ike saw John to the elevator, wished him well, and went to his desk, just in time to take a call from Robert's divorce attorney.

Joe had just parked his car in the underground garage beneath the warehouse building when his portable phone went off. It was Ike Vanden Eykel.

"Ken Fuller just called," Ike said. "He is already moving to get the kids."

"Get the kids and do what?"

"Give them to Robert, Joe. Robert is their father. Unless you can get some kind of court action to say different, he is the one who has got legal claim to them right now."

"Put him off," Joe said. "He's not touching those kids."

Ike hung up and muttered to himself. "Put off Ken Fuller. Sure. Why don't I put off a freight train, too, or stop a speeding bullet or something like that while I'm at it?"

Robert walked out smoothly, gliding across the parking lot as if he were on wheels, and climbed into his car. The instant his Cadillac slumped down heavily out of the parking lot exit, Mike Fiori put his car in gear and followed.

Forty minutes later, Robert was fuming. Normally he was always the last one to show up for a meeting. It was his trademark. His meetings with Colonel Young at the Howard Johnson restaurant on the Stemmons Freeway had been the exception, because Young was always even later than Robert. Today Robert had been waiting half an hour when Young appeared. Now Young had arrived, but he was standing at the door, as usual, waiting for the hostess to give him permission to enter. Robert wanted to jump up, grab Young by the scruff of the neck, and drag him to the table in the back, but he was even more afraid of creating a scene.

When Colonel Young finally got himself seated, he smiled at Robert sweetly and said, "How is your day?"

"My day? How is my day? My day is great, Colonel, except for the fact the FBI has been grilling me about whether I killed my wife."

"You told them no, I hope." He raised his eyebrows and waited for a response.

Robert turned his head just barely sideways and squinted at Young. He could never quite get a bead on the Colonel. Robert hunched forward and spoke in a hushed intent voice.

"Look, Colonel, I don't understand what the hell is going on. They said my wife's car was found abandoned up in Oklahoma. What the hell did you take her up there for?"

Young straightened himself. He brushed at his sleeves and lapels. He looked over and smiled at the waitress. She came to the table.

"Coffee for me," the Colonel said. "For you?"

Robert ordered coffee. After the waitress left, Young was silent.

Robert furrowed his brow. "I said, why did you take her up to Oklahoma and do it? I told you to do it in the garage or in the house and make it look like a robbery. So what's going on? Why would you cross a state line? Now the FBI's in on it. Did you know that would happen? Did you understand that crossing a state line would make it an FBI case?"

They stared at each other.

"Why did you go up there?"

"I did not," the Colonel said quietly, smoothly.

"Then how did her car get up there?"

"I am not sure. Apparently the man I hired to do it had thoughts of his own."

Robert looked away. He was still hunched forward with his fingertips pressing on the table. He sat up slowly to a straight position. He started waving at Young with one hand.

"Nah, nah," Robert said, shaking his head no.

"I hired a guy to do it," Young said, smiling broadly, shaking his head up and down as if waiting for Robert to get the joke.

"No, no, you didn't. Tell me you did not hire someone else to kill my wife."

"I did hire someone, Mr. Edelman. His name is Hitman Jack. He's good. He knows what he's doing."

Robert's breath was coming short. "Hitman Jack?" He reached for a glass of water, took a shallow sip, and then let the glass bang on the table. A man at the next table was startled by the bang, turned halfway toward Robert, and then turned back to his own conversation.

Robert hissed: "You brought someone else into this? You didn't tell me? Why in the hell did you not do it yourself, the way I thought you were going to?"

"I don't do them myself. I subcontract. It's okay. The guy is solid. He knows what he's doing. So it's done. Your wife's dead. I don't know why Hitman Jack took her up there. . . "

Robert winced, looking around warily. "Could you fucking call him something else?"

"He must have had some reason to do it that way. Maybe somebody drove up, and he had to get the body out of there. I don't know. It doesn't make any difference, Mr. Edelman. The job is done."

"I can't believe you brought somebody else into my business. I'm sitting here, I'm trying just to think what this means. I mean, I have no idea what's going on now."

"Sure you do, Mr. Edelman. Nothing is going on, because the job's done."

"No, no, I have no idea. I need to regroup. This is bad."

"Mr. Edelman," Colonel Young said, smiling broadly. "Everything is fine. You need to stay cool."

The store lady had seen Linda pull up in her little car with the rental agency bumper sticker almost half an hour ago. She recognized Linda. She was the woman Mr. Vanden Eykel had been buying groceries for two nights earlier.

Linda had been sitting in the car on the lot, motionless, staring out the windshield at the road ever since. The store lady stole glances out her side window at her every few seconds, eager not to miss whatever was going to be the next scene.

John almost missed the driveway into the parking lot next to the little store. He hit the brake and spun the wheel. The motor home floundered into the lot like a sea lion climbing a rock. John had some trouble finding a place to stop the motor home. When he did, the door of the motor home was on the side opposite Linda's car.

The instant the motor home came to a halt, the door exploded open, and Kathleen and Stephen came rolling out. They leapt to their feet, Stephen holding his little hands out catlike, Kathleen blinking through huge round eyes and turning slowly.

Linda leaned around one end of the motor home with a giggling smile and said, "Hello, children!"

They raced to her, screaming "Mommy, Mommy!" She reached, and both children plowed into her so hard she had to slap her free hand against the back of the motor home to keep from being bowled over.

John and Virginia stood a few feet away, holding each other's hands, waiting their turns, and smiling through tears.

✿   ✿   ✿

Joe Masterson was in the room with the electronic gear, wearing the headset, when he got the report.

"Our guy is not a happy camper," Fiori said. "Apparently he had no idea Young had subcontracted it."

"What?"

"No idea. Total shock. Young just told him at HoJo's."

"How upset is he?"

"Peeled out of here about ninety miles an hour. I would say very upset."

"So what's he up to?"

"Back to the office. Dunno after that. You gonna pull the plug?"

Joe ran his eye down a dense penciled checklist on a legal pad in front of him on the desk. "Not yet. We need a pay. We need sound and hopefully some photo on a pay. We've got to go on down the road a couple more miles, or we may lose him."

Joe hung up, dialed another number quickly, and reached two FBI agents who were fishing from a small boat in front of Ike Vanden Eykel's lake house.

"They in yet?" he asked.

One of the fishermen spoke into a small handheld telephone. "Nope. No sign."

"Where's she?"

"At the store. Waiting."

"We there?"

"Yessir."

"Keep an eye peeled. Things are poppin'. If something bad happens, this is when."

"Yessir."

Joe hung up. His phone rang. It was Ike.

"All right, Joe, we have definitely got problems," Ike said. "That was Fuller again. I just hung up. My ear is about burned off."

"Why?"

"Because he completely went ballistic on me when I told him I didn't know where the kids were."

"Why did you tell him that?"

"What do you want me to tell him? They're at the lake?"

"Don't even joke about that, Ike. This Edelman is a nutso. And he's pissed. If he finds out where she is or if he guesses somehow, then who knows?"

"Tell me about it. I know he's pissed. He wants those kids. And Fuller is extremely angry with me, as I would be in his position. He's taking us to court tomorrow to get the kids. And guess what, Joe?"

"What?"

"If that judge asks me where those children are, I am not going to perjure myself in front of him."

"Perjure?"

"Yeah, perjure. It doesn't make any difference why I do it. If I lie to the judge about something like this, it's perjury. Plain and simple. And I will not do it."

"Well, keep your shirt on, Ike. I got a couple irons in the fire here I need to take care of. We'll get everything straightened out for you in time for the court date. Not to worry, brother."

Ike hung up, muttering to himself. "Not to worry. Not to worry, brother."

Miriam and Jeanne were sitting in the library. Jeanne was reading a newspaper in an overstuffed armchair next to the cold fireplace.

Miriam sat nearer to the door on a smaller armchair, gazing down on Linda's Beatrix Potter figurines on the coffee table. She thought of how Linda looked whenever she sat in this same chair, gazing on the figurines in this same way. Miriam had come upon her more than once in this pose.

She did not really know where her parents or the children were. She did not know who might be out there prowling for all of them, who might come prowling into this house, for that matter. She longed to tell Jeanne, sitting right down there at the far end of the room, that Linda was alive, but she was terrified of the wires sticking down from the ceiling in the kitchen.

Jeanne, for her part, was beginning to be overwhelmed by the strange sensation that nothing around her was real. None of this situation—the FBI agents and the lawyers and the frantic neighbors, the terror, the sudden comings and goings, the talk of murder and kidnapping—none of it had any place in any world with which Jeanne was even faintly familiar, except on television. There had been moments in the last two days when she had even felt as if she had fallen into the land of television and was playing a bit part in a police serial.

The business with Virginia and the game of charades on the back step had thrown her for a loop. The more she tried to figure out exactly what Virginia had been trying to tell her, the more she wondered if she had imagined the whole thing. The stress of not being able to speak normally in the house was beginning to press on her every moment. She knew that Miriam knew something but that Miriam could not or would not tell her what she knew. She sensed that Miriam wanted to keep Merriellen and Janet at bay or under control somehow, but she could not imagine why.

Her son, Joe, had been calling all day with long complex theories about why the FBI story did not add up. Jeanne understood some of it, but did not understand what Joe was really saying. Was the FBI in on all of this somehow?

Even Linda's huge house was odd and frightening. The spaces were all too vast, like spaces in a public building, not a home. Jeanne shivered whenever she thought of Robert owning a machine gun and popping down into rooms from trapdoors in the ceiling.

There were moments when the combination of fear and strangeness made her want to run screaming from the house, but then she would look at Miriam, in all her pain, and the tug of family would prevail.

Jeanne put the paper down, walked over to Miriam, and asked if they might pray together. They both slipped to their knees in the middle of the library floor and bowed their heads.

Merriellen and Janet were sipping coffee together across the long table in Merriellen's kitchen. Neither had spoken in a long while. Merriellen's mother sat at the far end of the table, feeding a child and watching the two younger women confer.

Finally Merriellen said, "You're right. I know you are. There is something strange going on. John and Virginia are just not . . . I don't know. Not normal. Their daughter has been abducted, for goodness sake, and they don't know if she's still alive."

"Well, what about Miriam?" Janet asked.

"She was normal for a while."

"Yes, and then Ike Vanden Eykel said something to her, and she turned into a zombie, too."

They were both quiet.

Janet said, almost under her breath, "Vanden Eykel and that FBI agent seem to have them all under some kind of a spell."

"Yes. They do. They all know something we don't know. What about Rezilla?"

"I think she's like us. She's normal." Janet swatted her hand flat on the table. "I just don't understand why they all sit over there, Linda is missing, God knows what is being done to her, and they all take orders from this Goddamned divorce lawyer."

"Well, Janet, I think you'd have to say Ike is being pretty great about this."

"Great? He's a . . . he's a divorce lawyer! Linda is his client, that's all, his meal ticket. I . . . I love Linda! She is so . . . so good. So great. Such a great friend. She was so great for me, when I was going through pure unadulterated hell on wheels in my own divorce. My best friend! Maybe my only friend. God, I don't want her to be dead, Merriellen. I want to do something! It makes me so angry to have these stupid men telling me what to do, I could kill them!"

Merriellen was staring into her coffee. "You never told me your divorce was so bad."

"Oh," Janet said, with a careless flap of the hand, "you know. No worse than anyone else's. I trusted my husband."

They looked into each other's eyes for a moment. Janet rose, walked around the kitchen with her coffee. She paused and gazed out the window.

"I had a very bad time," she said softly. "The thing I don't understand about men . . . husbands, lawyers, even guys you just do business with. The most important thing to them, after sex, is that you trust them. I don't know why they bother with the trust part. That was always the trust part that did me in. It's like they lure you out, farther and farther, and then. . ."

She looked back at Merriellen with shining wet eyes and angry drawn lips. "Can you believe that rotten, stupid, vicious bastard, Robert?

"The luckiest thing that ever happened to that man, totally undeserved good luck, was when she married him. She has stuck with him, for God knows what reason, through his cruelty and his animalistic rages.

"All he ever had to offer her in return was the money. And you know what? He thought he was the one who was being taken. And now he's having her put away. The way you take a cat to the vet and have it put away. That's how it is for Robert. He's paying someone else to do it for him. You know he wouldn't have the balls himself."

Janet put her cup down on the table and then sank back into her chair. "Merriellen. He is having her killed. I . . . I don't know if I can handle this."

Merriellen came around the table and put her hand on Janet's back. "I'm so sorry, Janet. About your troubles. I think Linda is very fortunate to have you for a friend."

Janet looked up, her eyes brimming. "I have to go make something happen, Merriellen. It's the only thing that comforts me.

Miriam and Jeanne were at the long table in Linda's family room, sipping coffee, when Janet and Merriellen came in and slipped into chairs next to them at the table. They caught each other up on what they all had been doing in the previous forty minutes. Miriam tried her best to sound upbeat and confidant that everything possible was being done and there was no need for any change of plans. Jeanne listened and was noncommittal.

Then Merriellen and Janet walked up to the front of the house to confer together in the library without the other two. Alone in the library, Janet whispered to Merriellen, "They really are hopeless Okies. But I have this feeling they're plotting."

As soon as the other two were out of the room, Miriam snatched a piece of writing paper from the table and scrawled a note to Jeanne. She held it up for Jeanne to read.

The note said, THEY THINK WE ARE A COUPLE OF STUPID OKIES AND THAT'S WHY WE'RE NOT CONCERNED.

Jeanne nodded her agreement.

As soon as Jeanne read the note, Miriam took it to the stove, turned on the burner flame, and lit the piece of paper on fire. Merriellen and Janet came back through the kitchen on their way to the family room just in time to see the last inches of the page turning to black ash over the burner. Over her shoulder, Janet shot Merriellen an arch look.

Then Merriellen said, "Miriam, Janet and I are very concerned about how this is going. We don't think either of you realizes how important it is for us to make sure that everything possible is being done."

Jeanne looked up, listening.

Miriam shook her head. "No, no, Merriellen, I think you are wrong. I really think they are doing everything they can."

"Who is?" Janet asked sharply.

"The authorities. Ike."

"Miriam, excuse me," Janet said, "but, with all due respect, Ike is not an authority. Ike is your sister's divorce lawyer. He is not an authority."

"They are doing everything possible." Miriam said.

"Miriam," Jeanne said, "maybe Merriellen and Janet have a suggestion. Maybe we should listen to them."

"No," Miriam said. "Linda is my sister. I will not have you interfering with the proper work of the authorities."

Miriam got up and left the room.

Jeanne shrugged. Merriellen smiled back at her and said, "Your family is a tough outfit."

But Janet was not smiling. She got up and followed Miriam.

Suddenly, Jeanne needed to talk to someone she could trust. She decided to call her husband. She picked up the telephone. But there was no dial tone. She heard clicking and whirring noises. She was staring at Merriellen, who was staring at her. Then she heard Merriellen speaking on the telephone.

In a tinny, muffled voice, Merriellen said, "Janet and I are very concerned about how this is going. We don't think either of you realizes how important it is for us to make sure that everything possible is being done."

Jeanne gazed at Merriellen before her, who was silent, her lips unmoving. Jeanne's hand began shaking.

Then she heard Miriam on the telephone, saying: "No, no, Merriellen, I think you are wrong. I really think they are doing everything they can."

Then she heard Janet say: "Who is?"

Merriellen rose from her chair and came toward her. "Jeanne! Jeanne, what's wrong?"

Jeanne put the phone down. She had trouble getting the receiver into the cradle. She was shaking her head, backing away from the phone, wringing her hands. "I don't know. It's the bugging. It's something about the bugging. Now it's in the telephone. They can hear us through the telephone, even when it's hung up."

She turned and looked at Merriellen desperately. "I need to find Miriam." She hurried to the front of the house.

Janet had found Miriam sitting in the library in a chair, staring down on a table full of porcelain figurines and crying softly. Janet walked in front of her.

"Miriam! This isn't getting us anywhere. You can't just sit there and. . ."

She reached down and took Miriam by both shoulders and shook her hard. "Listen to me! You're from a small town in Oklahoma! You trust people! You can't do that here! You don't understand what's going on! There could still be a chance to save Linda's life, but you've got to get up off your bottom."

"Please," Miriam said, fending her away.

Janet stepped back, breathing hard, and gaped at her. "Please? Please, what? Miriam, do you understand that your sister may be being murdered at this very moment?"

Miriam rose and approached her. "Janet, please, I assure you, I understand everything. Everything is going to be all right. I assure you. It will all be all right."

Jeanne was watching from just outside the door to the library. Janet looked up and saw her. She walked around Miriam and went to Jeanne.

"Jeanne, what is she talking about? Do you understand what I'm saying, Jeanne?"

"Yes," Jeanne said. "Yes, I do. But, I don't. I don't understand what's happening. I don't understand . . . I think Miriam knows what she's doing. But I don't. I don't have any idea what's going on."

Jeanne turned and walked off toward the stairs.

"Where are you going?" Janet asked.

"I need to go to the bathroom."

Jeanne ascended the stairs slowly, deliberately. She felt oddly off balance—not quite dizzy but just a little uncertain of her footing. The business with the wires sticking down from the ceiling, their own voices echoing ghostlike on the telephone: it was all getting ahead of her. She was trying to remember why it was that they couldn't say things, what it was someone might hear, who it was who might be listening, what already had been said, who knew what, and who did not. The charades scene with Virginia on the staircase kept whirling back across her mind: she kept trying to work the puzzle, trying to figure out what it was that Virginia and perhaps Miriam knew, but were not telling.

She passed the hall bathroom at the top of the stairs and half-stumbled through Linda's bedroom to the bathroom. She had been using the small guest bathroom down the hall and had never actually stepped into Linda's master bathroom, having balked when she remembered the tales of Robert's descents from the attic.

When she did walk into the huge bathroom, it never occurred to her that someone had furnished it with opposing face-to-face toilets. She sat on the nearest one and simply assumed what she saw in her peripheral vision was a completely mirrored wall, reflecting her own side of the room.

She felt an odd creeping sensation in the flesh on one side of her face, then a chill. She turned very slowly—sweaty flashes of panic sparking up and down her spine as she turned. She looked. She still thought she was looking into a mirror. But in the reflection before her, the toilet was unoccupied. She was not there.

She gulped for air and felt her heart pounding. "This is it," she thought. "My mind has really snapped now."

Then in an instant it all jelled! She rose partially and squinted through the shower stall. "Matching toilets," she thought with absolute and angry disgust. "These people have matching toilets."

She ran down the stairs and marched into the kitchen. Merriellen and Janet had gone back to Merriellen's house.

"Miriam!" she shouted. "What on earth is going on? I want to know right now! What is going on in this house?"

Miriam took one look at her, then grasped her hand and led her out onto the front lawn.

"Jeanne," she whispered, once they were outside, "Linda is alive. It's a trick to catch Robert. That's all I know."

Tears sprang to Jeanne's eyes. She reached forward and squeezed Miriam's hand. "Miriam, I'm so . . . Are you all right?"

"Yes, I think so."

They stared at each other in silence.

Jeanne straightened, wiped her eyes, and said, "Let's go back in."

But just then a car pulled up at the curb.

Jeanne's son Joe and his fiancée, Mitzi, stepped out.

"Joe! What are you doing here?" Jeanne cried.

"I told you I was coming."

"I told you not to come!"

"Mother! Inside! I intend to talk to you."

Joe stalked ahead to the front door and waited on the porch. Mitzi, who was young, petite, with curly blond hair and pixie-pretty good looks, came along behind with a smile somewhere between sheepishness and total bewilderment. Miriam let them in.

Joe took a long look around the huge foyer, taking in the spiral staircase and dripping crystal chandelier in one long glance. He had heard stories about this house over the years, but this was the first time he ever had actually been inside it. He took a stance in the center of the foyer, with his feet planted wide and his arms folded in front of his chest.

He spoke in a booming voice of command. "All right, Mother! Miriam! I drove down here because I thought I had to. I have been reviewing a lot of the evidence in this case. A lot of what they are apparently telling you just does not add up. I think somebody is trying to spare you from reality, and now I think it's time for both of you to start facing the truth."

During a dramatic pause, he looked around at both of them. "Linda," he said slowly, enunciating each word carefully as he spoke it, "is not . . . going . . . to be found . . . alive."

Jeanne stared up at the chandelier with her hands folded in front of her face and exhaled a long sigh. Miriam stared at her feet, her mouth working and twitching slightly at one side.

"You women," Joe said, "have got to stop living in a fantasy world."

With his hands folded at his waist, he gazed around above him. He seemed to lose his train of thought for a moment. "Is this really Linda's house?" he said.

"Yes," Miriam said. "Joe?"

"Yes."

"Did you bring night things, to stay?"

"Yes."

"Let's go get your things out of your car."

"Now?"

"Right now."

Joe obediently followed Miriam out to the front curb where he had parked his car. He opened his trunk with the key and bent in to grab a small bag. Miriam leaned over the fender and dipped her head into the trunk next to Joe's.

"Joe," she said, inside the trunk, "Linda is all right. We cannot discuss anything inside the house, because we think Robert can hear us. Things are being taken care of."

Joe kept reaching for the bag, without even turning. He understood instantly. "It's a sting," he said.

"I don't know what that means, Joe."

He straightened up. "It's fine. I understand what's going on now. Now all of a sudden, everything makes sense. We'll stay the night with you, though, if that's okay."

"Fine."

Joe asked if it would be all right if he and Mitzi took off to do a little shopping at North Park. Miriam assured them she and Jeanne would be all right without them.

She made tea. Jeanne joined her at the long table. It was their first quiet moment together since Miriam had told her. Their spoons clinked in unison in Linda's bone china cups. The silence of the huge house lay heavily on them.

"Miriam," Jeanne said softly, "have you ever stopped to wonder if . . ." She looked up anxiously at the wires in the light wells.

"If what?"

"If . . . what if we're all wrong? About Robert?"

Miriam shrugged. Then she screamed, pushed back violently from the table, and sent her scalding tea flying over Jeanne's hand.

Jeanne pushed back, twisted to her feet, and gasped.

There was a man dressed in white standing in the kitchen behind them, staring at them, something glinting in his hand.

"Who are you?" Jeanne screamed.

"Damn!" he shouted. "I'm the milkman! Who are you?"

They looked. He was carrying a wire basket full of milk bottles in one hand and a billing book in the other.

The panic would not leave Jeanne. She gaped. Milkman! The words kept echoing around in her brain like shrieks from the madhouse. People don't have milkmen! Milkmen are dim memories from the 1950s!

"He is," Miriam said, finally catching her breath.

"He is what?"

"The milkman. They have a milkman."

"They have a milkman?"

"Hey," the young milkman said, "what can I tell you? It's the Park Cities. I'm the milkman. Geez, I must be a whole lot uglier milkman than I thought, though."

Jeanne, who had been skeptical of the house from the beginning, was making a silent but angry calculation: "One inflatable scarecrow in attic;

one set matching toilets in master bathroom; one milkman."

Miriam rushed forward to console him. She explained about Linda's disappearance.

"Oh man!" the milkman said. "She's been missing that long!"

"Yes."

"Well, it's her husband. That bastard would do a thing like that."

That evening, as Miriam and Jeanne and Joe and Mitzi were getting ready for bed, Hitman Jack was calling Colonel Young, insisting that he be paid off the following morning.

Ike Vanden Eykel was still in his office, plowing through case law on a computer and continuing to come up with the same answer—that if he lied to the judge the next afternoon about where the children were, it would be perjury.

Joe Masterson was in the room with the electronics, crowding more and more penciled notes onto the already almost black pages of a legal pad.

Linda prepared a small dinner for her family. None of them was especially hungry. They ate quietly in the strange house where Linda had found sanctuary.

Miriam had not been quite sure how to handle the fact that Joe and Mitzi were not married. She offered them Stephen's room and Kathleen's room, without suggesting what they should do with them. She figured they could do what they saw fit.

But at 9:30 P.M., Joe knocked at the door of the master bedroom and asked to be let in. When Miriam opened the door, she found both Joe and Mitzi standing in the hall in their nightclothes, dragging their pillows.

"Miriam, I'm sorry, but this place is too big and too spooky for me," Joe said. "I've never slept in a two-story house before, let alone a three-story house with murder plots going on. Can we sleep in here with you?"

Joe and Mitzi both got into the huge bed with Jeanne and Miriam for a while and watched television.

After an hour, Jeanne said, "I am sorry, Joe, but you know I can't sit up all night like this and watch television. Besides, this has been a very bad day for me. I have got to get some sleep."

Joe said, "Well, I'm sorry, too, Mother, but I am not going back out there into that haunted house and sleep by myself. You'll have to let Mitzi sleep here in the bed with you and Miriam, and I'll sleep over there on that sofa."

In half an hour, they were all snoring.

Joe Masterson called the lake house late, after the children and grandparents had gone to bed. Linda was sitting by the phone in the kitchen.

"We have to do it all tomorrow, Linda," he said.

"Why tomorrow?"

"Too many loose ends. Too many factors. We have got to get our pay-off on film and then arrest Young first, and then we've got to go get Robert."

She thought for a while.

"At least it will be over," she said.

"You bet it will. And we will have our case. Thanks to you, Linda."

"I didn't do anything but sit out here and cry my eyes out."

"No," he said, with real admiration in his voice, "you did a lot more than that. I've been through some tough cases, Linda. You're a hell of a soldier. I'd put my back to you any day."

"That means you trust me?"

"Yes. It means I trust you. I know you can go the distance. And now we're almost to the tape. The trap is open. Let's just hope no last little thing happens to spook Robert."

Joe said good night and then called Ike to tell him what the battle plan was for the next day.

After she hung up, Linda went to the tall stool behind the bar where she could look out through the plate-glass window in the front room. She took her position, staring at the black window and listening. She stayed there all night.

Janet lay on her bed at 10:00 P.M. with all of her clothes on, sobbing. She could not make herself stop crying. Finally, she reached for the telephone and called a friend's machine. It was midnight when Janet's friend came in, heard the message, and called Janet back. It was another fifteen minutes before the friend called her back again with the phone number Janet was seeking. Her friend said she thought it would be all right to call the number, in spite of what time it was.

"I call this person at two and three in the morning sometimes," the friend said, "and she always answers on the first ring. I think she never sleeps. I dread to think what she looks like."

"You've never even seen her?"

"Oh Lord no, Janet. None of us has. That's part of the deal. She's way the hell up in far North Texas somewhere, maybe in Oklahoma. I'm not even sure where that area code begins. But she only communicates by telephone."

Janet exhaled. "Pretty odd."

"Absolutely odd," the friend said. "But I have told you what she can do."

Janet thanked her friend, hung up, and then made the call. The woman answered on the first ring. Janet explained who she was and what she wanted. The woman was casual about payment. She said that Janet could send her whatever she thought it was worth. Janet's friend had told her it was worth $250.

Janet told the woman what had happened.

The woman said, "How big is she?" Layered beneath her Southwestern diction was an odd lilting cadence. Janet got the half-conscious impression that the woman might be Indian.

"She's small," she said. "She's very graceful. She's a dancer."

"I just have to know how big she is."

"Small. Not tiny, but smallish."

"That's enough. Okay. Just wait a minute."

Janet held the phone for what seemed eons. She could hear a sandy scratching sound, which she decided was the sound of the receiver at the other end being dragged across bed sheets. She thought she heard the woman talking very faintly, probably to herself, in a muttering distracted whisper.

"Yeah, okay," Janet heard her whisper a few times. "Yeah, right, okay."

Finally the woman came back on the line. Her voice was softer, more personal this time. "I have a picture of your friend," she said. "She is not dead. She is alive. She is somewhere very near a body of water. That's all I have for you."

Janet began thanking her emotionally, but the woman cut her off.

"It's okay, I have to go now. Just send what you think is right."

Rezilla arrived at the house at 7:00 A.M. and made coffee. She punched the intercom and woke the four people sleeping in Linda's bedroom, including Joe, who woke up with a whopping crick in his neck from sleeping all night curled on the small sofa.

Before the people upstairs could get down to the kitchen, Merriellen was in through the back door, and Janet arrived a moment later. Just as they were taking their first sips, Ike arrived.

"How is everyone this fine morning?" he asked cheerily.

Miriam, Jeanne, Joe, and Mitzi all sang back vigorous morning greetings to him.

Rezilla, Merriellen, and Janet exchanged puzzled glances.

After coffee, Miriam told Ike she needed to talk to him. She led him out through the back to the alley.

"Ike, I have told Jeanne that Linda is alive."

"I figured you might," he said. "It's okay. I understand. If everybody can stay cool for about another six hours, and if nothing happens to spook

Robert at the last minute, then I think we're almost to home plate on this thing."

"Oh, thank God."

The instant they reentered the family room, Janet told Ike that she needed to talk to him in Merriellen's kitchen.

Ike shrugged, not at all enthusiastic about it.

Janet was on her way toward the back.

"I'll talk to you here," Ike said behind her. "What do you want?"

Janet whirled. "Ike, what are you so cheerful about today? Do you know something?"

Ike paused and mentally reviewed his position. Miriam and Jeanne already knew. He wasn't about to admit anything to the other two. Things were basically under control. "No," he said. "I'm not cheerful. I just think we, we have to go on. Do the best we can."

"Do you know something?"

"No."

Half turning to Merriellen, Janet said, "I did something last night you will probably both think is absolutely insane. I called a clairvoyant. She's a woman who has helped several friends of mine. Her name gets traded around in society circles, and I know that she has been able to do some very amazing things for people."

Rezilla, Miriam, and Jeanne all began moving slowly toward Janet.

Ike snorted. "Well, Janet, I know you're under a lot of stress."

"Let me finish!"

Merriellen was listening intently.

"The woman told me Linda is still alive."

Ike was nodding indulgently with his eyes shut.

"She said Linda is somewhere near a large body of water."

Ike stopped nodding. He looked up. He looked closely at Janet. "Who is this woman? What's her name?"

Janet peered at him. "Tell me something, Ike."

"I don't know anything."

"Tell me something, Ike."

"I can't."

"Give me something, Ike. Is she alive and you know about it?"

"I don't know anything."

The phone started ringing. For two rings, no one moved to answer it. Then Miriam went.

"Ike," Janet said, "you had better tell me something, or I am going to blow the lid right off this thing. I have got friends at the newspapers and at the television stations in this town, and I am about ready to march downtown with Linda's picture and tell them I don't know which ones of you have got her but I think somebody has got her and is about to kill her if the media can't do something."

Ike came forward with his hands raised toward her shoulders, but she backed away and looked at his hands in a way that made him slap them back to his sides.

Miriam was seated at the table, speaking in very deliberate tones to someone.

"Janet," Ike said. "Twenty-four hours. Wait twenty-four hours."

"Why, Ike?"

"Twenty-four hours. Please. Please. I am begging you. Don't do anything for twenty-four hours."

Janet shook her head no, with tears in her eyes. She lifted a fist to her mouth and bit the back of her hand. "Oh, God, Ike. I really hope . . . I hope you're not. . . "

"I'm not what?"

"I hope you're not in on this, in some sick way."

Ike stared straight into her face. "Janet," he said, "you have got to trust me."

Merriellen moved between Ike and Janet, took Janet by the elbows, and looked up closely into her face. "He's right," she said. "You have to trust him. We have no choice."

Janet looked at Ike. She began slowly to nod yes.

"Janet," Merriellen whispered, "do you believe that Linda is alive?"

Janet continued to nod her head yes.

Jeanne and Rezilla both gazed at her, wide-eyed.

The phone call was from Dallas police department Missing Persons Investigator Patricia Canton, who was taking Miriam apart a piece at a time.

"But this is an FBI case," Miriam stammered.

"Yes, Miss DeSilva, the missing person case on your sister is an FBI case. But we are involved, too, because you called us in."

"I did not call you in."

There was a pause. Miriam could hear pages flipping on the other end.

"We were called originally by a Merriellen Lehner, the neighbor."

"Correct, but I did not call you."

The women were still talking to Janet about the clairvoyant at the far end of the room, but Ike had drifted over toward Miriam to eavesdrop.

"Miss DeSilva, I really don't see what difference that makes at this point. We're all working with the same goal in mind."

"Yes, of course. But I just don't understand what you . . . what it is you want, at this point."

"I thought I made that pretty clear at the beginning of this conversation, Miss DeSilva. I want to know where the children are."

"But why? Why does that concern you? I told you they're perfectly all right."

Ike was now seated across the table from Miriam, peering into her eyes and pointing with a finger.

"Miss DeSilva, with all due respect to the FBI, these domestic custody-related disputes are not really their show, and it's always possible we might even be able to see something that they might overlook. We might be able to help them, in other words, because of our experience and expertise in these matters. And I would assume that we would help you, because I assume you still want to find your sister."

"Of course I do. Why wouldn't I? But what can you see that the FBI can't see?"

"Well, Miss DeSilva, we see a mother in a very bitter, very publicized divorce and custody battle, and she has supposedly disappeared, but there is no body, just a car with blood on it, and now mysteriously the children have disappeared also . . ."

"What are you getting at?"

Ike motioned with his finger across his neck for her to get off the phone.

"What I am getting at is that I want to know where those children are. If your parents are in on this, then I hope they know that they could be subject to some very serious felony charges."

"Felony charges against my parents? If what? What are you talking about? What are you trying to get at?"

"If your sister is not really dead or even missing."

Miriam gasped.

"I have to go!" she said. "Why don't you ask the FBI where they are?"

"I intend to. But I wonder if Mr. Edelman might have some thoughts about all of this, too?"

"You . . ." Miriam had to stop. Her breath was out of control. "You're going to call Robert? I really wish you would not do that. Not now. If you could just wait."

Investigator Canton said goodbye quickly and hung up.

Colonel Young had been waiting half an hour. He sat on a stool at the end of the coffee counter in a suburban truck stop restaurant on the freeway. Gerry Hubbell was crouched inside the dark interior of a surveillance van in the parking lot. Through a view-hole in the side of the van, another agent was watching Young inside the restaurant with a telescope. A third agent sat at a communications console wearing a headset.

The telescope was divided in a T. At one end of the T, in the agent's hands, was a 35-millimeter camera. At the other end was a dual-lens eye-piece, to which the agent had his eyes glued. Every five or six minutes, the agent would take a picture; the camera's muffled motor drive made a barely audible humming sound; then the van was silent again. Gerry Hubbell sat with his forearms on his knees, staring at his shoes.

"Moving," the agent at the telescope said softly.

Neither of the other two moved or gave any sign they had heard.

"Pay phone," the agent said.

Twenty seconds later, the agent with the headphones said, "He's call-ing Zabitosky. Wants to know where the hell Jack is. Zabitosky's telling him Jack is on the way."

The agent with the headphones waited until the call was over, then punched a phone number into the console. "Joe," he said, "did you hear that? Yeah? Okay. All right. Will do."

He turned away from the console to Gerry Hubbell. "Masterson says they've got the warrants. You can go in."

Gerry Hubbell slipped out of a side door in the van, on the side facing away from the restaurant. He stepped around his own car, which was parked right next to the van. Then he walked briskly up a line of cars. He snaked between two cars and came back down the line on the other side, this time in view of the restaurant. When he got within 100 yards of the front window of the truck stop, Colonel Young saw him. The Colonel got off his stool and came out through the front door to meet him outside.

"Where the hell you been?" Colonel Young said to Hubbell.

"Got lost," Hubbell said. "You got it?"

"Yeah, I got it. I will pay you in the bathroom. Come on in."

"Well, I want to show you the jewelry, make sure it's right."

"I don't care about the jewelry," Young said. "You're late. I will look at the jewelry later. You want me to pay you or what?"

"I'm not going to carry that shit another day. You come look at it now, if you want to see it."

Hubbell led Colonel Young back to his car. He opened the trunk, unfolded a towel, and showed Colonel Young Linda's watch, locket, ring, and other jewelry. Then he handed Young a photograph of the jewelry.

Young compared the photo with the jewelry. He slipped the photo into his pocket. "I will show this to my banker," he said.

Then Colonel Young reached into his pocket, pulled out a thick envelope containing $5,000 in cash, and handed it to Gerry Hubbell. Hubbell squeezed the envelope, looked inside, and saw the cash. Colonel Young was facing away from him, surveying the lot nervously.

"Everything right?" Colonel Young said, with his back turned to Hubbell.

"Except for one thing," Hubbell said, slipping his I.D. out of his hip pocket.

"What's that?" Young asked, turning back quickly to face him.

Gerry Hubbell held the I.D. in front of Young's face. "I am an agent of the Federal Bureau of Investigation, and you, sir, are under arrest."

The van opened quietly behind Colonel Young. Young turned and found two more FBI agents standing behind him with guns.

Gerry Hubbell began reading him his rights.

At one instant, the street in front of Cedar-Maple Plaza was filled with what looked like normal weekday traffic. At the next, large American sedans, all with three small aerials protruding from their roofs, began snapping out of the line of traffic in front of the building, heaving themselves up over the driveway ramp and into position in a perimeter around the parking lot behind the building. Another line of cars pulled up in front of the building.

Inside, in the plush offices of WelMarc Housing Corporation, a receptionist was fielding a telephone call.

"Yes, I assumed you wanted to talk to Mr. Edelman, since that's who you called for," she said. "But Mr. Edelman will want to know what business you have with him before he will take your call, Officer Canton. Is it about security work at one of his job sites?"

The instant the cars began arraying themselves outside, Joe Masterson stepped out of a car already parked at the curb. With Agent Fiori and two other young agents walking quickly behind him in a flying wedge, he went in through the front door. One of the agents stayed in the lobby while the other three went up in the elevator.

Joe let himself into the front reception area of Robert's offices.

"He's not in," the receptionist said, holding the telephone receiver aloft in one hand.

Joe walked quickly past her. Another agent stayed in position in the reception area.

"Oh, shit," the receptionist said in a tiny voice.

The secretary in the next room said, "He can't see you now."

Joe walked quickly by her. A third agent took a position next to her desk with a gun drawn.

"Oh, God," she gasped.

Joe pushed open the door and found Robert seated, cross-legged, on the sofa at the far end of the room, smoking a cigarette , with his hand on the telephone. As soon as Robert saw Joe and Agent Fiori, he slowly pulled his hand to his lap. He gazed levelly at Joe without saying a word.

Joe informed him he was under arrest and read him his Miranda warning. Robert stubbed out his cigarette carefully in the crystal ashtray while Joe spoke.

Agent Fiori handcuffed him and led him to the elevator. Robert never said a word.

The moment Fiori had departed with Robert in his car, Joe called Ike from his car. "Bring 'em home, Ike. It's a done deal."

Ike dialed Caruth. Miriam answered.

"This is Ike. Let me speak to Rezilla."

"What is it, Ike?" Miriam asked.

"Let me speak to Rezilla, please."

Rezilla came to the phone.

"Rezilla, this is Ike. Linda is alive. She is not hurt. She is fine. She is on her way home now. I will be there in a minute."

Rezilla hung up the phone, walked to the long table, and leaned on it with one hand. She felt faint for a moment and had to wait for her head to clear. Then she said, "Oh, thank God. She is alive."

When Ike arrived, he assembled Miriam, Jeanne, Rezilla, Janet, and Merriellen in the library. Joe Pearsall and Mitzi had already left for Oklahoma. Talking quickly, gesturing with his hands, pacing up and down the room, Ike explained the sting to the women.

Midway through the explanation, Janet rose. She approached Miriam.

"Miriam," she said, "do you mean to tell me that you knew about this? All the way through?"

"Not all the way through," Miriam said. Tears sprang to her eyes. "Oh, Janet, please believe me, I hated lying to you, I hated the lying, I hated it, it has been tearing my heart out, but I was afraid for my sister's life, for my parents' lives, for those children."

Merriellen came and stood behind Janet with her hand touching Janet's elbow. "Janet," she whispered. "They had to do what they had to do."

Rezilla held out her hands and shook her head. "Miss Lesser," she said, "you surely know what a mean man Robert Edelman is. They had to play a lot of tricks to catch a man like that."

Janet sank back to her chair, shaking her head and crying. "Oh, thank God she's alive," she said. "Oh, thank God."

The word flew up and down Caruth, and the front doors of houses flew open. People began pouring out of the houses with bags of cookies, casseroles, flowers, bottles of champagne, six-packs of beer, and six-packs of soft drinks. And from houses up and down the street came rags and scraps of yellow fabric, yellow ribbon, yellow pillowcases torn in strips, even yellow trash bags.

When the huge old motor home finally turned onto Caruth, Linda looked out through the windshield and saw a sea of humanity all across the lawn and partially out in the street in front of her house, cheering and raising glasses in toast. And everywhere she looked, up and down the block, the trees and shrubs and fence posts were tied with fluttering yellow ribbons.

The children crowded up under her arms at the front of the motor home and gazed on their welcome with wonder and awe.

Conscious that she had only seconds left before they would arrive at the house and the door of the motor home would be yanked open, Linda squeezed her eyes shut and offered an urgent prayer of thanks to God.

"I thank you for sparing these children," she said out loud. "I thank you for sparing my parents. I thank you for life."

EPILOGUE

The trial in late winter 1988 was not going especially well for the prosecution. U.S. District Judge Barefoot Sanders, one of the most distinguished jurists in the Southwest, was a stickler on evidence. For a variety of reasons, the prosecution had not been able to get any tape of Robert actually ordering Colonel Young to kill Linda introduced into evidence.

In hiring lawyers to defend him, Robert had spent his money well. His lawyers told the jury that Colonel Young was a freelance opportunist and nutcase who had come up with the plot to kill Linda on his own. Robert, they said, knew nothing of the plot. Linda, meanwhile, was painted as a spoiled Park Cities ditz—a self-centered immature woman who couldn't tell the difference between real life and operetta.

Because Linda and her parents were witnesses, they could not sit in the courtroom and watch the trial. Miriam sat in the room for them and served as the family's eyes and ears.

Even though she could not watch, Linda sensed from the reports she received that it was not going well. She was terrified of what would happen if Robert went free. Miriam did her best to bolster her sister's morale. But as she watched the trial unfold, she realized in her own heart that Linda was right.

It was not going well. The prosecution was having difficulty forcing its way through the dense underbrush of rules and privileges that protect defendants. The defense, meanwhile, was having a heyday—presenting Robert Edelman as a prominent and distinguished member of the Dallas business community who had made the grave tactical error of trying to divorce his bitter, ruthless, maniacal wife.

After a while the words of the defense began to melt together, and Miriam had trouble making herself concentrate. She sat on the hard wooden bench with her eyes half-focused as the defense attorney went on and on about Robert: Why would he even want to murder his wife, the lawyer asked rhetorically, when the principle bitterness of the divorce was already behind him?

Miriam could not suppress a smirk at that.

A trial date had been set for the divorce, the lawyer told the jury. Soon it would all be over. Texas had passed a new joint custody law, which would have guaranteed Robert at least partial access to the children.

Why would Robert risk having his wife murdered? The differences had been settled. Robert had announced plans to remarry in November. He and his fiancée had planned a trip to Europe with the children. Why would he do any of what he was accused? It simply was not in his interest.

Robert managed somehow—through dint of intensive coaching, no doubt—to present a fairly reasonable persona to the jury.

Miriam watched the faces of the jurors. She could see them agreeing with Robert's lawyer. She could see that they found the lawyer persuasive.

And then an alarm went off in her head. Wait a minute! What had the lawyer said? Robert had announced a November wedding? The divorce would be final by then? Aha! Robert must have lied about it to his own lawyer.

Miriam rose brusquely from her seat, pushed past other onlookers to the aisle, and hurried out into the corridor. With trembling fingers, she dropped a quarter into a pay phone and dialed Caruth. Virginia answered. Miriam asked her to put Linda on.

"She's doing laundry downstairs," Virginia said.

"Mother, get her! It's very important."

Miriam explained to Linda what had just been said in the courtroom and then explained why she thought it was wrong.

Linda listened intently. "No, Miriam," she said, "you're right. I did tell you that. It was bifurcated. Only the custody was to be tried. The property was still totally unsettled, and that would have taken maybe years, Ike said. The property settlement also involved Ike finally getting his hands on Robert's books, which he had never been able to do."

Miriam and Linda quickly worked out a plan of action on the phone.

As soon as she hung up, Miriam rushed back into the courtroom, walked down the aisle, and opened the gate that allowed her into the area where the lawyers sit.

A bailiff started toward her with his hand on his holster. Assistant

U.S. Attorney Mark Nichols held up a hand, and the bailiff backed off. Miriam leaned forward and whispered hurriedly to Nichols. Nichols nodded, then told Miriam to return to her seat. He rose, approached the bench, and asked Judge Sanders for an immediate delay. Sanders granted his request.

Linda called Ike, then left for his office. When she got to the Galleria, Ike was waiting in the parking structure with the file. He jumped in the car with her, and together they drove downtown to the Earle Cabell Federal Building.

Nichols called Robert back to the stand and showed him the bifurcation agreement.

The instant Robert saw it, the hours of coaching evaporated; Robert's nice-guy exterior melted away and the ugly, sneering, arrogant Robert Edelman of real life emerged.

"I have never seen that agreement before," Robert said.

"Is this your signature?"

"It could be," Robert said, as if bored. "I sign so many things. I don't read everything that comes across my desk."

Miriam peered deep into the faces of the jurors.

It was there! In their eyes! They knew Robert was lying. And now they knew he was a man who had tried to murder his own wife, to murder the mother of his children, to murder the grandparents of his children. And then he coolly planned his remarriage.

They knew what Robert Edelman was.

There were seven women and five men on the jury. They deliberated less than four hours before returning a verdict of guilty. Ten days later, Judge Sanders sentenced Robert Edelman to the maximum penalty provided in the conspiracy statute under which he had been prosecuted—ten years in federal prison.

Colonel Young, who pleaded guilty and then cooperated with the prosecution, was sent to prison for seven years. He told his defense attorney some years later that his life in federal prison was better than he could ever have expected in retirement.

Even after his federal trial and sentencing, Robert still faced state charges. The Texas prison system is a far more frightening place than the federal prisons.

Robert's new lawyer came to Linda with a proposal. If Robert agreed to legally "de-parent" himself—to forsake and revoke forever any and all of his parental rights or claims on the children, including visitation of any kind, for the rest of their lives—would she give her blessing to a deal for Robert on the state charges?

She agreed. Robert went to court and admitted that he had

attempted to have his wife murdered. The court sentenced him to nine years on the state charges, which he was allowed to serve "concurrently" while in federal prison, which meant that he would never see the inside of a Texas prison and no law enforcement official would ever see the inside of his books.

At about the same time, Robert's original defense attorney sued him, because the $70,000 that was supposed to have been earmarked for legal fees in the divorce settlement was never paid.

Linda moved to a smaller house.

Surrounded by their grandparents, their aunt, and their mother, Stephen and Kathleen thrived. Stephen blossomed as an athlete, excelled in school, and threw himself into children's activities at Park Cities Baptist Church. Polite and respectful with adults, Stephen developed an uncanny gift for mimicry that made him the favorite stand-up comic of his pals. His special love was drawing and animation, and his dream was to draw for Disney.

Little Kathleen grew into a beautiful girl, with a singing voice so exquisite that she was tapped again and again to sing solos in church and for school productions. Her mother could not help thinking of Kathleen, the stage, and New York all in the same languid daydream.

Linda walked to the front of their new home one evening and saw Kathleen standing alone on the circular drive, staring off at the horizon.

"Oh, Mother," Kathleen called, "come and see this sunset. It is so wonderful!"

The calls come late at night now, when the children are in bed and Linda is awake by herself, sitting in the kitchen. There is breathing. Then the caller hangs up.

Linda goes to their rooms and looks in.

Here are her children, sleeping like angels.

She knows what this is. This is the real dream.

She knows exactly what this is.